ISBN: 978-0-86690-688-3

Cover art: Celeste Nash-Weninger

Front CoverZ: Shutterstock Photo ID: 391759417

Back Cover: NASA-JHU-APL-SwRI-ZLDoyle

Requests and inquires may be mailed to the publisher:

American Federation of Astrologers, Inc.

6553 S. Rural Road

Tempe, AZ 85283

www.astrologers.com

Before I begin, I would like to take this opportunity to 'thank you' for buying this book. I hope you find it to be an enjoyable read, as well as a useful source of information.

Blessings to you Dear Readers,
Alan Richards-Wheatcroft

Acknowledgements

Thank You…

There are only three people I need to personally acknowledge in this publication. The first is Maria Stiopei, the second is Christina Richter, and the third is Celeste Nash-Weninger. I would like to thank them all for their valuable and compelling contributions that have made this publication possible, and perhaps more importantly, for making it complete. However, in the case of Celeste, I would like to thank her, as an editor, for her amazing contribution and timing that made the publication of Pluto's brother Neptune possible — namely Discovering Faith in Neptune's Ocean of Dreams.

Firstly, and with regards to Maria, the hidden ability that I spotted in you, that represents your inner strength, brilliance and purpose has blossomed, and now signifies the fruit of your labors. I sincerely hope that we can continue to benefit from our cosmic collaboration — continuing to work together in the future. This powerful union of Pluto-orientated minds and hearts has proved to be a highly successful, worthwhile, as well as an extremely advantageous undertaking.

Maria is a true pioneer of life — possessing many remarkable physical, psychological and spiritual attributes.

Christina is a fellow Scorpio, and a brilliant medical astrologer — possessing remarkable insight. She is also coupled with a gifted intellect. The wisdom you have acquired in life is clearly unique and priceless. It has been an honor to work with you on many occasions.

Celeste Nash-Weninger is a truly shining star; hence she is a very gifted and accomplished soul. I feel your lustrous future has just begun. Your exceptional mindset has without doubt been fashioned from the evolutionary junctures that are bound by the delicate but anchored threads of spirituality. God bless you!

Alan Richards-Wheatcroft

Author's Note:

It is important to point out that at the time of compiling this publication Wikipedia was considered to be a reliable source of information.

Contents

Foreword

By Christina Richter, Medical Astrologer
Author of: *Learn to Self-Heal and Your Astrological Health*
www.christinarichterauthor.com

When my colleague Alan Richards-Wheatcroft contacted me to write the foreword for his latest book, Pluto's Season for Ashes, I was absolutely thrilled. I had to laugh however when he said to me "as a Scorpio, I feel that you will get the depth of this book", and he was right. As a consulting astrologer, I had already read his previous books, Astrology for Self-Healing, and One Body Many Illnesses, and found them both to be an excellent source of reference in my work.

This is not a book for beginners. You do need to have an intermediary level of knowledge in astrology to get the full benefit of this book.

Pluto is powerful and persistent, and it demands you pay attention. It will often trigger your natal planets three or four times over the course of two to three years, until you learn to integrate the energy that will support your evolution.

Pluto is two-fold in nature. The energy it brings is one of creation through destruction, and then transformation. Pluto packs a powerful punch on a magnitude that can only be appreciated in hindsight. The process is often painful and therefore requires self-reflection and understanding of the self. To achieve this, something in you must die in order for you to become the most amazing person you were born to be.

Out of all of Alan's books, I enjoyed this the most. His chapter on Coronavirus is relevant and insightful. He really does speak about the evolution and progression of our planet Earth, and its inhabitants. I also loved the way Alan has written about the positive change, and why COVID-19 had to happen, and where this new era is taking us.

Personally, I appreciated how the use of William Lilly's critical degrees were included and explained in many of his health charts. I had not seen this practice before and it prompted me to research this technique further, and include them in my own assessments of my clients. I found this technique a valuable tool, thank you Alan.

Everyone has Pluto somewhere in their natal charts; therefore we are all affected, and to understand the healing and transformative influence, especially with regards to health is important for holistic living.

Alan brings his decades of experience, wisdom and knowledge around psycho-spiritual health, which clearly shines through as you turn the pages. With his knowledge, he has created a beautifully-written and well-researched book that is a useful addition for any holistic practitioner. His passion and integrity are self-evident, and I feel this book will enhance the reader's knowledge and choices, as it did mine.

In conclusion, we are all a combination of body and soul on the path to personal growth. Personal evolution is noted by many things in the astrology chart — with Pluto being the main driving force. For all those born under the sign of Scorpio, or those who have Pluto strongly aspected in their charts, this book is a must-read.

SECTION 1

The Ashes of Pluto

The Ashes of Pluto

Pluto affirms that new thoughts and new age terminology refer primarily to the practice of positive thinking and self-empowerment — fostering a belief that a positive mental attitude will achieve success in creative endeavours'. Written by an unknown source, this, in my opinion, pertains towards the symbolic meaning of transformation, which is Pluto's primary characteristic.

Pluto's Sphere (Nucleuses) of Possibility

I have heard it said that 'planets in the cosmos constitute as a conscious entity; therefore, with this in mind, each planet must then be representative of a multiple cell organism'. This notion is a collective belief adhered to by those who are especially versed in the esoteric framework of both astrology and quantum sciences. So, if we were to split open the cells of every planet we would be able to release each cell's nucleus. Thus, an emancipated planetary nucleus symbolizes the potential for limitless possibility. And, the outer planets Uranus, Neptune and Pluto demonstrate the greatest potential towards an assemblage of limitless possibilities.

Pluto and Synthesis: In my previous teachings, I make reference to the fact that 'Neptune and Pluto can be viewed as one, hence one conscious organism'. This is because some believe (including myself) that Pluto was once a natural satellite of Neptune; and soon will be again. Hence, they are synthesized bodies with similar purpose and intentions. For example, the principle cornerstones of these planets are: Neptune-transcendence, and Pluto-transformation. Essentially, they are one of the same design structures. So, I would have to conclude that Neptune represents a multiple cell composition, and Pluto represents its multiple cell nucleuses. This is because Pluto is deemed as a microscopic body with regards to the cosmos. Uranus however, represents a single multiple cell organism that has its rulership over the extensive functions of the brain.

If then Pluto represents the most distant but distinct nucleus of the cosmos —recognizing its sole purpose of psychological and evolutionary transformation, surely this planet would be one of the most important and powerful spheres in the cosmos. However, with that said, it is important to point that every planet is important in its own unique way.

Transmutation: Pluto is equipped solely for the task of multiple cell redevelopment, hence transformation. Furthermore, Pluto is capable of 'appropriating an ability' to split open the cells of the other planets in the natal chart, in order to release the planet's nucleuses towards limitless possibility. Moreover, Pluto is particularly effective at splitting open the nucleuses of the planets that are in aspect to it in the natal chart, particularly via the conjunction and the opposition aspect (see table of planets below). Appropriately then, this intricate but intense procedure represents the authentic meaning of evolutionary transmutation.

The Potential for a Released Planetary Nucleus:

From a natal point of view, Mercury, Venus and Mars are the inner cosmic spheres that are strongly influenced by the conjunction to Pluto. Jupiter and Saturn however are intensely influenced by the conjunction and the opposition both in a natal capacity, and via a Jupiter or Saturn transit to natal Pluto. Be that as it may, the opposition will invariably inculcate tension, which in itself, builds psychological barriers, and thus prevents the onset of transformation — the quintessential ethos of Pluto. Aspects to the luminaries represent a potential for transformation. However, and in many cases, a period of illness and disease will ensue before soul and psychological transformation can be achieved. I have explained the consequences and conclusions of Sun and Moon conjunctions and oppositions to Pluto in greater depth in Part 3, where there are many case studies to examine.

Illness and Disease: Meanwhile, I have discovered in all my years of study that the prevention of 'inborn transformation' gives rise to the onset of illness and disease. In which case, the planets that conjoin or oppose Pluto will simply exacerbate Pluto designated illness and disease (see Part 3 for more information). Therefore, when the nucleuses of the planets concerned are released illness and disease is finally eliminated. Here is a brief summary of Pluto's natal conjunctions and oppositions:

Mercury

When the nucleuses of Mercury are released under the powerful and transformational impact of Pluto, the potential for releasing more of the brain's capacity towards 'power creation' becomes a distinct possibility — bearing the words 'out of nothing something comes forth'. Coupled by the capability for developing a supreme intellect, this analogy establishes that a Mercury–Pluto conjunction signals a powerful force to be reckoned with.

In the natal chart, a Mercury–Pluto conjunction displays enormous potential in both an evolutionary magnitude, and in a highly developed cerebral capacity. Thus, an alignment of this proportion denotes an individual who possesses a complex mind, but in the same sense, it shows someone who is perfectly capable of exploring the relatively unknown recesses of the brain. Hence, a Mercury–Pluto conjunction indicates a person who can gaze beneath the surface of conventional boundaries

— similar to looking into a deep lake and being able to see the bottom. Likewise, this is an individual who displays an intense curiosity in order to elicit the legendary fountain of knowledge.[1]

This unified alignment indicates the presence of a powerful and a conceptual intellect. Thus, Mercury conjunct Pluto signifies the innovator, the inventor and the designer — given the potential to see beyond the conventional — and with the ability to see something taking on a specific form — and well beforehand. Possessing an ability towards the power of persuasion is also likely when Mercury conjuncts Pluto.

Uranus: All in all, these interpretations would be equally relevant when Pluto conjuncts Uranus. Although a Uranus–Pluto conjunction is relatively uncommon, therefore a similar set of scenarios would be likely when transit Uranus opposes natal Pluto. With a Uranus–Pluto opposition however, a direct line to the cerebrally–cultivated sphere in the spiritual world would maintained at all times, even though this alignment is potentially thwart with tension, which would, on accession, psychologically impede this indispensable connection.

Venus

When the nucleuses of Venus are released under the powerful and transformational influence of Pluto, the potential for releasing more of the brain's capacity towards the honing of 'unconditional love' is the intended outcome of this alignment. However, a Venus–Pluto conjunction also brings tremendous potential for 'power creation'; and in addition, both of these capabilities are infused with a heavenly purpose, meaning that divine assistance is always available if required or recognized. Furthermore, this gentle but equally powerful and polarized alignment embraces the potential for self–awareness, self–development, and it intensify the capacity towards emotional and psychological depth — learning to love the self.

So, when the individual begins to love the self, and learning to love the self, releases more of the brain's capacity, outwardly and inherent sexual desires will slowly begin to dissipate. Moreover, any obsessional tendencies that are traditionally attached to the Venus–Pluto conjunction will also begin to disappear. Thus, the need for synthetic love will no longer be relevant, leaving the individual unimpeded in his or her pursuit for creative and psychic endeavours, which will be sought out in an impassioned way. In the long term, a Venus–Pluto conjunction will represent a source of soul and cerebral conversion; and this will be of great benefit to humankind, particularly in a way that will regenerate the art of social discourse.

Neptune: All in all, these interpretations would be equally relevant when Pluto conjuncts Neptune, although a Neptune–Pluto conjunction is relatively uncommon. Therefore, a similar set of scenarios would manifest when transit Neptune opposes natal Pluto. Thus, with a Neptune–Pluto opposition a powerful spiritual connection to the divine manifests, which is always on hand if needed — a connection that can only be maintained once any self–doubt and inhibition subsides — a customary theme of the Neptune-Pluto opposition.

Likewise, a Neptune-Pluto opposition would encourage the development of telepathy and ESP. Thus, to awaken the dormant part of the brain that holds within it recesses this deep potential.

Mars

When the nucleuses of Mars are released under the powerful and transformational influence of Pluto, the potential for releasing more of the brain's capacity towards psychic strength and inner courage becomes possible. Likewise, the Mars–Pluto conjunction represents 'transformative power' — to seek out soul and psychological transformation in a manner that is simply unrelenting. Naturally stimulated by the process of challenge and subliminal obstacles the transformative power of a Mars–Pluto conjunction is capable of 'psychologically moving mountains'.

Thus, when the energy emitted by this dominant and powerful alignment is refined and administered into a particular creative and innovational endeavour, the desire to achieve the impossible becomes ever possible.

Similar to the primordial effects released by a Venus–Pluto conjunction, when the individual hones this configuration to its highest good, there is no more need for outwardly inherent desires and in particular transfixations, particularly those of a sexual, and or of an aggressive and belligerent nature. Thus, when the brain releases more of its potential via a Mars–Pluto conjunction these base elements will be purged and therefore eradicated from the psyche.

Moreover, when this planetary unification has been purified, those bedrock emotions such as fear, hate and jealousy can also be eliminated from the psyche. Furthermore, the fear of, coupled with the experience of physical pain and psychological suffering, will also be absolved.

In addition, self–confidence is heightened. This is often via a belief that immortality is a very real concept; and one that is worth fighting for. Esoterically speaking, Mars is meant to be the lower vibration of Pluto, meaning that this planetary combination blends itself perfectly.

Jupiter

When the nucleuses of Jupiter are released under the powerful and transformational guise of Pluto, the potential for releasing more of the brain's capacity towards psychological expansion becomes increasingly possible here. This potential is strengthened exponentially by an intense need for an 'accumulation of knowledge'. Potentially, this is a very favourable aspect; and one that can improve the quality of life significantly, because buried within the nucleuses of Jupiter and Pluto is an 'inner treasure trove' of mental, spiritual and evolutionary abilities that can manifest via a single thought. One such example would be to evoke the evolutionary and spiritual component of wholeheartedness.

Helping others to feel whole and complete is one of the attributes associated with this heavenly alignment. This is especially so once the individual feels whole themselves. Thus, Pluto's soul and psychological transformation can occur in others as if by magic — simply by the Jupiter–Pluto individual having to adopt a convivial approach towards anyone who falls in their range of vision. Essentially, this is what the Jupiter–Pluto conjunction is directed to achieve. This is its evolutionary purpose, hence its cosmic charter.

Wholeheartedness is mostly connected to spiritual pursuits, which we have all experienced at some point in our evolution. But because societies have become fragmented, it remains an extremely uncommon characteristic. Furthermore, wholeheartedness represents soul expansion, which in turn expands the brain's psychological capacity and heightened potential.

The Opposition: When an opposition occurs between Jupiter and Pluto, either through a natal alignment, or through a transit, additional work on eliminating the inherent and inner tension must take place before any sense of unconditional joy becomes apparent.

The fall: When Jupiter tenants Capricorn in the natal chart, or when it transits this sign wholeheartedness and joy become difficult attributes to achieve in life. Jupiter is in its fall in Capricorn. A Jupiter–Pluto conjunction occurred at the height of the coronavirus pandemic in 2020, and a distinct lack of joy was evident throughout many societies.

Saturn

When the nucleuses of Saturn are released under the powerful and transformational influence of Pluto, the potential for releasing more of the brain's capacity towards an intense need to break free of its psychological limitations and restrictions becomes apparent. Furthermore, there is a pressing need to liberate the soul from its karmic shackles, which is essentially representative of an evolutionary barrier, and one that denotes a lack of conscientiousness. This is perhaps the truest aspect that denotes the Phoenix rising out of the ashes of its earlier existence. Restriction limits the brain's capacity, and once this hurdle has been overcome, the potential for achieving Pluto's higher objectives becomes possible.

A Saturn–Pluto conjunction holds within its combined matrix the greatest potential for cerebral and soul transformation; and furthermore an allotted amount of time has been provided in order for this to be achieved. Potentially, this alignment signifies a combination of arduous and hard cosmic supreme forces. However, a Saturn–Pluto conjunction represents an alliance that has the potential to penetrate the evolutionary boundaries that remain invisible here on the material–orientated plane of the Earth. Thus, once the brain has released more of its potential a Saturn–Pluto conjunction is able to view the seemingly indistinguishable abstractions that are contained within a solid framework of energy. One such example would be to detect the energy patterns at work within the Earth's rocky and hard surfaces, such as trees. Thus, to view energy compositions that are evolving, especially in elements that are considered to be inert.

Also, once the nucleuses of these planets are released the raw and repressive emotions that are kept under strict lock and key can be finally purged. Unfettered emotions prevent the soul from remembering its right to immortality; therefore once the emotions are suppressed slow but definite transformation can take place. Gradual transformation to a higher plane of existence is the modus operandi of a Saturn–Pluto conjunction.

The Opposition: The opposition between Saturn and Pluto can however give rise to a distinct but intense fear, which will reside deep within the psyche. This must be eliminated before transformation to a higher plane of perception and duty to the self can take place.

The Fall: When Saturn tenants Aries in the natal chart, or when it transits the sign, irresponsibility is often an issue; and will need to be balanced before the limitations and restrictions that are put in place by Saturn at birth are uplifted.

Inherent Capabilities

As I have indicated in the relevant sections below, releasing each of the planet's nucleuses is only possible via stillness, contemplation and visualization techniques. Furthermore, and because of Pluto's substantial influence, the task is also achievable and maintained through intense creative endeavours. Of all the cosmic probabilities the Saturn–Pluto conjunction is perhaps the best placed for achieving the task of nucleus release. This is because patience, determination and resilience are often attributes that have been tailored into this workable alignment. Distraction, hindrance and temptation are often relevant determinants, which have been anchored to a large percentage of the other cosmic associations.

Pluto Dimensions

Human beings only use 'up to'10 per cent of their brain's capacity. This is a proven fact that is frequently contradicted — confirmed as early as the classical period by the Greek philosopher and medical physician Aristotle, who in all likelihood had a pronounced Pluto in his natal chart. If only his birth details were known!

In essence, our brains have turned to ashes; and this is why there is so much corruption, violence, greed and contradiction upon the Earth at present, because we are not using the extensive range of our brain's capacity. If we did the Earth would be a very different, accessible and suggestable point of origin in the cosmos. The fact however remains that we are not evolved enough yet — physically and psychologically. Pluto's ashes symbolize a residue of Pluto's past potential, hence the last remnants of an obsolete but retentive existence. This is reminiscent of cell death; or cell dieback — when the dead cell is replaced by a healthy one. This scientific analogy is similar to the legend of the mythical Phoenix, which rose out of the ashes of its earlier life. The Phoenix represents transformation and rebirth from the old life; the old life being symbolized by fire and brimstone, hence the ashes.

Cosmic Stimulus: Those who possess intercepted houses and planets in their natal chart have in effect 'released' more of their brain's potential — either in previous incarnations, or whilst in spirit. However, the evolutionary potential contained within the realm of intercepted houses has to be 'reawakened' by transit Pluto — transiting these intercepted zones. In a recent astrological study carried out by the reverend Alice Miller and written into one of her books, it highlights that 'transit Pluto will always move through intercepted houses at some point in the individual's life, gradually awakening these zones'. Therefore, by moving through the intercepted houses Pluto will begin to release more of the brain's potential. However, this will only become possible if and when the recipient becomes aware and is in total agreement.

Further Indicators: In addition, when Uranus, Neptune and Pluto are in hard aspect to the Sun in the natal chart the potential for channelling more of the brain's capacity is equally possible. Hard aspects to the Sun from these particular planets are often evident in autism and epilepsy charts; and those who suffer from the likes of autism and epilepsy often have access to the so–called fragments of the brain that are deemed redundant — portions that access greater levels of suggestion, psychic programming and comprehensive idealism.

Uranus, Neptune and Pluto regenerate cerebral and spiritual consciousness — stimulus that is required for accessing more of the brain's function. Thus, they are awakening planets.

Uranus provides a 'light bulb moment'. Neptune stimulates the unconscious with a program of transcendental visions, and 'Pluto' transforms them into reality, for the purpose of additional awareness and power.

Pluto and Power: So, if we had access to 20 per cent of the brain's capacity for example, we would have complete control over the body and metabolism — procuring the capability for genuine self–sufficiency. Therefore, we would be able to eliminate illness and disease once and for all.

Acquiring 20 per cent of the brain's capacity will only become possible when Pluto's nucleuses are split open via the esoteric level of consciousness. This course of action can be successfully achieved through stillness and contemplation, visualization and intense creative endeavours. Achieving self–sufficiency would be an entirely possible endeavour.

Interestingly, the concepts of illness and disease will always be superior and potent forms of influence on Earth, providing of course we continue to access this very low percentage of the brain's capacity and potential.

Summarization: Sources of Illness and Disease

Before I begin my analysis, many people have asked me how I came up with such a curious title for this book. In simple terms, think of a lifetime, hence a cycle of evolution as a collection of ashes, or in this case memories:

1. Ashes left over from childhood,
2. From adolescence,
3. From midlife, particularly ashes of a sexual and monitory nature (power play),
4. Memories are in effect a last remnant of Pluto's potential.

Pluto's nucleus is comprised of several components, including those that represent our deeper and more significant memories. It is important to remember that whereas the Moon reflects the very essence of our memories, it is Pluto that submerges them — deep within the soul. It does this because Pluto is the planet that 'doesn't like to let go of anything', especially manipulative and obsessive tendencies it considers to be of monitory, and of sexual value (see diagram 1). These particular facets make up a very small percentage of Pluto's enormous power it wields over the psyche. However, there is often a price to pay for the over usage of Pluto's godfatherly dominance and authority, which not only resonates at the physical and psychological level of consciousness, but also on an evolutionary scale.[2]

Power Play: Obsession and manipulation go hand–in–hand. So for example, when manipulation becomes an obsession and visa versa these elements invariably create a physical imbalance deep within the psyche; which can only be readdressed via the Pluto archetype. Thus, Pluto views this imbalance, which is essentially representative of an abuse of power, as a karmic debt that needs to be repaid.

However, Pluto doesn't always expect the debt to be repaid in monies alone, but it does expect the debt to be paid back in full, especially in a psychological capacity. As a result, the debt is often required to be recompensed at the expense of the soul. Anal, prostate, vaginal and colon cancer are extreme examples that highlight an abuse of Pluto's power, which appears as a karmic dent within the evolutionary bridleway of the soul (the aura) — for those who are able and are fortunate enough to be able to view this auric field of energy.[3]

The case studies I have chosen to portray in Part 3 represent prominent Pluto figureheads who have held, or continue to wield power in one form or another; and who have taken enormous psychological risks with the use of this power. Ultimately, the exploitation of Pluto's power in the natal chart meant that they paid a high price. Significantly, the price has not always resulted in physical death. In some cases however, the intermittent psychological profile has become distressed and unstable.

Meanwhile in the interim, Pluto is often associated with the devil incarnate. This demonic influence is merely a reflection of both the current physiological and psychological state of mind, especially when the mind, body and soul succumb to illness and disease — deemed as the ultimate price for the overexertion of Pluto's karmic power.

Illness and Disease: Illness and disease, and even the effects generated by physical and mental forfeiture, are negative characteristics that invariably damage the soul, especially in a psychological capacity. This is why Pluto–orientated illness and disease represents the 'devil in disguise' because they draw out energy (power) from the soul for the purpose of iniquitous rebirth, similar to the purpose of the mythical vampire. Literally, illness and disease consume the very essence of the soul. This is especially the case where viral illnesses are concerned, as the world witnessed throughout 2020 with COVID–19 (refer to the next section).

Viruses, especially in their current state of consciousness (see next section for more information about the consciousness of viruses), have essentially been transmuted into microscopic vampires, whereby they represent the 'ultimate abuse of power'. Viruses are therefore prime examples that denote an unnatural and perhaps gothic rebirth into poisoned physical matter, because viruses have become catalysts for physical and psychological illness and disease, when their true purpose denotes something entirely different. Thus, these microscopic organisms represent seeds for new spiritual growth, which they were intended to be.[4]

In recent years, viral infections have become more commonplace and prevalent. Unfortunately, a global virus pandemic has been evident recently with the onset of coronavirus. Interestingly, this virus became active at a time when the world was steeped in abusive power play and apathy. Viruses initially belong to the Neptune archetype; however the way in which a virus transmits and alters the body's DNA belongs to the Pluto archetype.

Karmic Redress: Pluto afflictions are often lingering and long–lasting. Initially, it can be perceived that during a period of illness or disease * Pluto is 'calling in' all of his pending debts. This notion is often very relevant when an illness or disease proves to be terminal and therefore fatal. Pluto–type illness and disease leaves within its wake impairment within the soul; which continues to affect the physical body throughout the course of future evolution. This means that weaknesses within the physical organs that have been afflicted throughout previous incarnations become evident throughout the soul's current incarnation, unless transformation (rebirth) at the soul (heart) level systematically occurs.

Ashes (Memories): Lunar memories are translucent and often fragmented. That is often the reason why we cannot hold on to, or remember our dreams in the morning, because the Moon presides over our dreams during the hours of sleep. Neptune transmits the dreams in the state we call unconsciousness. Pluto's memories however are much more defined. Thus, they are often latent and meaningful, and they often display ways to achieve rebirth (transformation). Pluto–orientated memories invariably occur when the physical body, the psychological profile and the soul have been afflicted in some way; this is when the term Pluto's ashes become more significant. This is partly why nightmares, and highly charged emotional and reclusive guilt dreams are frequent occurrences during extensive periods of illness and disease.

Dreams that involve sexual intercourse sometimes leading to premature ejaculation and orgasms when in the unconscious state of sleep are orchestrated by Pluto via Neptune. This type of dream can often be the result of sexual dysfunction, dissatisfaction or even frustration in the here and now, which can, in the long term, have a drastic effect upon the psychological bodies (the crown chakra). In addition, this type of dream is representative of karmic fragments that have become lodged within the long–term memory; and therefore denote sexual encounters from a previous incarnation. Realistically, these pleasurable but obsessive memories can leave an emotional imprint within the psyche, which can eventually transmute into ashes that are representative of loss and depression. Achieving rebirth via contemplation will help to distil these kinds of memories.

Many of us retain our memories indefinitely, thus making them the principle foundation for the present and in some cases for the future. Reliving our lives especially in a bygone era, rather than embracing the present, is essentially the psychological cornerstone that spawns disorders such as dementia and Parkinson's disease, as well a litany of other psychological disorders, and even heart conditions.

* *At this point it is important to point out the difference between illness and disease. Conceptually, illness is a psychological feeling of being unwell with or without the presence of a disease, whereas a disease is a diagnosable condition that is characterized by the condition of the body.*

Conversion

Pluto's nucleus, as with all the planets in the cosmos, is comprised of many leading facets, which are all touched upon throughout Part 1. Thus, these Pluto dimensions are intended to nudge the psyche towards psychological progression and spiritual advancement, hence the power of transformation. Transformation is Pluto's sine qua none at the evolutionary–spiritual level of consciousness (see diagram 1 below).

However, when the flow of life begins to stagnate, it is often at the transition of physical and psychological deterioration that illness and disease begins to envelop the body — highlighting the onset of Pluto–related infirmities.

Diagram 1: Pluto's Sphere (Nucleuses) of Evolution

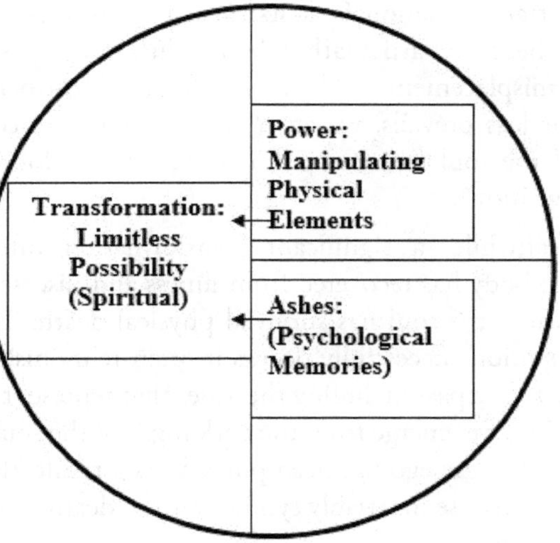

Preserving the Ashes

In a high percentage of cases, many unwittingly conserve Pluto's ashes; and this becomes especially noticeable during the third phase or cycle of physicality — memories representing an assemblage of temptations that once presented themselves upon the path of life. This is particularly relevant during the teenage and twenties years.

The third phase or cycle represents the period leading up to the (third Saturn return), hence maturity.[5] In simple terms, the ashes represent our deeper and more significant memories — holding on to them for the purpose of reminiscing — particularly in the final phases of physicality maturity. The final phase of physical life is the period or cycle that transgresses beyond the (third Saturn return).[6]

Maturity is more often than not the transitional period when we recollect our thoughts, reflect and thus submerge ourselves in the latent depths of these memoiristic ashes. It is also the cycle when Pluto's influence via its ultimate element of significant transformation is at its most powerful. Reflections of the past become particularly relevant during periods of illness, disease, misplacement and loss. Therefore, in those periods when illness or loss prevails, we enter into what is termed the dark night of the soul (see Part 3 for more information about this deep transition).

Meanwhile, a significant transformation often follows when the body has recovered from illness and disease, and even loss, because the soul has survived physical death. Thus, when transformation successfully occurs it often relinquishes all connections to the past including the ashes that represent our memories. When we emerge from the dark night of the soul, we do so knowing that the ego has been purged. As a result, the onset of illness and disease invariably symbolizes the death or the absolving of the ego.

The Spiritual (Evolutionary) Significance of Maturity: Maturity represents the portion of physicality when realistically we are destined to reclaim, in the name of remembrance, our spiritual heritage — preparing for our return to the spirit world. Once again, this is what is meant by 'rising out of the ashes of the earlier life,' as told throughout the mythical legend of the Phoenix, which is a very Pluto–orientated and transformational notion. Ideally, maturity is the segment of life when we are bound by conscience to relinquish our bygone memories, because the memories of all our past doings are automatically recorded in the matrix of the spiritual heart (soul) — intended for the life review. The life review occurs once we re–establish our power, and our connection to the world of spirit. Unfortunately, when the body has passed from a lingering disease or illness it drains the soul of its fundamental power.

Psychologically, it is no easy feat to relinquish the past. Pluto, similar to its shadow planet Mars, represents the power of courage, determination and strength of character, but at a much higher level of consciousness. Therefore, it takes courage and determination to 'let go' of the past.

Unfortunately, once dis–eases such as dementia, Parkinson's disease and sexual transmissions such as AIDS get a grip so to speak (see Part 3), which they do by significantly altering and transmuting the body's DNA, the natural process of physical renouncement is suspended in physicality, and is reflected this way once in spirit.

The Power of Past Events

Holding onto the past in physicality represents power that is controllable; and it is power that is safe, because for the most part, the past signifies a collection of concealed images that add a sense of jubilation to the life. This is a measure that is only temporary, and has little or no solidity, therefore it represents illusion. And illusion (involution) is a characteristic of Neptune (Pluto's mythical brother), whereas Pluto symbolizes evolution, the very foundation for transformation, which requires awareness and strength of character.

The power associated with past events is a further example of why Pluto–orientated illnesses and diseases are often long–lasting concerns in the here and now. Furthermore, the indiscernible seeds representative of illness and disease are transmitted throughout many generations of lifetimes, and often throughout eternity. This is why we can often relate to an illness or a disease in the present as karmic déjà vu; because we have no doubt experienced something similar in the past. By the same token, this is why I have blended medical matters with the concept of evolution.

The Ashes of Destruction: In addition, Pluto–orientated infirmities are often triggered by lingering memories that have become psychologically snared and fragmented in the buffers that house the long–term memory. Lingering memories, particularly those of a negative disposition (the ashes of destruction), pervade the body in much the same way as those toxic emotions that are Neptunian in nature. Hence, negative memories are often the catalyst for gastro intestinal problems (see Part 3 for more information). Psychological snared memories prevent us from accessing more of the brain's capacity.

Illness and Disease Examined Further: Dementia sufferers in particular retain defined, and in some cases confused memories of the past, which they hold on to relentlessly — often taking them into the spirit world. This will, in turn, prevent the soul from progressing onwards. Metaphorically speaking, and because of their confused memories, dementia sufferers have brains that have simply 'turned to ashes'. Undertaking a lifetime of intense creative endeavours will prevent the brain from turning to ashes.

The Psychological Power Net

It can also be said that holding on to memories is reminiscent of Pluto's familiar and psychological power net that is always karmically attached to the body, and which is for the purpose of physical containment. As I indicated previously, Pluto doesn't like to let anything go. The only problem with this power net is that when the soul chooses to, or obsesses over returning to physical incarnation, as opposed to remaining in spirituality; it brings with it the evolutionary memories [ashes] that set a precedent for the onset of illness and disease, and in most cases, psychological disorders caused by the abuse of power.

However, when the soul chooses to remain in the spirit world the ashes (memories) are purged and thus contained in what can only be best described as a kind of spiritual funeral urn.[7] Once again, this scenario is the true representation to the Phoenix that rises out of the ashes; and in this case the ashes represent physicality. Once transformation (higher awareness) occurs in the life of an individual, illness and disease will never become a troubling factor again. This is Pluto's foundation for core truths. For more information about core truths see section 1 in Part 3.

In addition, 'not letting go' of the past in the here and now can not only lead to a litany of psychological distresses, but it can lead to problems relating to the gut, which are all infirmities concerned with Pluto; and are explained in detail throughout Part 3.

The Power of Renewable Power

Pluto is the planet that rarely renounces anything that contains hidden or buried power (truths). Instead, Pluto's power increases exponentially throughout its cycles of evolution. Pluto's cycles and purpose of evolution is representative to each sign it tenants in the zodiac (see Part 4). Furthermore, Pluto's power is renewable — renewing its power at the beginning of an evolutionary cycle — plugging itself in to an entirely new sign of the zodiac — hence a season for ashes (see Part 4 for more information about Pluto's tenure of the signs).

During the course of an average lifetime, Pluto traverses roughly four signs of the zodiac. So, from the moment we are born to the moment we leave the Earth plane Pluto's power is steadily being renewed, meaning that we should have grasped the need and importance of transformation by the time we reach sixty years of age. The quality of the sign Pluto tenants at birth indicates how we can best achieve transformation in our lives. The sign Pluto tenants at death determines the qualities and purpose of the spiritual realm that the soul will ultimately frequent.

Modus

The Pluto mission (should we chose to accept it) is to rise from the ashes and leave them behind where they belong — in the past. Moreover, we have the opportunity, courtesy of Pluto, to alter our genetic coding via its generational program of transformation. This is achieved through Pluto's journey through the particular segment of the natal chart it frequents during the course of a physical lifetime. Ultimately, we can orchestrate transformation through the development of higher reasoning and awareness, which can be honed within every life cycle (the periods between the Saturn returns). Thus, the principle of transformation allows us to progress physically, psychologically, and perhaps more importantly spiritually. These three constituents are the fundamental cornerstones for evolution.

Ascending from the ashes signifies the evolutionary provocation of the mythical Phoenix — Pluto's emblem of transformation. Today, the classical tale of the Phoenix is merely a metaphor for hope. Hope symbolizes physical, psychological and spiritual transformation, as the keys that will unlock the evolution of the soul. These are points in question in which Maria emphasizes most descriptively in the forthcoming Part 2 of this publication.

Transformation and Evolution

Transformation or soul conversion is Pluto's genetic code; and represents by far the largest segment that comprises its nucleus (see diagram). Furthermore, transformation from illness and disease, which transmutes as higher reasoning, is the subject matter of the entire book. So, acquiring both the will and the necessity that will implement this cosmic overhaul is explained in both a medical, and an evolutionary capacity.

Briefly I would like to return to my original question of why I have blended medical matters with the concept of evolution, which is a self–generating force? Simply speaking, illness and disease have always been prevalent throughout civilization; therefore illness and disease are considered to be evolutionary factors. A classic example of when evolutionary transformation occurs is in the aftermath of an illness or disease — when the body is in recovery. Thus, there is often a gradual but powerful shift in thinking; and in the psychological outlook on life. In some cases, especially after a brain related injury, there is a shift that takes place allowing more of the brain's capacity to be accessed.

Recently, a psychological and an evolutionary shift of this very nature occurred; and one that transpired en masse (see next section on coronavirus for more information). Psychologically speaking, what was taking place during this unprecedented period throughout evolution was a psychological and healing transmutation, hence a juxtaposition in individual and collective consciousness, which was all part of an overall shift within the generational framework of humankind.

Conclusion

Compiled in two separate and compelling parts, Pluto's season for ashes has been assembled not only in evolutionary format in order to aid spiritual progression, but it has been formulated for use as a medical and diagnostic tool; and as a way of indentifying Pluto–orientated obstacles in the natal chart. The book also examines ways in which we can contemplate certain Pluto–based therapies that act as a prevention for illness and disease, and as a major catalyst for transformation.

Examined in utmost detail are the congenital and synthetic infirmities that are associated with Pluto, such as colon and psychological disorders, and which are backed up by the appropriate case studies. This journey into the heart of Pluto from a medical viewpoint has been examined by me.

In addition, in the forthcoming Part 2 of this book, An Evolutionary Viewpoint, it examines the soul's purpose and its evolutionary journey, and its eventual destiny as spirit. It looks at the evolutionary dimensions of both expansion and contraction — components that have brought the collective and the Earth to its current state of transition.

Moreover, it examines significant world events that have shaped and reshaped the course of history. Part 2 features many of the iconic figures and world leaders who have orchestrated global shifts in power that again have brought us to our current state of evolution and potential extinction. This intrinsic journey throughout the heart of evolution has been examined by my guest astrological writer Maria Stiopei, and will be published in due course. Maria's evolutionary knowledge and insight is nothing short of exemplary.

References

1. The fountain of knowledge or the fountain of wisdom as it is mostly referred to have mostly been considered to be a mondegreen.
2. Long–term memories or ashes.
3. Reference to the innate abilities of Christina Richter.
4. Information source the Akashic Records.
5. The first Saturn return occurs between 28—30 years of age. The second Saturn return occurs between 57—59 years of age.
6. The third Saturn return occurs between 86—88 years of age. It is highly unlikely that a person will reach a fourth Saturn return.
7. Information recorded in the Akashic Records.

Section 2

Covid-19

Covid–19

"In every crisis, doubt or confusion, take the higher path — the path of compassion, courage, understanding and love".

Amit Ray, *Nonviolence: The Transforming Power*

Before I begin it is important to mention that this feature was compiled during the spring of 2020, when the progression of the virus was at its global peak.

Throughout 2020, the world gave rise to the onset of a so-called deadly phenomenon adeptly named Covid–19, or as some would prefer to call it coronavirus. Perhaps, the main reason why Covid–19 established such a 'powerful foothold' in such a justifiably short space of time is because of a distinct absence of spiritual light (heartfelt joy) in the world. Heartfelt joy requires no external stimulus; it simply exists through the power of unconditional love, which is also absent in many parts of the world today. Unfortunately, a large percentage of humankind prefer to invest in the negative components of greed, arrogance, apathy and aggression, which only exacerbates the negative effects of illness and disease, and in particular Covid–19, which in this case was influenced for the most part by Pluto.

Primarily, Covid–19 affects the lungs, therefore making it difficult to breathe properly. In addition, Covid–19 brings about prolonged periods of coughing. In severe cases however, a persistent spell of coughing can lead to overall blood loss. The virus also affects the body's senses; particularly with the sensations of taste and smell — rendering them neutral. Covid–19 also bombards the body's DNA — altering its genetics. It is important to point out here that these are some of the classic symptoms normally associated with radiation sickness, a definitive characteristic of Pluto.

According to my understanding from the *Akashic Records* (see footnote), Covid–19 is an evolutionary condition that dates back over 68,000 years — to the conclusion of Atlantis — initially spawned via the process of cloning. Cloning is a process that creates copies of organisms from cells and DNA fragments.

It has been widely suggested that China was responsible for the outbreak of Covid–19; and China, according to many historian minds, has close links to Atlantis. It is interesting however that Covid–19 first became evident during the conjunction of Saturn (cells) and Pluto (DNA) in 2020. Hence, this powerful cosmic system of hierarchies was particularly *prevalent* in China's chart. Because of the generational effects that are generated by Saturn-Pluto conjunctions and oppositions, they are often experienced long before the culmination point. Therefore, it is quite possible that this virus has been around much longer than originally anticipated. The following are my observations on the effects of Saturn's conjunction with Pluto.

Footnote: Reference to Edgar Cayce, H Blavatsky and Theosophy were all users of the *Akashic Records*. The *Akashic Records* are an infinite source of knowledge.

Organisms

COVID–19 is an organism; or to be more precise, it is a microorganism.[1] This particular microorganism is unique because it *emulated* the violence and the greed that is widespread upon the Earth. Many people became more aware of this underlying factor when Mars conjoined Pluto in mid-2020. This is perhaps further evidence suggesting why the virus killed so many in such a terrible way. The solution to altering the negative effects of COVID–19, as with all organisms and microorganisms, is to alter its genetic code with love (Venus, Pluto's polarity planet); and transform it (Pluto) to co-exist in harmony with the Earth and its inhabitants. However, this can only be achieved through raising collective consciousness (Neptune) and heartfelt contemplation (Pluto).

Deep breathing exercises (Pluto), such as breath meditation and colour visualization (Neptune), will help to realign the virus. These spiritual and ancient techniques will also help the body to protect against the effects of Covid–19.

Origins and Augmentations

On reflection, COVID–19 is commonly believed to be a genetically modified dis-ease. Furthermore, it has left an epidemic of fear, suppression and death in its wake. The disease has also accelerated the evolutionary changes that were occurring around the globe long before the onset of this crisis, such as financial meltdown (Pluto). Similar to all viruses, Covid–19 will no doubt mutate.

However, in light of some recent and perhaps more credible information that came to the forefront of the media in September 2020, and which has been drawn up by the resourceful and respected climate scientists and climatologists who coordinate their findings with the *World Health Organisation* (WHO), the long-term effects of coronavirus have 'most likely' been amplified by the deleterious circumstances associated with climate change.[2] Likewise, this evidence suggests that Covid–19 will mutate, because the warmer it gets the better the virus thrives.

There is very little evidence to suggest that Covid–19 will simply disappear. There is strong evidence to suggest however that this disease *will* remain an extant and powerful influence. Thus, it will prevail in the shadows for long periods of time before remerging in the form of new variants, whereby it will orchestrate a new wave of fear and panic. Furthermore, its impact upon society will continue to sow the seeds of suspicion, especially concerning its dark and pathological origins.

As a result, this dis–ease will continue to spawn the negative characteristics of uneasiness and apprehension, especially throughout many governments, for generations to come. Therefore, Covid–19 will be considered to be representative of a *defective* evolutionary pattern evident in the greater domain of Pluto — given rise to by the Saturn-Pluto conjunction of 2020.

Statistics and Repercussions

In the initial aftermath that followed the first wave of the disease, occurring between March and September 2020, many succumbed to depression, anxiety and other mental health disorders. Medical astrology determines that these negative characteristics are designated as both Saturn and Pluto afflictions. With both of these planets in close proximity to each other for the greater part of 2020; this pivotal year that heralds the beginning of a new decade would therefore prove to be a period of unprecedented change and transformation — unlikely to be forgotten. Transformation in typical Pluto style often comes with a price tag attached to it. Never before in our 'modern evolution' have we, as a collective consciousness, experienced deep-set fear quite like this.[3]

Meanwhile, and long before the advent of social distancing became the recognized normality, humankind *had* become extremely *distanced* from his/her collective and spiritual roots. This transition continued to occur throughout generations. Interestingly, the wholly new concept referred to as 'social distancing' belongs to the Venus-Pluto polarity; hence Venus (social) and Pluto (distancing). In effect, Covid–19 became the transitional element that began *prodding* at this stagnating period in our evolution. The after-effects from this disease will, I'm sure, begin to secure the infirmed roots of civilization once again. As a result, a new era of unity and awareness will eventually dawn from the mire of uncertainty; hence, seeds of transformation. Perhaps this will be the transitional point of the much-prophesized Age of Aquarius? However, some would remark that this marks the end of civilization.

Planetary Mechanisms

Looking ahead, Covid–19 will no doubt prove to be the 'major catalyst' for a worldwide underlying adjustment. The cosmic instruments for this transformational impetus, as previously indicated, were most likely Saturn and Pluto, with the inclusion of 'Neptune'. The influence of these planets was slightly maximized by a fallen (weak) Jupiter from a Capricorn station. The effects from a closely-connected Saturn and Pluto were stirred up further by a very determined and fiery Mars in exaltation — transpiring throughout the latter half of 2020.

Saturn-Pluto

The Saturn-Pluto transit of 2020 was considered by many to be the principal catalyst for the Covid-19 outbreak. Moreover, Covid-19 has been biologically *manufactured* in such a way that its ultimate purpose was to 'wake up the world' from its unconscious slumber. In China, where the virus was first detected, Saturn was notated, gradually traversing a path towards omnipotent Pluto — ready to conclude their monumental conjunction from their combined Capricorn station. Thus, the ensuing exactitude would trigger the presence of the virus worldwide. A solitary exactitude of this transit occurred on the 12th of January 2020 at 22 degrees of Capricorn.[4] According to the late Ivy Goldstein-Jacobson, 22 degrees of any sign raises the prospect of public awareness. Later, Jupiter would *solidify* and *unify* the dominant effects of the conjunction.

Throughout the pandemic, consensus suggests that COVID–19 has been around longer than previously thought. It is therefore conceivable that the disease first made its entrance when Saturn entered Capricorn at zero degrees — zero is an anaretic degree (the degree of fate). This makes perfect sense because Saturn was the architect of pandemics and plaques before Neptune was awarded this prominent disposition, and Saturn did connect with Neptune before it conjoined Pluto. However, with regards to the disease being around much earlier, I was personally debilitated with a mysterious viral infection in January 2019. Whatever it was it most definitely carried with it all of the physical hallmarks of coronavirus, including the inability to breath properly.

Imprecision=Mutation

In most cases, outer planetary transits provide three durations of exactitude, similar to transiting planets impressing upon natal planets. There is a saying in astrology, and that is: 'the third time pays for it all'. In effect, the third exactitude secures the potential that is emitted by the aspect; and thus it releases a window of opportunity. The first exactitude is often the worst, and depending on the planets concerned, it strikes like a bolt from the blue, because we are often *unprepared.* By the onset of the second exactitude (the retrograde phase) we have become more aware, and this phase often allows us to return to where it first began, and make corrections and enhancements. By the time the third phase occurs we should be beginning to improve the situation or circumstances, hence we are beginning to *absorb* the message being imparted by the aspect.

In the case of the Saturn–Pluto conjunction, there was no second and third phase. Some refer to this as imprecision. Thus, the impending consequences are still continuing to emerge, as a result. Throughout 2020, the UK experienced the upshot of

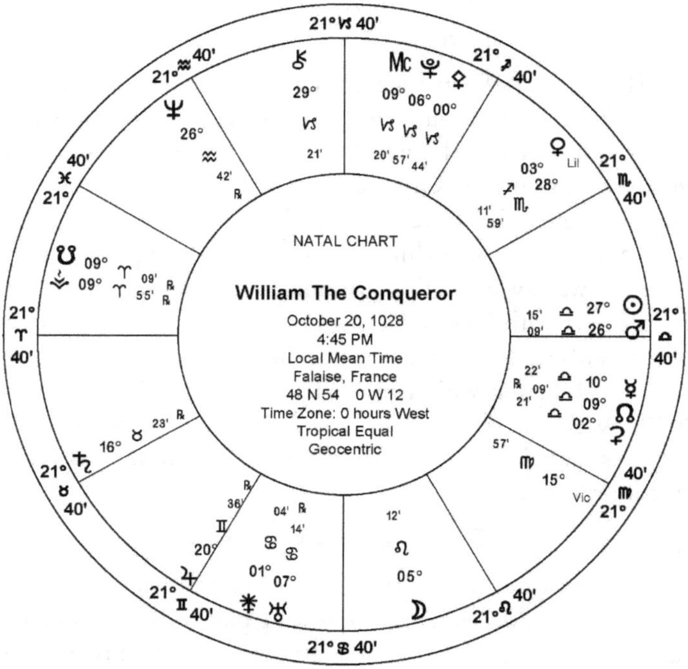

imprecision via an unprepared government — proving later to be reckless and foolish. This alignment occurred in the United Kingdom's domicile tenth house. I prefer to use the 1066 chart (see chart). It is fair to suggest that the UK will suffer more than most nations because the government were simply indisposed, and it remained that way all through the crisis.

Meanwhile, I think it's quite likely that the virus will mutate *significantly* in the UK. This is due in part to the fact that there was only a single exactitude of the Saturn-Pluto conjunction. As Mars entered it retrograde phase from its Aries station in August 2020 — moving across the UK's Ascendancy, and then squaring Saturn and Pluto in September, through to October, anger and unrest towards the UK government increased exponentially. However, this also became a worldwide characteristic.

Jupiter-Saturn-Pluto

During the initial stages of the pandemic, a distinct lack of joyfulness became ever noticeable when Jupiter, the planet of joviality, made its conjunction to Pluto in April 2020. Jupiter, from its Capricorn station, was merely projecting an alarming image of the deep division and the hopelessness that was magnified throughout the world since its last passage through Capricorn in 2008. Thus, from its debilitated station in Capricorn, Jupiter, the planet of abundance and good fortune, is *unable* to express itself easily. Instead, a deep sense of fearfulness and panic began to *expand* throughout the world — creating a confluence of apprehension and pathological dis-ease. Hence, this marked a vexatious period in our collective evolution that would prove to be noticeably *incurable*.

It wasn't all doom and gloom, however. The Jupiter–Pluto conjunction meant that humankind was presented with a 'period of prolonged contemplation', which, for some, led to personal expansion and transformation. Thus, for the most part, an overall shift in *thinking* occurred. Hence, this psychological swing in consciousness would, in time, prove to be the key to unlocking the pandemic. Alongside Saturn, Pluto effectively fractured the heart of societies by destroying the world economy. Pluto also gave rise to political and environmental rebirth. More and more people preferred to work from their home environment, which meant less pollution in towns and cities. In addition, governments began to flounder, as their sublime incompetence and inequalities were exposed.

Pluto has shifted its energy towards exposing greed, gross materialism, suspicion and totalitarianism. Perhaps the big question now is: will Saturn's steady but concretized influence begin to slowly rebuild the foundations of the world, beginning in the latter half of its Capricorn station? From its Aquarius station however, and alongside Jupiter in December 2020, Saturn has the potential to gradually rebuild and reinfuse with cautious optimism the fragile infrastructure of our collective consciousness.

An Evolutionary Farewell

The onset of Covid–19 may well also be attributed to Pluto's grand finale in Capricorn, thus in the final degrees of this sign. However, before the planet of regeneration ploughs its furrow in Aquarius and emphasizes our need to create deep and lasting collective connections, this concluding transition in the final degrees of Capricorn may prove to be one that gives rise to an overall sense of awareness and reckoning. Perhaps these characteristics weren't noticeable before but may come to light when Pluto reaches the anaretic twenty-ninth degree of the sign. Twenty–nine degrees of Capricorn might mean that we begin to learn to *think* from the heart before orchestrating any action that would prove to be damaging.

China

The triple conjunction of Jupiter, Saturn and Pluto was the initial 'trigger' that projected the virus on a *global* capacity. In China, however, where the virus had first occurred, the conjunction took place in China's twelfth house of karma and stealth (see equal house chart). Many countries have blamed China for the proliferation of the pandemic. The twelfth house would prove to be the 'breeding ground' for this chronically-induced virus. In medical astrology the twelfth house is concerned mostly with chronic illness. Traditionally, the twelfth house reveals other underlying factors. For example, it was also widely reported in the media that the authorities in China covertly 'blanketed' the actual death rate, and in addition, they covered up the length of time they had actually been under the influence of the virus. These falsifications are cloak and dagger reverberations directly concerned with the twelfth house of secrets and lies.

Other impending factors include Jupiter's tenure of the twelfth house, which is debilitated in Capricorn. Overall, this means that a lack of joy is evident within the nation. The sign of Capricorn

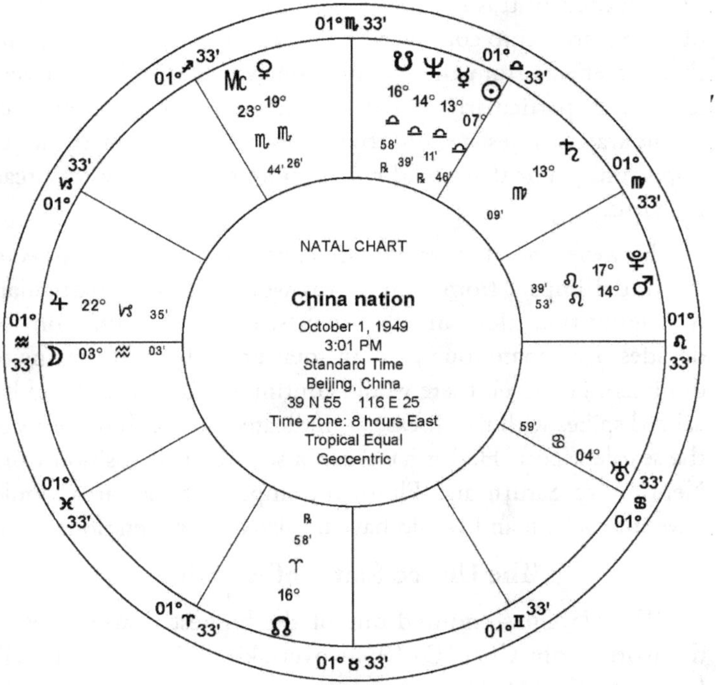

Neptune and Pluto are in what is termed as a 'parallel of latitude'.[5] This type of configuration can indicate that the effects of the virus will mutate further, or the deception will go on longer than anticipated. Before Neptune was deemed the modern ruler of viruses, Saturn was the overseer of plagues, epidemics and pandemics. Transit Neptune resided at 18 degrees of Pisces in China's second house of security when Saturn and Pluto made their historic sextile connections in December 2019. This was around the time China first made the headlines about the virus. Neptune is of course the natural ruler of the twelfth house.

It is fair to say that during the pandemic, China's security was compromised and weakened (Neptune). According to William Lilly, 18 degrees of Pisces is a dark and afflicted degree[6].

The darkness of this particular degree tainted the overall effects of the Saturn-Pluto conjunction further via the sextile, meaning that the effects from the conjunction would be felt for a very long time, particularly as the impact would occur in an economic way. Sextiles are concerned mostly with the emergence of opportunity, but that could represent an opportunity to spread the virus.

However, because sextiles are considered to be *soft* aspects, the initial impact from coronavirus would not be a particularly lengthy transition; in other words, it wouldn't drag on for decades. I estimate four years in total until the virus begins to diminish. However, there would continue to be isolated and localized spikes with the disease, as indicated on the four points of the sextile aspect. Had it had been a square or opposition from Neptune to Saturn and Pluto, the impact of the virus would have intensified; and would have persisted for generations.

The United States of America

The USA has endured one of the highest deaths rates in the world from COVID–19 — overtaking China and Brazil. In my analysis of the USA, I have used the Rudhyar chart in order to specify why the death rate has been phenomenal (see inner wheel below). At the time of writing this the USA was experiencing a Neptune opposition and a Pluto return (see outer wheel below). As a result of these major planetary configurations, I would ascertain that the USA chart is in fact a Covid–19 projection chart.

Looking further at the transit chart (outer wheel) the Jupiter-Saturn-Pluto transiting conjunction took place in the USA's second house, which denotes the nation's finances, possessions and security. Medically speaking, the second house represents the throat, but in the case of America it represents its infrastructure, hence the skin that holds the nation together. COVID–19 breached and tore a big hole in its powerful armour — catapulting the nation into an enormous recession — throwing millions

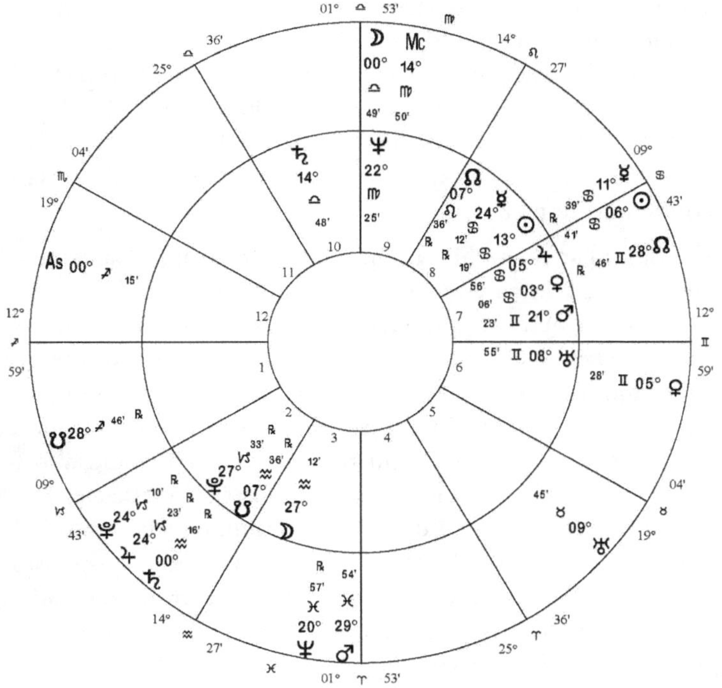

Inner wheel: Dane Rudhyar USA natal chart: 7/4/1776. 5:13 PM LMT, mean node
Outer wheel: Transits 6/27/2020, 9:39 PM Koch houses, mean node

into mass unemployment. Many spoke out about the way the virus was managed, many demonstrated, and many spoke out about racial abuse. Alas, this collective expression of the nation's throat chakra fell on deaf ears, because no one in authority was listening.

On the 12th of January 2020 the Saturn–Pluto transit conjunction opposes the nation's Mercury at 22 degrees of Cancer, after previously opposing the Sun and Jupiter. Right from the beginning the powers to be never took the crisis seriously, because the USA does not advocate the use of *limitation*. This was even after it was reported that the USA could become the nation that incurs the highest rate of deaths from coronavirus in the world, the country still dismissed it as mere propaganda. On the 27th of June, an exact conjunction of transiting Jupiter and Pluto opposed the nation's Mercury. Furthermore, transit Neptune opposed its natal position from the third house of communication.

So, what does this mean? Firstly, it means that America speaks loudly in an erroneous manner, because the USA has an inflated and obsessive president in the form of Donald Trump. He 'mistakenly' fails to acknowledge the true extent of the situation and has been in self–denial from the very beginning. The expression of self-denial is projected further by woolly Neptune's opposition and its position in the chart, which would also seriously affect the nation's tourism industry. In essence, fewer people would freely visit due to the continuing spread of COVID–19. Secondly, the Neptune opposition could be responsible for causing a split; hence a divide of opinion within the nation, which is already fragmented, and which would be catastrophic for its future relations with the rest of the world. We have already witnessed this trickery and deceit in the polls — leading up to the November 2020 presidential elections.

Potentially, all of this planetary movement could severely *weaken* America's power and dominance in the world. Consequently, very few nations will even flinch when the USA flexes its muscles. This would be particularly so when the Pluto return reaches its exactitude. Donald Trump however is correct in as much that "America must become great again", but Neptune and Pluto may well have other ideas about this!

Transmission

The cosmos doesn't impart illness and disease upon the people; the planets merely project the overall current level of consciousness upon the Earth at any given time. However, speaking metaphorically, Pluto contracted the virus from Neptune via the spirituous sextile, and transmitted it to Saturn. Confusion (Neptune), fear (Saturn) and death (Pluto) would then proliferate similar to the virus. At the peak of this crisis, which occurred at varying stages throughout the world, Pluto remained at 24 degrees of Capricorn. According to William Lilly 24 degrees of Capricorn is a dark and pitted degree[7], which ordinarily will 'stretch out' Pluto's dark shadow pathological effect.

Emergence

According to Hippocrates[8], "all disease begins in the gut". Furthermore, and according to the World Health Organisation (WHO), 'Covid-19 starts initially in the gut' or the second brain. The Pluto-ruled colon is the primary organ in the gut, and the colon is a magnet for viruses. In effect, all viruses are 'transformed through default' in the colon.[9] Scientifically speaking, a virus is a submicroscopic agent that replicates only inside the living cells of an organism. It contains alternate codes that reconfigure the body's natural genetic coding; and as we are now aware, genetic coding falls under the transmissional guise of Pluto.

Rebirth

The evolution of humankind is about to change; and undergo a monumental transformation. This will become more of a reality once Pluto begins its sojourn of Aquarius in 2023-2024. Meanwhile, the world has to adapt to the changes imparted by coronavirus. It will no doubt be an upheaval, but it can also be a fulcrum (the seed of collective consciousness). Similar to the AIDS virus (Pluto) and the flu (Neptune), we will have to simply learn to live with COVID–19.

Chart Data:

- Event chart, Coronation of William the Conquer UK chart, 25 December 1066, 12:00 Noon, Westminster, London, UK, Placidus Houses, Mean Node.
- People's Republic of China Natal Chart, 1 October 1949, 15:01 PM, Beijing, China, Equal House system, Mean Node.
- Inner wheel, United States Rudhyar event chart, 4 July 1776, 17:13 PM, Philadelphia, USA, Koch Houses, Mean Node.
- Outer wheel, transits 27 June 2020, 21:39 PM, Boulder, Colorado, USA, Koch Houses, Mean Node.

References

[1]: Microorganisms (organisms) are sentient, and have been on Earth longer in some cases than humans; therefore their spiritual roots are set firmly in the evolutionary soil.

[2]: Climate change is a sensitive subject, and one that pervades the hearts of many an in-depth and motivated soul; and who has the good of future generations at heart.

[3]: The duration deemed the 'modern evolution' is the period that began when Pluto entered Leo in 1939 — the beginning of conservative activism. This current period in evolution will be *modernized* further when Pluto enters Aquarius in 2024 — beginning a wholly new evolutionary phase that characterises conservative intellectualism.

[4]: A single exactitude of an outer planetary alignment is fairly unusual but not unheard of.

[5]: Parallel occurs when both planets are equidistant from the equator in the same direction.

[6]: Christian Astrology page 116.

[7]: Christian Astrology page 116.

[8]: Hippocrates was deemed the father of modern medicine.

[9]: Information courtesy of The World Health Organisation (WHO).

Pluto's Long-Seated Associations Congenital and Synthetic

Pluto (DNA) requires a biological template in order to characterize its congenital method of human sequencing

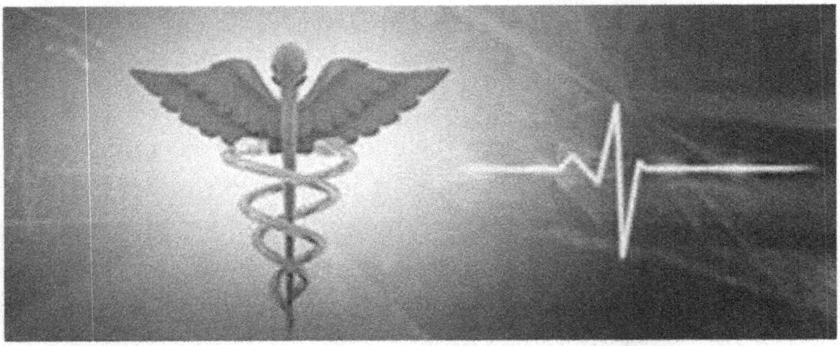

Pluto: Death and Rebirth

"Pluto explores uncomfortable themes like madness in the family, abuse, violence, the seriously disturbed, insanity, prostitution and amputation".[1]

"Sensitive people usually love deeply and hate deeply. They don't know any other way to live than by extremes because their emotional thermostat is broken".

Shannon L. Alder

Following on…when the emotional thermostat is broken, Pluto casts a dark mire of indignation upon the natal chart. This displeasure often represents an underlying cause for illness and disease, particularly psychological illness. The key is to repair the thermostat by purging the emotions, and to transcend the Pluto archetype with the assistance of Neptune; thus projecting its dark energy towards the light of hope, truth and positive idealism. Hence, these are the seeds through which progressive evolution germinates. This in-depth section outlines how this can be best achieved.

Evolutionary Transits

Pluto transits symbolize *transformation* of the mind, body and the soul. Thus, in medical astrology Pluto transits mean that the physical organs, particularly those under Pluto's rulership like the colon, for example, are undergoing powerful changes. However, if the physical and mental bodies are out of condition at the time of any incurring transits, illness and disease will establish a powerful grip over the entire body. In the case of the colon, cancer and other infirmities will become evident.

Medical conditions that reverberate from the heart of a Pluto transit are essentially congenital signatures, meaning that somewhere in our ancestral past there was someone who possessed similar genetic sequencing to our own. The aim during a Pluto transit is to alter our genetic coding in order to sever its vital link to illness and disease.

The Dark Pathological Cauldron

In medical astrology, Pluto represents the dark pathological cauldron – a cauldron that is being 'steadily fired' by omnipotent Pluto. Pluto brings to mind purging, exorcizing, and releasing buried power or core truths – core truths that are initially immersed within the recesses of the shadowy and tenebrous cauldron. Thus, if this buried power is not emancipated and brought into the light, it perishes, and illness and disease are born from the ensuing blackness housed within the cauldron. An example of buried power that had perished within the heart seed (nucleus) of so many souls was recently displayed by the high percentage of deaths during the COVID-19 outbreak in 2020 (see Section 2). In Pluto terms, this was unprecedented.

In practical terms, Pluto's core truths represent a bottomless structure that holds within it the evolutionary transcripts of the mind, body and the soul.

The Colon

The colon, can be deemed as the body's pathological cauldron, because according to statistics, ninety percent of all illnesses and diseases are *seeded* in the bowel. When conceptual power and emotional truths remain buried and trapped in the colon, diseases such as bowel cancer, IBS and diverticulitis are spawned; and thus they become anchored in this prodigious physical organ – extending their dissentient influence outwards to affect other organs and soft tissues. Being a major part of the reproductive system, the colon is the most sensitive organ in the body and is therefore easily compromised by negative thoughts and emotions (for more information about the colon see Illness and Disease further on).

Similar to the purpose of the pathological cauldron, the colon represents a storage facility; and in this case the body's emotional responses such as hate, anger, envy and jealousy all accumulate in this organ. Thus, Pluto brings to the surface the deeper and perhaps the darkest of all the emotions – to be transformed within the light of truth – regenerated into love, passion and endearment – the emotional cornerstones for keeping the colon and the body in perfect health.

Medical Conspectus

Popular consensus concludes that Pluto is the planet most associated with physical death. However, Pluto is perhaps most associated with the death of the psychological and emotional propensities, especially during lengthy periods of illness and disease. The psychological/emotional propensities are *housed* deep within the colon; they include the body's internal strength and will power – employed mostly for the purpose of physical and spiritual resurgence. Moreover, the colon is often referred to in some quarters as the second brain; hence the secondary brain that allows the individual to experience passion and emotional pleasure at a deeper and a more intense level of understanding. After all the Pluto-ruled sexual organs that are the catalysts for intense passion, and which denote physical pleasure are situated close to the colon. But similar to the physical brain, the colon is extremely *susceptible* to deep and disturbing pathological disorders.

The Dark Pit of Change

Pluto is firmly anchored in the mastery of transformation, which is an epitome of a higher emotional consciousness. Transformation is often deemed as unnerving to many because it means that some form of alteration and change must take place, especially from the everyday normalities and complacencies of life, before a new life can begin. However, for a great many of us, even the very thought of transformation can bring to the forefront of everyday physical reality the prospect of illness and disease, not to mention a mire of psychological and emotional distress.

The Death of the Ego

Unfortunately, when an individual descends into Pluto's dark pit; hence the dark pit that symbolizes the lowly and obscure predicament of change, the soul inevitably perishes. This psychological decline represents the death of the ego, which is one of Pluto's habitual penchants. The death of the ego diminishes the soul's energy throughout the physical body, thus causing dispirited disorders such as clinical depression. Today, clinical depression is by far the most common form of psychological/emotional inactivity to impose itself upon the will of the individual, and that of the collective consciousness. Depression, or psychological stagnation, is the root cause to a raft of other mental and physical infirmities such as Alzheimer's dementia and Parkinson's disease.

This section was written in early 2019. Thus, I anticipate that when Saturn, that symbolizes depression, and Pluto, that symbolizes the deeper emotions that can be a catalyst for depression, align in the first of their conjunctions in early 2020, it will act as a trigger, instigating a wave of depressive disorders that will proliferate, particular in the United Kingdom, which will propel an already fragmented NHS (National Health Service) into further meltdown and chaos. This powerful transit will be *elevated* in the UK chart, hence the tenth house. I always use the 25th of December, 12:00 Noon, 1066 for the UK chart (see relevant chart).

As a global evolutionary shift in consciousness is predicted to take place in 2020, the slow transformation of the NHS will be a part of an overall transformation that is occurring throughout every corner of the UK, and indeed the world. Gradual and circumspect transformation in the form of turmoil and instability is *steadily* transcending the rest of the world. The slow demise in overall health facilities will in turn create more depression and mental/psychological disorders. Thus, we are all being pressed to reclaim our real power, and no longer must we rely on outdated recourses.

The Measured Effects of Evolution

Pluto is considered to be an evolutionary planet, meaning its energies pertain towards slow development, prolonged advancement and measured growth. However, some would consider that slow development translates merely as the death of the earthly ego, because the earthly ego demands that everything in life must transpire with immediate effect. However, slow development is necessary for evolutionary growth because it *absolves* the ego.

Because we all exist in a fast-paced world, where impatience is widespread and extensive, illness and disease proliferate. Nowadays, the world is a swamp of emotional uncertainty where the intense yearning for abject requirement knows no bounds. This is perhaps why there are so many colon-related disorders present in the world today. Individually, many are simply not evolving. The concept of evolution (growth) has perhaps been augmented by the theory of natural selection – penned by Charles Darwin in The Origin of the Species.

Darwinism

While Darwin's Theory of Evolution is a relatively young archetype, the evolutionary worldview itself is as old as antiquity.

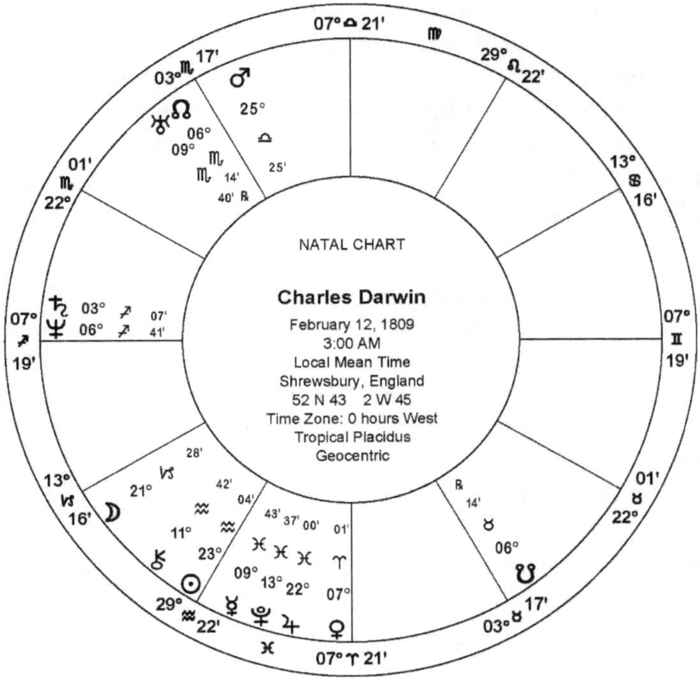

Not surprisingly then, Charles Darwin had a very pronounced Pluto in his chart, tenanting his third house of communication and writing, at thirteen degrees of intuitive Pisces (see relevant chart). Thirteen degrees of Pisces is extremely fortunate, according to the Christian astrologer William Lilly. This auspicious staging point would prove to be favourable in some way, especially in his later years. Darwin was fifty years old when The Origin of the Species was first published.

Darwin's evolutionary message, being circumjacent to his third house, had to be deep, resourceful, enlightening and meaningful, if it had any chance of being understood, and eventually accepted. In essence, his message was expressive, because he believed that all life is related and has descended from a common ancestor. I wonder whether this expanded belief and idealism was due to Black Moon rising on his Gemini descendant – a past life notion perhaps? Gemini, does after all, descends from a common ancestry, and in this case it is the Twins, which have become interconnected by a cosmic birth. Darwin also presumed that the development of life from non-life is purely naturalistic; hence he believed it is purely undirected. Gemini is the sign that is often *undirected*, and therefore one of its challenges is to be pivotal in thought.

In addition, Pluto squares the Ascendant; therefore, Darwin continually pressed home his theories onto an incredulous world. The third house is also a medical zone. Pluto is also besieged *loosely* between the natural polarity planets of Mercury and Jupiter; which also tenants the sign of Pisces on the cusp of the medical third house. In esoteric astrology, Pluto is the ruler of Pisces – transcending the third house into a very inventive and prolific zone. However, this heavily tenanted third house was also responsible for spoiling his health, which is often the price for achieving brilliance and insight.

Impoverished Health

Unfortunately, for most of his life Charles Darwin was an extremely sick man – enduring a raft of pathological and psychological disorders throughout life. Some of the conditions he suffered were chronic intestinal disorders, cyclic vomiting syndrome, and autonomic dysfunction that caused him to sweat *excessively*. These are all deemed as Pluto disorders; and the trigger was no doubt Pluto's besieged square to the Ascendant, which is lame and deficient according to William Lilly. Thus, Darwin had no success with conventional therapeutic treatments. In 1849, after being recommended, he indulged in a course of water therapy, which included cold salt baths. Although it had no direct success on his overall health, Darwin nevertheless believed that it helped to balance his psychological and his overall emotional health (Pluto).

Psychological Expansion

Pluto is the last known planet to exist in the physical cosmos; hence it is a trailing sphere. Esoteric studies determine that this 'cessation of the physical cosmos' is where the emotional and the psychological intellect are *spawned*. Therefore, Pluto's primary objective is to *hone* the phrenic intellect, and to purge the internal lake of psychic response. This internal lake is perhaps best described as a bottomless well in the infinite heart that gradually brings to the surface those deeper and metaphysical components such as extrasensory perception, paranormal consciousness and supernormal awareness. Purging this internal lake is considered, in the esoteric world, to be a 'rebirth of the soul's psychological faculties'. However, once this rebirth takes place the soul has a much better prospect of rising up from the dark vibrations that are invariably associated with illness and disease.

More often than not the purging of the emotions occurs during and after the soul/individual has experienced a period of psychological death known in some quarters as the 'dark night of the soul', which is explained in greater detail further on. The potential to hone one's psychological/emotional abilities occurs throughout the evolution of Pluto's more *pronounced* transits, which are considered to be a major rebirth, hence cosmic resurgence.

Cosmic Resurgence

Once the psychological/emotional faculties have been reinitialized (rebirth), through the reclaiming of Pluto's power, they can be further energized with the help of Mercury. Mercury is the leading sphere in the physical cosmos. Moreover, once the emotional and psychological bodies have been absolved, they can be re-energized with the assistance of Venus. Venus is for all intents and purposes an intermediary sphere in the cosmos; it is also Pluto's polarity planet. Mars, which is also an intermediary sphere, provides the soul with the determination to succeed in the on-going evolutionary transformation of rebirth.

Cosmic resurgence is a monumental part of the life plan, and it is the presupposition for the prevention of illness and disease.

Psychological Observations

Clinical depression transpires mostly because of a distinct lack of creativity (joy), awareness (love) and renewed idealism (innovation) that is absent in the life of an individual – including a litany of other psychological, emotional and physical disorders that maybe present. A complete scrutinization of Pluto's pathological and psychological disorders is outlined further on. When these accomplished attributes are absent, the soul's energy diminishes; and in effect it withers. This is because the soul is *energized*, in part, via the application and motivation of love, joy and innovative endeavours. Thus, depression is a purely synthetic condition; and the pathological effects of this disease are often evident in the physical eyes – displaying them as dark, sombre and often lifeless bodies.

The reason depression and other similar disorders such as anxiety are proliferating is because there is an overall dip in unique worldwide creativity, and in overall levels of awareness. Similarly, many people *emulate* the mannerisms of others, particularly those of celebrity figures. Paralleling another person's characteristics is not advisable because, for one thing, it inhibits evolutionary growth. It is also reminiscent of Neptune's lower vibrations. Interestingly, Elvis Presley and Michael Jackson are perhaps the most imitated celebrity figures that are forever pronounced in this way. Both celebrities had pronounced Neptune and Pluto in their natal charts.

There is also a dark shadow enveloping the world at this time, which is reminiscent of the 'dark realms' (lower astral regions) in the spirit world. This has become more evident since Pluto began its sojourn of Capricorn in 2008. It's as if these lowly regions are influencing our way of life, hence the upturn in overall crime. They are not, it is our perceptions of events, which make this conception appear real. And that is what depression is, a perception of events – seen through the eyes.

Ocular Perceptions

The physical eyes are often referred to as the 'windows to the soul'; and therefore they can be a frequent indicator to the soul's demise, and alternatively to the soul's ultimate transformation. Therefore, the expressions and reflections that are displayed in the eyes belong, in part, to the rulerships of Neptune and Pluto. However, overall jurisdiction of the eyes must surely belong to swift Mercury, because the eyes move like quicksilver.

The eyes of criminals and murderers (Neptune) that encase the dark and dismal energies that are connected to the underworld (Pluto) are often transfixed and lifeless – like they are starring into a deep and empty void of nothingness (Pluto). Lifeless eyes are also an indication to the absence of love, which is the cornerstone to all forms of physical, psychological and emotional illness and disease, such as clinical depression and anxiety. *

Meanwhile, eyes that are a channel for love and creativity are usually enhanced with light, meaning that they sparkle; and they shine with such brilliance. So, observing the condition of the eyes must gravitate towards Pluto's jurisdiction, because observation is a most powerful attribute connected to the planet of evolutionary transformation.

* It is important to point out that the psychological/mental/ emotional bodies are one of the same thing.

Being Unobservant

So, as we have ascertained, observation is an atypical Pluto characteristic. However, when an individual becomes *unobservant*, due to a lack of awareness, opportunities, especially for constructive and superior financial gain, are often overlooked as a result. Many astrologers have remarked that "no one has more money than Pluto". Furthermore, and speaking purely in a medical capacity, when an individual remains unobservant, he or she will ill-judge the condition of his or her health – compromising the immune system – leaving it vulnerable to the stringent and unrepentant effects of pathological illness and disease.

Expiration

Throughout evolution, the *protracted* psychological demise associated with the inner spirit, both individually and collectively, has always occurred. Today however, psychological death, especially in the form of mental breakdowns is at an all-time high. Psychological death (Pluto) is responsible for an assemblage of physical illness and disease, such as Alzheimer's dementia and Parkinson's disease, which are also at an all-time high.

Prem Rawat, the Indian teacher of spiritual wisdom and knowledge, said in an address to his followers that "there are many dead people on Earth at the moment, completely void of any new ideas". It is fair to suggest that this spike in 'uncreative unconsciousness' has become very evident throughout the world today. Moreover, the slow death of the psychological propensities is the root cause of illness and disease, such as Alzheimer's dementia and Parkinson's disease (already mentioned), but also disorders such as schizophrenia, and psychosis.

Alternatively, other pronounced disorders such as autism occur via the opposite equation to that of psychological death. Thus, autistic souls are being pressed to *trigger* (rebirth) their extraordinary centers of reasoning and intellect. Autistic souls are often considered as the opposite of intelligent. This is yet another Pluto observation coupled by the misdiagnosis factor that emanates from Pluto's mythical brother Neptune.

Global Prognosis

Alarmingly, there are too many people on Earth who are simply not progressing in the way their souls intended them to do throughout evolution; and, as a result, they are failing to *augment* their psychological and emotional capabilities, especially in an evolutionary capacity. Furthermore, this lack of evolutionary progression is also responsible for why there is so much illness and disease sitting on the collective seat of humanity. To put it in a rather quaint Pluto dialect, if this trend continues a large percentage of mankind will literally be *flushed* down the evolutionary toilet. 5

Psychological demise, which, in some cases can often be proceeded by evolutionary transformation, hence the death and rebirth prognosis (Pluto and the mythical Phoenix), was a crucial part of the teachings imparted by the many adepts and seers that have been seated upon the Earth plane throughout the course of evolution, such as the Gautama Buddha. *

*Gautama is the primary figure in Buddhism.

The Natal Chart

Repeatedly, this marked deterioration in consciousness, hence the psychological demise that the soul has conveyed throughout evolution, and which often leads to the onset of illness and disease, is frequently displayed in the natal chart. One such example of psychological decline is characterized by the quincunx aspect (adjustment and rebirth). The quincunx is a quizzical aspect of 150 degrees orb. Thus, from the eighth house (Pluto's natural domain) to the first house (a primary medical zone), it measures 150 degrees.

The potential for psychological demise is especially relevant when Pluto receives a quincunx from a personal planet or a luminary. In the case of a luminary it is showing that an adjustment needs to take place between the concepts of light and dark. In a previous incarnation, the soul was obscured in darkness (Pluto); but the soul needs to move from the dark and back into the light, displayed by the aspecting luminary. A further example of a required adjustment from the darkness is shown in the natal chart as a Sun-Pluto combustion (conjunction), see further on for more information about combustions. Here, Pluto's energy is concealed by the sheer size and magnitude of the Sun; therefore, for a positive outcome to occur, Pluto's energy needs to be absorbed into the positive light of the Sun.

Supercilious Aspects

Quincunxes are often undervalued, and so the tangled but perplexing energy of this aspect is often minimized as a result. Literally, quincunxes need to be 'straightened out'; hence they need to be balanced via soul contemplation. Quincunxes do often feature in physical death charts, because in most cases death is anything but orderly and respectable, especially when death occurs from illness and disease. Moreover, if we were to examine the decumbiture chart of a depression sufferer, for example, the quincunx would no doubt be evident. This is because the center of logic, hence the objective mind, is confused and mixed up.

In addition, I have frequently viewed the presence of the quincunx in the charts of my depression-afflicted clients. For them, they feel as if they continually experience the death of the psychological faculties. However, with Pluto's assistance, quincunxes offer a way to transform the soul from psychological death to emotional rebirth – symbolizing the adjustment characteristic of this aspect. Quincunxes also pose as an important source of authority in medical astrology.

Renascence

Many would agree that the solution to *reactivating* the wheel of evolutionary progression, especially after it has ground to a halt because of the onset of physical and mental health problems, and more importantly keep it rolling, is to embrace the concept of rebirth. In order to do this we must understand the deeper meaning of Pluto in the natal chart via contemplation. This is why it is also important to understand the deeper meaning posed by the quincunx aspect, especially if this puzzling aspect is 'influencing' the planet of death and rebirth. If we embrace Pluto's energy at a deeper level of consciousness, illness and disease will no longer be issues on the life path. At a deeper level of experience Pluto acts as an evolutionary conduit for the protection of the mind, body and the soul.

As a result, the necessary adjustment initialized by the quincunx can be successfully orchestrated, which is 'backed up' by other key elements in the natal chart, and the soul and the psychological faculties are reborn. Adjustment and rebirth are also key factors when Pluto opposes or squares a luminary in the natal chart. Medical astrology determines that squares and especially quincunxes are deemed 'bad' for the health. However, this is far from the truth. Squares get things *moving*. After an initial setback, so do quincunxes and oppositions. However, as a worst-case scenario, these aspects can exacerbate the progression of an illness or a disease.

Intercepted Houses (Suppression)

There is a further evolutionary component sometimes present in the natal chart. This polarized element 'conceptually' symbolizes psychological and emotional death – indicating a significant part of the soul's consciousness that has been restricted or supressed in some way. This 'psychological death' often occurs in the name of karmic progression. Thus, it is deemed necessary for additional soul growth and spiritual progression by the Elders or Lords of Karma.

Availing one to the Placidus and the Porphyry house systems, physical, psychological and even spiritual (evolutionary) consciousness that is *concealed* is highlighted in the natal chart by the presence of intercepted houses. Even though it is perceived, mostly by the esoterics, that souls who possess intercepted houses and planets are 'highly evolved', they have little or no access to their spiritual memories once they have become *reabsorbed* into the heavy vibration of Earth plane physicality.

For them, possessing intercepted zones in their charts is not necessarily deemed as a form of psychological death, but more like a form of psychological suppression, because they find it difficult to access the energy that is contained within their fields of resistance. The purpose of these 'intercepted souls' so to speak is to elicit their spiritual memories; in order to redeem the essence (knowledge) of their souls (Neptune and Pluto), thereby projecting the soul onto a much higher plane of spiritual and mental consciousness, whilst conscious in physicality.

Notwithstanding, intercepted souls are much more sensitive to the negative undercurrents that encompass the Earth plane than, for example, those souls who are not so evolved. Therefore, intercepted souls are much more *responsive* to contracting illness and disease, such as bowel and nasal disorders, especially when Pluto/Scorpio/Venus/Taurus is intercepted. The effect of this interception, for example, is similar to a Pluto combustion (see next section). The reason interceptions are connected to Pluto is because they require reawakening (rebirth-Pluto). When they lay dormant in the chart the individual often succumbs to colon disorders, because the colon is the primary objective that seeks to influence intercepted houses.

Intercepted planets merely act as channels or distributors of energy – providing the intercepted house/sign polarity with the ability to express itself. An intercepted house where there is no planet present expresses itself via the presence of transiting planets, most notably Neptune and Pluto – both of these planets *reawaken* these dormant domains.

Pluto's Universal Objective

The ultimate objective of Pluto on all levels of consciousness is to reinstate and replete the psychological potential within the soul — replenishing it with renewed vision and creativity. This is transformation at its peak intensity; and furthermore it symbolizes Pluto's rebirth potential. It is also a major part of the birthright of every human being. However, please be aware that despite whatever level of personal evolution and awareness attained, we all function via the energy of the soul, whether we are aware of this fact or not.

The soul is the *spark* of life, and it represents solely who we really are. This is partly why so many souls find, for example, Neptune a difficult planet to work with, because Neptune *administers* the wellbeing of the soul; and so many individuals are literally *disconnected* from their souls. Disconnection from one's soul is s further factor for the onset of illness and disease. Pluto merely reconnects us, hence it rewires the soul.

Mythology

Pluto's penchant for rebirth is the same to that of the mythical Phoenix – that transcended from the ashes of its earlier condition. This marks the true symbolism for spiritual rebirth. However, rebirth, hence transformation, can only occur through the realization of heightened awareness, which creates an inner awakening, and a willingness to embrace the presence of the soul. Moreover, illness and disease can then be perceived as integral symbolizations – merely intended to reawaken the inner spirit. This was the verifiable message imparted by the narrative that relates to the mythical Phoenix.

Transgressions

Pluto's evolutionary influence in the natal chart conveys wholly new transitions of resurgence, renewed awareness and rigorous development (rebirth). These generational transgressions are necessary for regrowth, especially when the physical body undertakes a cycle of healing from the effects of illness or disease. Regrowth is absolutely crucial, especially in physicality, because the negative effects of illness and disease remain as a part of the soul once it returns to the spirit world – reverberating indefinitely throughout eternity – until soul transformation occurs. Spiritually speaking, this is a well-documented fact, which is widely reported throughout a legion of past and present spiritual literatures.

Tenebrosity (Darkness)

When an individual succumbs to the effects of illness or disease, this afflicted cycle of transgression is referred to by some in the medical astrology world as the 'dark night of the soul'. Further, the dark night of the soul (see further on) can be described as a manifestation of psychological and emotional death, caused in part, by the onset of illness and disease.

Pluto Combustions (Dark Sun)

Pluto combustions can often be described as pathological and chronic experiences in the natal chart. In addition, Pluto combustions can be important significators – pointing towards the potential for illness and disease – especially in the later years of the life. Chronic (Pluto) combustion occurs when a planet is situated within eight degrees of the Sun, and in conjunction. Combustions are significant because the planet that is nearest the Sun becomes *obscured* by the Sun's rays, thus rendering the planet's influence as *weak* and *indisposed* in the natal chart.

In psychological-based astrology, hence Pluto-based, the Sun is deemed as a natural malefic force. This is because his solar energies scorch and dry out the planet closest to it. Therefore, being too close to this great ball of fire, particularly when Pluto is involved, is not a pleasant experience. Because of its distance from the Sun, Pluto is deemed an icy world, so a close Sun-Pluto conjunction would ordinarily cause internal steam combustion, as its surface ice melts away. Thus, Pluto would trap a certain amount of heat within its mainframe. Therefore, the individual would be susceptible to a wide range of psychological disorders, fevers and even spontaneous combustion, which was proven to exist. In essence, combustion would cause Pluto to influence more like its predecessor Mars.

Pluto cannot comport *independently* as a result of combustion, and thus it loses some of its power. Furthermore, Pluto will not seek pleasure in the experience, because the Sun will drown out his powerfully-aligned energy with his effulgence – exuding Pluto's power further.

If left unchecked, in other words, if this conjunction is not honed, a Pluto combustion can lead to an array of physical and mental health problems, including cancer, heart problems, and even tumors of the bowel. Considerable significators towards the onset of poor health are when Pluto receives hard aspects from other planets – accelerating the process of combustion. These transitions towards impoverished health occur primarily because the body has renounced its power – relinquishing it to a greater source, and in this case, it is to the Sun.

The key to overcoming the negative effects of Pluto combustions is to reclaim the power of Pluto through contemplation – gradually drawing it back from the calefaction of this great luminary. Hard aspects to Pluto in particular represent an opportunity to reclaim the planet's authority.

Exacting in a positive light however, Pluto combustions are quite literally a death and rebirth configuration. Therefore, moving the life beyond the natural order of things through evolutionary transformation will help to achieve the 'reclaiming of Pluto's power'. Once Pluto's power has been reclaimed the body will be better equipped to fight off the effects of illness and disease.

In rare cases, Pluto combust souls will often experience a 'very long dark night of the soul', especially if they have already succumbed to the damaging effects of illness and disease, which is terminal, or life-altering in some way.

The Dark Night of the Soul

"Remove the dark from in me and give me that which I have lost".

George Harrison

The dark night of the soul is essentially a 'psychological' and a 'pathological' experience. It is also important to point out that during the dark night of the soul the potential for social collapse, drug and alcohol problems and accidents fall crucially under the gloomy spotlight of Pluto and his mythical brother Neptune – producing far-reaching consequences.

In most cases, the dark night of the soul is *initialized* mostly as a result of a hard Pluto transit – gradually occurring in the natal chart. Thus, the dark night of the soul is not a sudden occurrence. So, under the influence of a difficult Pluto transit, it will feel at times as if there is an indeterminately supple and uneasy shift taking place, and one that denotes internal psychological apprehension. This psychological shift is coupled by a complete loss of control, especially over all of the seemingly important aspects of life, such as the loss of personal life direction. Dark thoughts are often abundant at this time.

However, during a period of illness or disease, or due to an injury, the loss of control and personal power are by far the most common themes that are experienced. The loss is often accompanied by a lack of insight – with absolutely no clear sign of what lies ahead. This notion was very evident during the coronavirus epidemic of 2020. So, to reiterate, loss is the significant transition that is commonly experienced during the dark night of the soul. However, what is really occurring is that the road of life is being diverted to a wholly new location. Furthermore, an opportunity for personal contemplation (recapturing power) is always presented at regular intervals during this psychological transition.

Illness and Disease

Anxiety and depression are also common occurrences experienced throughout the dark night of the soul. However, illness and disease are always common occurrences during the presence of hard Pluto transits, particularly diseases of the colon (see further on). Meanwhile, hard Pluto transits denote a rebirth within the soul's cognitive and rotational (aspiring) abilities. In so many cases however, and because of these *unfamiliar* changes, the somatic body seems to gradually descend into emotional and psychological meltdown. Sometimes the body will recover from these stresses, and thus the soul is reborn as a result. In a large percentage of cases, deaths from illness and disease or from an accident are all too common. However, death brought about by illness and disease during a hard Pluto transit is representative of the 'familiar death factor' that Pluto is widely associated with.

Psychological Rebirth

Speaking in a language that contains elements of the psychological and of the evolutionary, conditions such as Alzheimer's dementia occurs in order to reset the psychological pathways. This is mostly overlooked because of the loss of memory associated with this disturbing and debilitating disease. Besides, this notion would *not* be generally accepted by the populace – rather it would most likely be viewed as a crazy notion.

Essentially, those who have fallen victim to dementia are being called upon to *hone* their faith (Neptune). It's as if they are being given one last chance before they leave the realm of physicality. Honing one's faith by working closely with the Neptune archetype (Pluto's mythical brother) is a common theme that is always required during the dark night of the soul experience. However, the only way faith can be truly obtained during the dark night of the soul is when the soul/individual embraces the concept of transformation (Pluto). Dementia patients would naturally heal themselves if they embraced the concept of transformation, especially within their mindsets.

Evolutionary Assessments

Evolutionary assessments that are carried out during the dark night of the soul, which are initialized by a hard Pluto transit, are cosmically designed to be a supple undertaking; however, psychologically, they can prove to be arduous and powerful concerns. The dark night of the soul is a Pluto 'testing ground', which stimulates the soul into thinking exactly what is happening in its immediate environment. Thus, Pluto helps the individual to focus and contemplate on the changes taking place within the emotional and the psychological bodies. Perhaps more importantly, Pluto calls upon the soul to *recognize* and *accept* the changes that are taking place – emotionally, psychologically and sometimes environmentally.

Evolutionary Perspective

Further, during the dark night of the soul, Pluto advocates that the external perceptions contained within the mindset are directed to focus *solely* on the internal changes that are occurring. This is so that the gradual and necessary shifts in power and consciousness take place without any form of repercussions, such as the onset of illness and disease. It is worth remembering however that the *fear* that is generated during the process of change (transformation) is the psychological foundation prevalent in all forms of physical and psychological illness and disease.

Transposing

Pluto's gradual shifts in personal power and in consciousness are also necessary for the body to overcome the debilitating effects dealt out by illness and disease. When applied via the act of serenity for example, Pluto's power merely represents gentle healing energy. Hard Pluto transits symbolize major changes that are taking place within the psyche, and similar to a Saturn transit, they are designed to strengthen the body's responses to them.

One such example of this internal change during Pluto, and particularly Neptune, transits is the inner [spiritual] eye is activated; and is therefore opened. It is generally recognized by esoterics that heightened awareness that represents the sight of the spiritual eye is enhanced further during the dark night of the soul.

Courage and determination (Mars/Pluto) are attributes that must also be honed during the dark night of the soul. This is often the case when transit Pluto squares Mars in the chart. Courage and determination are the essential requirements that allow the soul to recognize the changes that are taking place – embracing them as cycles of positive and necessary growth. This being the case, the soul will emerge from the external darkness much stronger and wiser than before it initially entered into the dark night of the soul experience. In which case, the generalized effects associated with illness and disease should begin to subside as a result, especially if they are psychological. These supple but powerful shifts in power symbolized by hard Pluto transits highlight the ascendancy of the mythical Phoenix that rose out of the ashes of its earlier existence.

The Personal Experience

During the evolutionary cycle that symbolizes the dark night of the soul, especially if the cycle is concerned solely with illness and disease, you will need to ask yourself some very important questions such as: 'what it is I actually stand for', and 'what really matters right now', especially when everything, including the death of the cognitive abilities has been consumed by the effects of a particular disorder. These precepts were tested during the coronavirus epidemic of 2020.

And, as we have previously established, the dark night of the soul cycles are all about reclaiming Pluto's personal power – power that has been purged – power in its purest form – recycled power. This type of power is what replenishes the soul with so much healing potential. Redeeming the soul in this way is the only way to vanquish the effects associated with the deadly effects associated with illness and disease, particularly dementia and Parkinson's disease.

Enlightenment

Once illness and disease have been purged from the body,

the soul can *ascend* towards the light of hope; and it carries with it the potential to digress from the darkness of despair, which was essentially the hidden message that is being conveyed behind the legend of the mythical Phoenix. In the natal chart, Pluto provides the ability, through its supple and resilient power, to defeat the effects of illness and disease by *powering* the chart. I know from personal experience, that this notion is one that bears the majestic fruits that symbolize understanding, and of course the truth.

Upshot

During a Pluto dark night of the soul, the individual is instinctively *coerced* into visiting the dark abyss of the underworld. Once there, and with supple persuasion from the planet of obsession/transformation, the individual must decide to either remain in the darkness, or project his consciousness towards the light of truth. Criminality is born from the darkness. In most cases, criminals who commit appalling crimes have entered the dark night of the soul. Equally, healers who send out light to heal the sick have entered into the dark night of the soul, and into the light of truth and transformation. Whatever decision the individual arrives at, will in a psychological capacity, continue to have a major influence on the long-term health.

The dark night of the soul is a purely synthetic experience. However, if the soul is *absorbed* into the dark realms of the spirit world (the lower astral plains) when its physical life concludes, the transition into spirit becomes a continuation to the dark night of the soul; therefore it becomes congenital (Pluto). This is because so many who are absorbed into the dark realms believe they are still very much alive in earthly incarnation. In effect, this can be deemed as a form of emotional and psychological illness. Furthermore, it is also an illusion projected on behalf of Pluto's bigger brother Neptune.

The Capacity for Hidden Transformation

In the cosmic hierarchy of planets, Pluto is deemed the 'great discloser'. For the main, this is because the planet *unravels* the twisted and hypogean (concealed) threads that obstruct the emergence of that which is connected to the hidden truth. This is factualness that is always recognizable within any situation, and a condition that essentially points to the prevention of illness and disease.

By *intuitively* relaying a question to the soul via meditation, for example, such as: 'what is the best possible way to overcome the effects of my illness or disease' and the answer that is transmitted via instinct (the hidden truth) is Pluto's penchant for the absolute truth. This is the point with which the soul can begin the process of transformation. However, the answer that is received will be purely *instinctual*, meaning that there will be a *knowing* with regards to the correct course of action that is needed. This is Pluto's capacity for hidden transformation.

Evolutionary Potential

Pluto's evolutionary potential for revealing the *truth* is regarded as a powerful attribute in the chart; and has earned Pluto its ultimate seat of power within the great cosmic hierarchy. Thus, Pluto's power is *unearthed* from the deep recesses of the soul – power which is renewed between its generational cycles of the zodiac – power that is considered to be from the realms of the spirit world as a necessary *rebirth*. Hence, this is regarded as the *reawakening* of the soul.

Initially, Pluto *powers* the natal chart and transforms it into a wholly new form of energy, via its often dark, supple but powerful transit cycles. As we have previously established, there is a dark night, a death, thus the end of a cycle, to endure before the rebirth of the soul can take place. It is at this point of transition that illness and disease gain a foothold. A case in point would be to highlight the recent surge of Alzheimer's dementia and Parkinson's disease that has afflicted the mainly older generation.

Mostly, they are those who were born with Pluto in Cancer (1914-1939). This is because they have reproduced as the generation who are dealing with the consequences of repressed (buried) emotions and emotional preconditions. You will note that these dates represent the beginnings of the first and second world wars; hence cycles of time where the emotions were often repressed due to survival (Pluto). It is, in part, repressed and restrained emotions that are the impetus for the onset of dementia and Parkinson's disease evident in later life of this particular group. Ordinarily, emotions are meant to be expressed (released).

Pluto's current transit of Capricorn (Cancer's polarity sign) has proved to be the *trigger* – firing the outpouring of these diseases – diseases that have been unleashed into the mainframe since Pluto began its transit of Capricorn in 2008. Capricorn and its ruler Saturn are also archetypes that signify suppression. At some point these souls will have experienced a Pluto opposition to itself.

Medically speaking, a Pluto opposition transit to its natal position often signifies the transition between death from, in this case, illness and disease, and a potential rebirth into an entirely new cycle of form. Moreover, a Pluto opposition to itself can be a favourable aspect; and one that allows the individual to come to terms with an illness or a disease, after the initial period of tension. Conceptually speaking, this is an aspect of contemplation, in which case Pluto begins purging and preparing the soul for its onward and inevitable return to the spirit world. However, as Pluto is a generational planet, this transition can take time to ultimately achieve.

Reawakening

Pluto's hallmark is one that denotes rebirth. Pluto constitutes as the release of the soul's evolutionary power – power that it has acquired throughout the course of evolution. According to *The Akashic Records*, it is a similar power that created the Earth, the cosmos and the physical universe.

Perhaps more importantly, rebirth determines the end of a cycle, or the old life. Hence, it is a cycle of physical and mental expansion that is now complete; and therefore new evolutionary shoots must emerge from the intense undergrowth of physicality in order to create a new cycle of growth, preferably spiritual. However, some may view this notion through the eyes of fear, such as bringing to bear the death of complacency, when in fact rebirth signifies *reigniting* the eternal flame of hope. So, when rebirth is perceived purely out of fear, it is at the end of an evolutionary cycle in which illness and disease drop an unyielding anchor in the body.

Cessation

Illness and disease represent physical disorders that all too often become prevalent at the beginning of, or at the culmination point of a Pluto cycle. This is because there is often an instinctive *wondering* as to whether the life has reached its ultimate limits and cannot progress any further as a result. Mostly, this kind of thinking occurs because there is a lack of new ideas or creativity present.

An absence in original thinking or creativity is especially noticeable at the start of a hard Pluto transit. This is often perceived as a death. Furthermore, this lack of idealism or creativity is congenital; and it has always been present throughout the evolutionary journey of the soul. One such example that determines this way of thinking occurs during retirement from the workplace. In a high percentage of cases, death from illness and disease, particularly from heart problems[2] is often swift during retirement, particularly within the male population.

Renewal

At the culmination point of a Pluto transit, the release of Pluto's elaborate and renewed form of power signifies the rebirth of the soul, whether in physicality, or whether the soul has been released from its physical restraints, and thus returned to the spirit world. Pluto's power signifies the capacity for psychological potential; and this marks the planet's subsequent purpose in the natal chart. It is the 'evolutionary power' that is submerged deep within the soul that needs to be realized. Suppressed power, however, is often considered as the 'core truths' behind the many fundamental reasons for the soul's return to physical incarnation.

Dissention and Development

Continuing on, and significant in most cases, the release of this submerged power is usually during the point by which the soul transcends the experiences associated with the dark night of the soul scenario. Therefore, Pluto's power is released as a form of protection. However, the lasting effects of the dark night can also corrupt Pluto's power (dissention), which is why many turn to crime or power play (corruption) during a dark night experience – crime and corruption can, after all, be considered as displaced and psychological forms of synthetic illness and disease.

Pluto oversees elementary, psychological and environmental annihilation. This occurs so that new spiritual shoots can emerge, necessary for the evolutionary progression of the soul, which is evident during a significant Pluto transit. Pluto transits can seem almost like extended ordeals of emotional and mental pain, and even torture. Furthermore, they can even signify a slow death of the life force energy. Pluto transits, particularly frictional transitions, represent the 'art of acquiescing', meaning that we shouldn't fight against that which we cannot change. Change happens naturally, and change symbolizes the 'rebirth of evolutionary potential' (development).

Notwithstanding, if and when the soul rises like the mythical Phoenix, particularly after the extensive dark night dealt out by a particular transit, a new and richer life is forthcoming; and thus it is assured. This transition is deemed as a new evolutionary cycle of progression, in which case illness and disease will no longer be prevalent issues.

Corruption and Rebirth

When Pluto is under duress in the natal chart, which is caused primarily by the presence of frictional aspects, its dominant energy often becomes corruptible, and its power is feared by the incorruptible as a result. This corruptible effect can often create a dichotomy within the psyche of those concerned; hence it is a separation that moves between the powers of good and evil. Furthermore, it is a division that highlights one's greatest fears of being destroyed (death), and the pursuit of the deepest longing in the heart (rebirth). Moreover, it is the division between love (good) and hate (evil) that orchestrates the prospect of illness and disease.

One such example of this division that has been created is noted by those harrowing and tragic disorders known as HIV and AIDS (for more information see case studies below). HIV and AIDS are often created from a corrupted and subverted soul that is under the duress of a hard Pluto transit. Hence, HIV and AIDS are true representations of a negative dark night of the soul.

Power Deception of a Hard Pluto Transit

The use of corrupted power is yet a further indication that the ego is attempting to reinforce its fragile defences (death), in order to regain control of its psychological faculties. When Pluto demolishes the ego during its difficult and Herculean transits, the soul has the potential to experience rebirth, thus surrendering to a new and spiritual life (rebirth).

However, a corrupted [sullied] soul is a prime example of illness and disease, whether it is a psychological, emotional or physical disorder. Pluto is considered to be a generational planet, so frictional Pluto transits, especially to personal planets or the luminaries can often determine how long an illness or disease will ultimately linger. '

There is a spiritual maxim: "die many times before you die". *

This is a true representation of an undemanding fact that naturally unfolds within the hierarchy of Pluto. Pluto teaches about the effects of *perishing* in the physical flames of the ego (death), and emerging as a wondrous, cleansed and progressive spiritual force (rebirth). Being moribund [dying] is essentially another word for elimination. Pluto's power of elimination, especially the elimination of toxins from the body, can in effect help us to rise up like the mythical Phoenix from the negative undertones that are placed in motion, especially by the effects of illness and disease.

Currently, illness and disease in every known type and form, and with the addition of many synthetic forms, are pandemic and unbridled upon the Earth, and across all its avenues of diversity and experience. However, very few souls manage to rise up and ascend from the ashes of their injurious experiences – transmuting as an analeptic and progressed soul. Ascension is Pluto's organic penchant; and its evolutionary presupposition is the elimination of illness and disease.

*Julius Caesar is commonly quoted as making this statement.

Illness and Disease (Elimination-Based)

Typically, illness and disease, especially those 'hidden' disorders that are strongly associated with Pluto, symbolize a prominent cycle of elimination, which is considered by the esoterically-minded to be in the category of death and rebirth. Thus, Pluto is associated with the immune system and the reproductive system, and diseases transmitted via the sexual organs, and particularly the organs associated with the process of elimination. Therefore, common Pluto afflictions are mostly associated with the colon [bowel], all of which have a tendency to *obstruct* the elimination of detritus from the body, which can be very dangerous to the overall anatomy.

Pluto and Scorpio also have their rulership over the sweat glands, which are a major part of the body's elimination process. The disease hyperhidrosis (excessive sweating) is examined in the case studies further on. Pluto's element of suppression is a concept that rules over the disease known as anhidrosis, this is a condition where a person has an inability to sweat normally, and this is also examined in the case studies. Some of the least significant of Pluto's physical disorders, that are mostly triggered by psychological stress, are diarrhoea (colon toxification), and irritable bowel syndrome (IBS), and which are both examined in the case studies further on. Of course, both of these disorders are associated with the colon.

Thus, Pluto has its rulership over the colon or large intestine. More often than not, the colon is referred to in a medical capacity as the second brain. Thus, the colon is referred to in this way, in part, because of its brain-like appearance; and its ability to process bodily responses at the emotional/psychological level of consciousness. The brain is the center of logic, whereas the colon is the center of emotion. Therefore, the colon is susceptible to the fallout from external psychological vibrations, for example, from pestilential and toxic foodstuffs, and from randomized energies – tethered to negative thought patterns. Hence, these negative vibrations that are discarded and otherwise absorbed into the colon are the essential *triggers* for the onset of illness and disease, such as food poisoning and psychoparalysis.

Pluto possesses the capability to absorb all of the negative and injurious emotional/psychological influences that resonate from external influences, such as hate, jealousy and anger, which are mostly damaging to the colon, and to the immune system. Cancer and other related dis-eases such as Crohn's disease, which is considered as being the first stage towards the onset of cancer, can often be the result of this 'emotional undermining' within the colon.

Colon Destabilization

Once all negative and psychological emotions have been absorbed directly into the colon, they become imprisoned, and they will continue to threaten, compromise and to destabilize the natural balance, and the congenital rhythms of the entire body. Crohn's disease for example is triggered by negative emotions that are highly toxic in nature such as anger, and which become trapped and absorbed by the colon. Thus, the body's natural balance and its congenital rhythms are overseen by Pluto, and its polarity planet Venus. In the long-term, the continual absorption of toxic emotions such as anger will destabilize the inborn functions of the colon, which is solely concerned with the body's metabolization and elimination processes, hence its equilibrium and its rhythmic cycles.

Innate Functioning

The primary purpose of the Pluto-ruled colon is essential, because it oversees the wellbeing of the entire body. The colon nourishes the body with renewed energy [power] from metabolized foodstuffs that in turn *wield* emotional responses. This is why it is so vitally important that the individual consumes good and healthy nutrition. If, for example, we chose to live a life solely on consuming innutritious food, the body will respond by creating negative emotions, and in the worst-case scenario, illness and disease. If, however, we chose to consume healthy and nutritious food, the body will be purged with positive and regenerating energy, hence the renewing potential and intense power of Pluto.

Further, when healthy and nutritious foodstuffs are successfully metabolized by the colon, the energy that is realised as a result is vital for the natural balance, its functions, and the organic and synthetic rhythms of the body. So, if the diet consists of nothing more than harmful and unhealthy nutrition, the body will become susceptible to the onset of illness and disease, particularly colon-based. Furthermore, the colon eliminates what the body doesn't require and converts it into waste, which is eliminated through the appropriate orifice, whether it is Pluto's anus, or Taurus's mouth. However, when the colon continually eliminates waste, that is the after product of innutritious foodstuffs, the colon and its interconnected organs become susceptible to illness and disease.

Interestingly, when undigested foodstuffs are purposely eliminated via the mouth, it is often a sign that the disease anorexia nervosa is beginning to take a hold in the body. Anorexia is a Pluto-ruled disease, because anorexia signifies that the physical/psychological and emotional bodies are beginning to degrade and perish. In addition, the colon will naturally eliminate unabsorbed waste if the diet consists of unhealthy foodstuffs – starving the body of vital nutrients – producing malnutrition. This, in itself, is a type of anorexia.

Concluding with Illness and Disease

As we have ascertained, the colon is the primary organ that oversees the body's death and rebirth process; and initially, the seeds of illness and disease are firmly set in the colon. Furthermore, if the body fails to eliminate the body's waste because of a colon-related illness, such as bowel cancer, it will deteriorate, and it will eventually die. Appropriately, the colon can be referred to as the body's 'underbody organ'.

Elimination (Pluto) represents the process of death and rebirth, because in a physical capacity the body is *reborn* after the elimination of the body's waste; and all the body's chemical toxins (Neptune). The primary function concerning the condition known as diarrhoea is to *expunge* the poisonous chemical elements from the body that have become unsuitably housed in the colon.

The colon is the organ that is most susceptible to bodily corruption (illness and disease) – corruption caused by waste products that have metastasized. Furthermore, colon corruption is the catalyst for the onset of most types of cancer.

Pluto's Chemical Elements

Pluto also rules over the liquefied substances that are fundamentally 'concealed' within the physical framework of the body. Thus, one of the biological elements that Pluto oversees, alongside its exoteric understudy Mars and its mythical brother Neptune, is bile – a dark green to yellowish brown fluid produced by the liver that is stored in the gallbladder. Pluto also rules over the gastric acid that is produced in the stomach, which is comprised of hydrochloric acid and potassium chloride. Pluto oversees insulin – a lifeblood biological chemical that is produced in the pancreas. Finally, Pluto also oversees bone marrow, which it co-rules alongside its exoteric understudy Mars.

Furthermore, we can also conclude that disorders such as bowel, bladder, prostate and pancreatic cancer, with the inclusion of pancreatitis, which is often a catalyst for cancer, are all typical Pluto infirmities, because they are all conditions that are subjected to chemical impedimentation[3]. In addition, Neptune is mostly responsible for the overall development of cancer (for more information about cancer refer to my previous publication *Discovering Faith in Neptune's Ocean of Dreams*). Whereas the many different types of cancer are divided up and categorized under their designated and respected planetary rulerships, such as pancreatic and colon, these infirmities, as we have now ascertained, are firmly categorized under the rulership of Pluto.

Further Chemical Imbalances

It has been suggested that hiatal hernia (acid regurgitation) is primarily a Pluto-ruled disorder. I do however agree with this concept. Urinary tract infections are part ruled by Pluto, especially when this chemical imbalance causes kidney infections. Initially, urinary tract infections begin in the kidneys – the kidneys are ruled by Venus and Libra; and Venus is Pluto's polarity planet. All of these chemical imbalances are deemed as mostly congenital. However, they can also be synthetic, caused primarily by external and environmental conditions.

Pluto's Classic Infirmities

Diverticulitis and particularly IBS are consummate Pluto disorders. For example, diverticulitis (inflammation of the diverticulum) occurs when small bulging pouches form in the lining if the digestive system. Diverticulitis also impairs bowel function. IBS (irritable bowel syndrome) is caused by increased sensitivity in the bowl. Anxiety and depression are often triggers for IBS. However, IBS can often signify a *purging* of toxins from the body, which is considered as a Pluto rebirth. Colon disorders such as IBS are mostly categorized as congenital conditions, but they can be equally deemed synthetic. Furthermore, infirmities such as IBS are often triggered by deep-set and underlying fear – fear being ruled by Saturn. According to the *World Health Organisation* (WHO), unfettered emotions such as fear and stress that are triggers for IBS and diverticulitis have increased in the last ten years. This would be comparable to Pluto's sojourn of Saturn-ruled Capricorn, thus orchestrating internal conflict, which will reach out through the approaching generations.

Retroviruses

Retroviruses such as HIV is also a Pluto-ruled condition. HIV or human immunodeficiency virus is a retrovirus that causes AIDS or acquired immune deficiency syndrome.[4] Retroviruses such as HIV come under the guise of Pluto because, in part, it is a sexually transmitted virus, whereas AIDS, which describes a number of potentially life-threatening infections, falls mostly under the dominion of Pluto's mythical brother Neptune (for more information refer to my previous publication *Discovering Faith in Neptune's Ocean of Dreams*). HIV and AIDS are deemed congenital and synthetic disorders – brought about by external and environmental conditions. Interestingly, Neptune and Pluto are synthesized planets, meaning their combined influence is *one*. This will all be explained in my forthcoming publication *Synthesis, The Twinned Rulerships of Neptune and Pluto.*

Manufactured Disorders

Acute radiation syndrome (ARS) is very much a Pluto-ruled illness, and is mostly synthetic, caused primarily by environmental and chemical conditions. However, ARS can create further implications, such as physical and mental deformities in offspring. Therefore, ARS can be congenital by design. ARS is also known as radiation sickness, or radiation poisoning, and the end result is always terminal (death and Pluto).

We will now examine some, if not all, of the above conditions via the appropriately-judged case studies.

HIV/AIDS

"I enjoy being a messenger for God (Neptune) in terms of letting people know about HIV (Pluto)".

Unknown Source

Recently, HIV has made its underlying presence known once again – reported in a news review. However, in truth, HIV has always been foreshadowed; hence it has always remained in the background. HIV returned to the news mostly because of the recent announcement in August of 2019, made by the former Welsh rugby player Gareth Thomas. Thomas announced that he is now living with HIV. The exact birth time for Gareth Thomas is unknown, so it is not possible to give an accurate reading in order to determine the actual conditions surrounding this disease. I will therefore provide alternative case examples of well-known figureheads in order to illustrate Pluto's proliferous connection to HIV in the natal chart.

Further, and according to *The World Health Organisation* (WHO), "HIV and AIDS are inherent gender issues, and a decade ago women seemed to be on the periphery of the epidemic;

today however they are at the epicentre of this epidemic". This is why I open my case analysis with a well-known female figurehead that shocked the world, at the time of her demise.

Facts and Figures

Statistics reveal that 47 percent of the 36.1 million people living with HIV are women, and this proportion is increasing. In undeveloped countries, poverty exposes women and girls to abuse (Neptune), and to higher risk behaviour such as Female Genital Mutilation (FGM), which is overseen by Mars, Neptune and Pluto. Moreover, sexual exploitation of girls and women has become a family survival strategy in most cases, in which case HIV and AIDS are transmitted to their offspring – fabricating them as congenital and synthetic conditions.

Let us now open Part 3 with a series of case studies, beginning with a well-known female model that died of HIV/AIDS related conditions.

Case Studies

Gia Carangi

I begin my in-depth analysis of the case studies with an American model that rose to fame in the 1970s and 1980s. Gia Carangi was considered to be the very first supermodel, and she featured on the covers of fashion magazines such as *Vogue* and *Cosmopolitan*. She also appeared in advertising campaigns for fashion houses such as *Armani, Christian Dior* and *Versace.*[5] On November 18th, 1986, Carangi died from HIV/AIDS-related complications, after being found in an alleyway, badly beaten (Mars/Pluto), and raped (Neptune). Appropriately, it should be remarked upon that this cycle of despair she endured most definitely occurred during Carangi's 'dark night of the soul'.

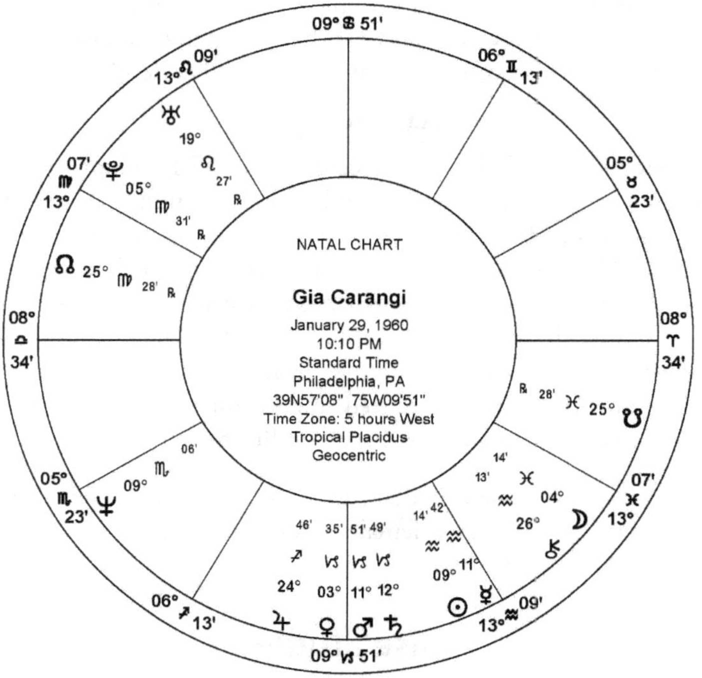

Gia Carangi was one of the first women to die from complications related to HIV. At the time of her death transit Pluto was tenanting its natural rulership sign of Scorpio (dignified), and conjunct natal Neptune. Venus was square to both Neptune and Pluto. Ordinarily, this powerful transit would attach additional weight and influence to a significant rectangle pattern, which was the cornerstone of her entire chart (see analysis below). In brief, the likelihood that her death (Pluto) was caused by an infection-based disease that was initially set in motion by the transference of drug-related implements (Neptune) – in this case it was the sharing (Venus) of hypodermic syringes.

The Natal Chart

Before I begin, it is important to point out that the Chart Shapes self-evident in these chosen health charts are only devised from the nearest relevant patterns. In effect, they can vary. For more information regarding the more *defined* and *definite* chart shapes, I would recommend you reading *Chart Shapes, The Key to Interpretation* by Wanda Sellar.

In this splay-type chart Pluto is a dominant force (see relevant chart). The splay pattern often determines an individual who possesses a dynamic center that is clearly displayed within the personality.

Firstly, Pluto is displayed in a tight opposition to the Moon. Speaking purely in medical terms, the presence of this opposition meant that Carangi was susceptible to infection-based diseases, because for the most part, the Moon tenants Neptune's sign of Pisces. For all its creative capability, the Moon is Pisces is vulnerable to infection, which is often the result of a depleted immune system. In this case, the immune system has gone into meltdown because of the aftereffects associated with drug and alcohol abuse. Pluto also has a tendency to *intensify* the presence of a disease. As a result, any foreign bodies (Pluto) that entered her body, especially in the form of viruses (Neptune), would eventually cause the spread of infection, which would compromise both the fluidic and lymph systems (Moon).

Contraction

Carangi contracted the HIV virus, even though initially she began her life with a strong and healthy immune system, which was the result of the Mars-Saturn conjunction, and which is also trine to Pluto in the chart. For the most part however, Saturn would actually *strengthen* the biological immune system with its conjunction to Mars. Moreover, because her lifestyle in middle age became governed by the necessity for drug addiction, transmitted in part, by the Moon/Pluto opposition, it was inevitable that the HIV virus would be compounded – only to manifest into AIDS. In her case, the AIDS virus would simply have reflected as the more 'dominantly-powerful condition' (Pluto).

This particular opposition can be deemed a *Hades Moon*[6], manifesting as the instrument for the absorption of harmful emotions, especially those imparted by other addicts, and HIV sufferers. Thus, her interaction with other addicts would prove to be a major and negative influence in her life. In effect, the Pisces Moon, powered by Pluto in this case, became the primary catalyst for this inimical catastrophe. In turn, this caused Carangi to nosedive into the opposing sign Virgo – becoming the victim.

Further Influential Frameworks

The opposition between Pluto and the Moon is a very presiding aspect, because it joins two corners of a mystic rectangle pattern in Carangi's natal chart. I fear, however, that this rectangle pattern represented an additional catalyst for the onset of HIV (Pluto) and AIDS (Neptune). The two other corners are connected by Mars's opposition to the MC – comprising the inner cross of the rectangle.

In most cases, the rectangle configuration would be representative of an 'instrument for progression'. However, in the case of Gia Carangi, it would act as the catalyst for her ultimate demise, partly because of the influence bestowed by the Moon-Pluto opposition. Also, Neptune is joined to the rectangle by way of a sextile to Pluto. In addition, Neptune sextiles the close conjunction between a dignified Mars and Saturn on the IC, tenanting the fourth house of the grave. In this instance, the window of opportunity posed by both sextiles would be dissentient.

Further, it was an opportunity to increase her need for the consumption of illicit drugs (Neptune). Consequently, her life ended in the most violent of ways, compounded by the Mars-Saturn conjunction. It was ascertained by the police (Pluto/Scorpio) that she was beaten to death in an argument concerning drugs. Thus, Carangi became a notorious heroin addict (Neptune), and she contracted the HIV virus by sharing needles and syringes with other addicts.

Rectangular Influences

The rectangle pattern is also powered by two quincunxes (adjustment), which connect the MC to a closely conjunct Sun and Mercury. The Sun and Mercury's conjunction also positioned in the house of the grave is weakened by the Sun's detrimental position in in Aquarius. Moreover, Pluto's oblique sextile to the MC provides additional power into the quincunxes. In this case, the quincunxes were, in my opinion, further catalysts – increasing her ultimate demise.

Susceptibility_

It is fair to suggest that these additional influences connected to the rectangle pattern would have created a surge in sensitivity, which would course through her veins, and at times, would have been overpowering and overbearing. Drugs seemed her only option to alleviate the suffering. All of this intense energy was coupled by an overwhelming need to be admired; a characteristic that is highlighted by the trine from Venus to Pluto. In order to mask out these negative responses, however, Carangi needed a regular *fix* (Neptune) in order to feel *good* about life. Also, Carangi had a powerful brain, but there was a tendency present not to use it. This is highlighted by the Sun-Mercury conjunction, which is square to Neptune in the chart. If she had plied her brain in the way she was capable of doing, she would no doubt have been able to 'think' her way out the harrowing situation she ultimately found herself in.

In addition, she could have successfully utilized the adjustment detail, which was representative of the quincunxes. Here, she could have put her extraordinary brain power and talent to good use, such as embracing the power of her inborn faith, instead of being deluded by her innate intense sensitivity – the fragile signature signed in part by the Cancer-ruled MC. Thus, it was this uncomfortable sensitivity that would play a major role in her ultimate expiration, because her drug addiction would 'blot out' this often-unbearable feeling.

Necessary Balance

Pluto's sextile to Neptune further highlights a reminiscent search for God; and the Ascendant lies at the midpoint of this lowly aspect. We can speculate that she possessed the opportunity to rediscover her spiritual roots in order to be at peace and harmony with herself and others. I have discovered that the element of balance is often associated with rectangle patterns. Carangi's natal chart is all about acquiring a healthy equilibrium, which was one of the primary elements of her life. Furthermore, she had the power (Pluto) at her disposal to attain it. Moreover, the Sun-Mercury conjunction would have assisted her with this divine quest for the accruement of inner knowledge.

Publicly, it was reported that Carangi was often disruptive and threatening in her behaviour, especially towards others. This would become prevalent when she didn't get her own way. This type of behaviour was clearly the result of an imbalance shown by Venus's wide conjunction to Mars, and Mars's opposition to the MC. The law of attraction (Venus) determines that we 'draw in' the same vibration of energies that we give out. Perhaps, if she had sought and acquired inner peace that *rings* out in her chart like some loud sonic bell, she may not have had to endure this terrible illness, as well as going through the ordeal of rape. To acquire balance would be the adjustment necessary demanded by the quincunxes – adding an additional nuance to the rectangle pattern.

Further Considerations

There would possibly have been great difficulties in her relationship with her Mother (Moon-Pluto opposition), perhaps a troubled and dishevelled childhood? The Moon-Pluto opposition would have, however, bolstered her ability to acquire determination, hence a determination to succeed in her life. But perhaps she leant a bit too far off the Pluto rectangular edge in her reckoning; and in her will to succeed in life.

Neptune's sextile to Pluto is pitted (deficient), because nine degrees of Scorpio (Neptune's degree) is lame according to William Lilly.[7] This geometric incapacitation would have strongly suggested that she fell from grace because of a weakly positioned Neptune. Essentially, she couldn't handle the pressure of fame (Neptune). Thus, she became addicted to drugs because of the hazy undertones of the Neptune-Pluto sextile that shrouded the rectangle. This was coupled by the Moon/Pluto opposition. In essence, all of this became the architect for the onset of HIV/AIDS.

Spuriousness and Deficiencies

In the case of Gia Carangi, the contraction of HIV/AIDS was purely synthetic. Had she had children however, the virus could have well manifested as a congenital condition. The MC at the head of the rectangle is also deficient. Ten degrees of Cancer is an azimene degree; and this is perhaps one of the reasons why she didn't have children. Thus, the concept of any children in her life had simply been eliminated from her life; but having children could have made a huge difference in her life. Not having children, however, may also have contributed towards her demise.

Overall, the oppositions and the quincunxes connected to the rectangle were simple too overpowering for her to *consciously* deal with – all powered by a very prominent Pluto. According to the lecturer and spiritual teacher Louise Hay, HIV and AIDS are the result of "sexual guilt" (Neptune/Pluto), and "a strong belief in not being good enough." This is most likely derived as an imprint of her troubled childhood, caused primarily by the position of the Moon-Pluto opposition.

Brief Conclusion

Gia Carangi lived only for a short season – not long enough to rise from the ashes of her earlier life of adolescence. She was 26 years of age when she died. Ordinarily, Carangi's life was a life driven by sexual guilt and drug abuse. Had she had acquired peace and harmony in her life, which lay *concealed* in the depths of her soul, she would no doubt have served humanity in some unique and humanitarian way. Instead, she perished in the viral ashes of her own self-perpetuated annihilation (Pluto). This was most definitely a reflection – denoting the influence of the dark pathological cauldron that coursed through her deeply-ingrained soul.

Rock Hudson

Rock Hudson was an American actor and a movie star. At the pinnacle of his stardom, Hudson rose to prominence both in the 1950s and the 1960s. Unknown to the public, Hudson was diagnosed with HIV on June 5th, 1984. This shocking news story emerged three years after the emergence of the first cluster of symptomatic patients in the US; and ironically only one year after the initial identification by scientists of the HIV virus that causes AIDS.[8]

The Natal Chart

In this locomotive-type chart, Pluto is very authoritarian, and perhaps peremptory. Thus, the locomotive pattern generally determines an individual who possesses a relentless drive towards their focused objectives. How they achieve their goals depends solely on both the leading and boundary planets in the chart. Boundary planets are the spheres that ay at the leading edge of chart's constellated planets and can be very influential in the way the chart plays out, particularly when the natal precepts are medical in nature.

Pluto's elevated position in this case means that it tenants the tenth house alongside the Black Moon (see relevant chart). This cosmic coalition evokes the presence of immeasurable and undisclosed secrets by which many of them are karmic in nature – dragging them through the murky depths

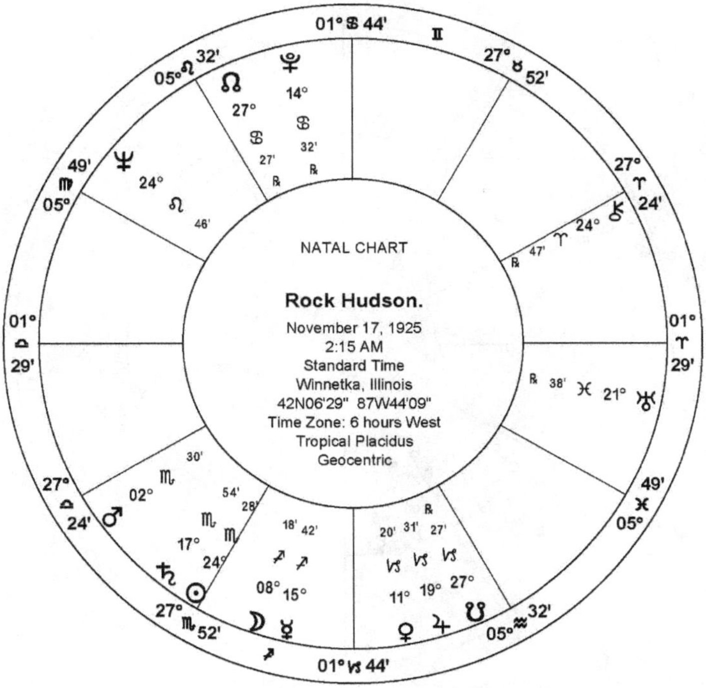

of the subconscious only to be further scrutinized by a suspicious Pluto.

Perhaps, the most profound and clandestine conundrum to spring forth and make its presence felt in a naïve world was the point at which Hudson announced he had contracted HIV/AIDS in 1985. Up to the point of disclosure, however, Hudson managed to conceal his long-time secret, namely that of being gay for many years. Likewise, he even managed to 'somehow' conceal it from his wife Phyllis Gates, who eventually confronted him about his tenebrous sexuality. Karmically speaking, and in my estimation, Hudson kept something very close to his chest, so to speak, in a previous incarnation, which was similar in nature to that in the here and now.

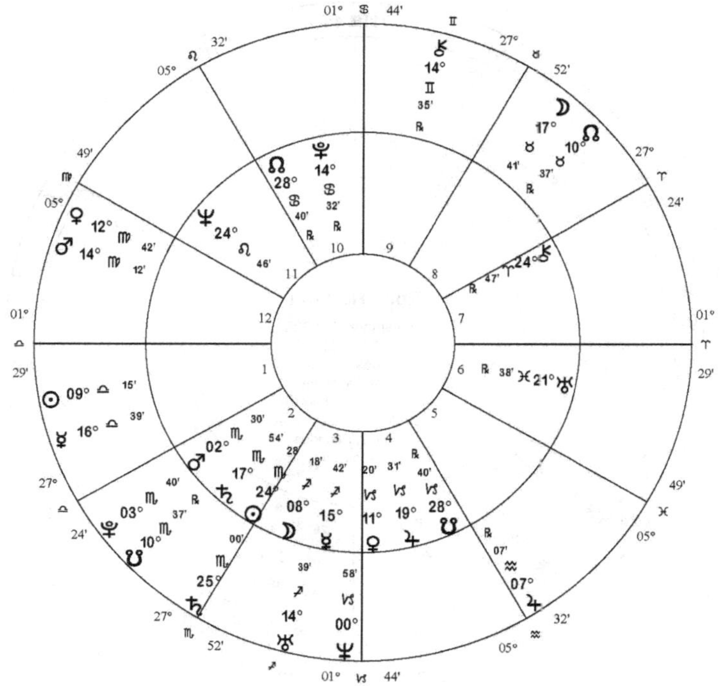

Inner Wheel: Rock Hudson Natal Chart
Outer Wheel: Death of Rock Hudson: October 2, 1985, 12:30 PM; Beverly Hills, California; Placidus Houses, Mean Node

Pluto's position at the top of the chart does, however, provide additional weight to his powerful Scorpio Sun. Although they are not linked directly by aspect, Pluto is nevertheless the natural ruler of Scorpio. Moreover, Pluto's impending overhang (elevation) at the top of the chart acts in this case as a kind of barbarian or even the Plutonian demon of the deep, in which case the planet harbours dominant secrets. However, Pluto's conjunction to the Black Moon would also create power struggles, especially with those domains where authority figures are prevalent, and it was widely known that Hudson had a secret loathing of those he considered to be more powerful than him.

Likewise, it was frequently reported throughout the media that Rock Hudson 'crossed swords' with those he considered to be officially *superior* to him. However, with Black Moon closely conjunct Pluto, the power struggles would most likely have taken place within his own subconscious, thus creating an imbalance between where his feelings and his loyalties lay. Furthermore, Hudson was uncertain as to whom he could trust. This is perhaps one reason why he kept his closely guarded secrets so close to his chest.

Elevations

Elevated planets are considered by many to be powerful influences in the natal chart. In some respects, they could even be deemed as 'accidentally dignified'. In the case of Rock Hudson however, his elevated Pluto created a dichotomy within his deeply-chastised persona. More likely this deep division was a battle between his desire for eminence and notoriety, which was partly powered by Neptune in the eleventh house in Leo, and conflicted with the cloak and dagger facade, projected by an elevated Pluto, coupled by his powerful Scorpio Sun. Combined with all of this was an extreme fear of the unknown. Ironically, this was a traumatic factor that persecuted the very foundation of the life of Rock Hudson. In addition, his deep-set fear (Saturn) extended to the deepest recesses of his soul. This was reflected in the natal chart by the Sun/Saturn conjunction.

Pluto's elevation in the tenth house of status and reputation, coupled by the Sun in the second house of sensuality, may have nonetheless created a much bigger issue, concerning his sexual orientation. His preference for being homophile is epitomized primarily by Pluto's *unchallenging* link to Uranus in Pisces. Let's not forget here that Pisces traditionally represents the sign of confusion. In the natal chart, the 'confusion factor' is augmented here by Uranus's wide and disassociated opposition to the Ascendant

– denoting the self. In essence, Hudson may have, at some point, been *confused*, as to which sex he was naturally drawn to.

Melancholy

There is yet another hidden agenda concerning Pluto's conjunction with the Black Moon. Thus, and for the most part, Hudson was *shouldering* a great deal of sadness. This sadness may have been generated by a deep shame concerning his sexuality – abashment carried over from a previous life perhaps? However, examining this powerful conjunction from a psychological capacity implies that in a previous life Hudson may well have died of a sexually transmitted disease, possibly syphilis, which was prevalent, especially during the Middle Ages. Likewise, the Pluto-Black Moon conjunction points strongly to the law of attraction, especially in the here and now; and this concluding factor points to the reason *why* Hudson died of a sexually transmitted disease. If lessons are not learnt in the here and now, the cycle of karmic law will undoubtedly repeat itself.

A further characteristic of the chart that points to the law of attraction is seen via the Venus-Pluto opposition. In addition, Hudson's Sun exactly squares a much-shrouded Neptune – shrouded by the Sun – because of the exact degree of this aspect. In reality, this square conveys that he *shielded* his sadness and the truth from public view extremely well indeed. Thus, throughout all of his movies, and in his private life, Rock Hudson always exhibited a well composed posture, coupled by a sense of coolness, which was spirited by his Sun-Neptune square.

Tenderness and Femininity

Throughout his life, Rock Hudson frequently displayed and projected a powerful form of tenderness and femininity, which was evident in his movies, where he mostly acted alongside female co-stars. In essence, the ladies loved him. According to the Christian astrology William Lilly 24 degrees of Scorpio, which is the degree of Hudson's Sun, is *feminine*.[9] We have already established that the sorrow Hudson was tormented with was because of issues surrounding his gender. I also suspect however he would have preferred to have been born a female. In addition, I suspect that this particular issue of gender may have had something to do with Uranus in Neptune's sign of Pisces, in a wide opposition to the Ascendant, and coupled by its close trine to Pluto, adding more confusion to the mix.

Lameness, Hence a Depletion of Power

At fourteen degrees of Cancer, Pluto is lame [azimene], according to Lilly. In laymen's terms, the lameness of Pluto's degree meant that in physicality Hudson's was *susceptible* and was also *sensitive* to the contraction of viruses, particularly those of a sexual nature. He was known to have frequent colds. The relative *ease* with which Hudson would nonetheless contract a virus is shown by the close trine from Pluto to Saturn. Essentially, this chart determines that his body was laid bare to the sudden contraction of disease. These medical predispositions were exemplified mostly by the Sun's exact square to Neptune (infection). In addition, the Moon at eight degrees of Sagittarius is also lame according to Lilly. The Moon tenants a medical house, hence the third. This combination would have seriously increased his susceptibility towards the contraction of illness and disease.

Mercury is also considered to be *lame*. Thus, the planet of communication is detrimental in Sagittarius; however, it is domicile in the third house. Therefore, this gives additional nuance to the flighty messenger; and Sagittarius on the cusp of the third house *epitomizes* further the dark influence of Pluto. Primarily, this is because the ruler of Sagittarius, Jupiter, opposes Pluto in the chart. However, because of these connected afflictions, the third house becomes essentially *indisposed*; and it is the point where the AIDS virus began to develop, and thus grow and expand (Jupiter and Sagittarius). In this case, Pluto (the significator of the AIDS virus) casts its dark and malign shadow over the medically-disposed third house – even though it doesn't lay at its natural polarity.

Looking at this combination from a different perspective, Venus and Jupiter, which Pluto opposes. are deemed as the benefic planets. This would, to a degree, cast *light* over a dark and deficient Pluto because of its conjunction with the Black Moon. In which case, the opposition from Pluto to a widely conjunct Venus and Jupiter would pronounce Hudson as a dashing heartthrob, thus projecting a man with a caliginous appearance. Moreover, the opposition from Pluto to Venus would also mean that Hudson possessed the power of seduction, and he would not take *no* for an answer. These characteristics were often displayed throughout his movies, especially when he acted with all his females. As a point of further interest, he initially achieved stardom for his role in *Magnificent Obsession* – obsession being associated with Pluto. An interesting conception!

Personality Characteristics: Inspiration and Creative Power

Pluto sits at the head of a Grand [Golden] Trine linking both Saturn and Uranus in Hudson's chart. What does this mean? Well, with continued hard work, this configuration would prove to be the potential 'diamond' in his chart, in terms of his earned wealth and prosperity, which was orchestrated by his trine from Saturn to Pluto. Although the planets configuring in this pattern would not have always been easy to work with, the scope of potential available to him was *limitless.* However, there were constrictions to contend with. Limitless potential was perhaps best seen with his rise to fame, which happened relatively quickly, which, in part, was the result of the Sun's trine to Uranus.

Equally, he would fall from grace just as quickly, which was also caused, in part, by the oppositions intersecting the Grand Trine. Thus, his fall occurred in the mid-1960s. It was reported that Hudson declined into a state of depression during this difficult time. In Hudson's chart fear and depression (Saturn) runs deep (Scorpio Sun). Both fear and depression are characteristics that became evident in his life in later life – deemed by the Sun-Saturn conjunction – Saturn overseeing maturity.

Desirability

Rock Hudson was certainly a prolific charmer displayed by the Venus-Pluto opposition. Charm, however, was perhaps displayed with an air of eccentricity thrown in for good measure, which was the result of the Sun-Uranus trine. Hudson's charm was no doubt infectious, thus infecting everyone who came into contact with him. Furthermore, Hudson also had the ability to 'charm' the male of the sexes, in particular Marc Christian, who would later become his long-term lover. This *unusual* (for the time of day) partnership was most likely the result of the Sun's trine to Uranus. This would be deemed as a very *male* aspect. Hudson also had an ability to bridge the gap between many cultural differences, such as rich and poor, wisdom and ignorance, scientists and poets. This ability was most likely the result of Saturn's trine to Uranus.

Moreover, Hudson was frequently viewed as a creative genius, especially within the movie industry hence, a further factor generated by the Sun-Uranus trine. Hudson was also a perfectionist (Saturn-Pluto), and he was particularly renowned for inspiring others, especially in later life, which would have most likely been due to the Sun-Neptune square. Thus, it would be wise to suggest that the Pluto-headed Grand Trine was the main catalyst that powered his enormous success, although it was to be proved 'short lived'.

Disintegration

It is fair to speculate that the Grand Trine also played a major role in becoming the instrument for his ultimate demise. Unfortunately, the 'easy approach' associated with the Grand Trine didn't *protect* him from contracting HIV/AIDS. To many soft aspects, particularly trines can render this effect in health charts.

In most cases however, square aspects strengthen the portion of the chart they stimulate and pose the challenge.

Regrettably, and speaking in medical terms, Neptune's square to Hudson's Sun that apportioned (drew in) his Ascendant, merely *weakened* his unusually powerful Sun. In further health terms this weakened effect would have been diminished further by Neptune's square to Saturn, which would have seriously depleted his immune system. In effect, there was always a price to be paid in terms of his health for this speedy and efficient rise to fame.

Death from HIV/AIDS

Death occurred around the onset of his second Saturn return – culminating his second Saturn cycle. This is discernible in the death chart (see below). In the death chart, Pluto's position can be described as dominant, at 3 degrees of Scorpio. Thus, in the natal chart, transit Pluto positions itself on Hudson's natal Mars in a very closely contested conjunction. The transiting North Node (ascension) in the death chart lies at 10 degrees of Scorpio, which according to Lilly is a lame degree. The transit North Node positions itself between the malefic planets of Mars and Saturn in the natal chart. Ordinarily, this Nodal influence *impose*s a death-related transformational influence over these remorseless malefic planets in the natal chart. It would have also brought into question the karmic significators surrounding his current life plan.

The transiting South Node (descending) tenants the eighth house of death and opposes Mars and Saturn in the natal chart. The eighth house is naturally ruled by Scorpio. Transit Saturn at 25 degrees of Scorpio closely conjoins Hudson's Sun (karmic). The transiting Nodes, Pluto and Saturn are also 'intercepted' in the death chart. The impact from these interceptions would instil a sense of shock and disbelief on a wantonly disbelieving world; because nobody would have believed that Rock Hudson, who was the number one heartthrob at that time, was in fact a homosexual; a fact solely concerned with a chart that is so dominated by Pluto and his brother Neptune (secrets and lies).

Expiration

Transit Neptune at 0 degrees of Capricorn is anaretic, is on the cusp on the fourth house of the grave and opposes the MC in the natal chart. Finally, the transit Moon at 21 degrees of Taurus opposes the Sun from the eighth house of death. With all of this planetary activity symbolizing death and transformation, it was without doubt Hudson's time to leave the Earth plane. Death from a sexually transmitted disease was clearly indicated by the array of authority asserted by the heavy Scorpio-Pluto presence – exemplified further by the Neptune (infection) opposition to the MC.

When Hudson passed from his life in physicality, many, especially those who were close to him in Hollywood, would have sincerely hoped that his transition was one of serenity and tranquillity. This notion would have been clear cut, despite the shame that was cast upon him because he died from such an exiled disease. Perhaps however, his passing was peaceful. Rock Hudson was nonetheless a kind and gentle man; and to coin the title from one of his movies: It's What Heaven Would Allow!

Meanwhile, the contractions of both HIV and AIDS were deemed both synthetic and genetic conditions, caused solely by inherent (karmic) and superficial influences.

Contracting both these viruses, however, would have been viewed as an *unfortunate* occurrence. Therefore, it could only be perceived as Hudson's dark night of the soul.

Asexuality

Asexuality is considered to be an illness in its own right. Essentially, asexuality stands for the *lack* of sexual attraction to others. Thus, asexuality is a condition *directly* concerned with Pluto; and therefore it can be an upshot of this planet. To better explain this connotation let us turn our attention to T.E. Lawrence (Lawrence of Arabia), who according to reliable sources (those closest to him), was asexual.

The reason I have chosen to highlight this very Pluto condition is that according to the World Health Organisation (WHO), 'those who consider themselves to be asexual are at further risk of contracting HIV'. This is because the immune system has never had the opportunity to build up a resistance against the bacteria and the microorganisms found in saliva and in the fluids that are transmitted via the act of sexual intercourse.

T.E. Lawrence (Lawrence of Arabia)

Colonel Thomas Edward Lawrence was a British archaeologist, army officer, diplomat and a writer. Lawrence was renowned for his role in the Arab revolt and the Sinai and Palestine campaign against the Ottoman Empire during the First World War. His activities and associations, and his ability to describe them vividly in writing, earned him international fame as the renowned personality known as Lawrence of Arabia.

Lawrence had a difficult childhood — experiencing persistent beatings and abuse from his mother. There is also considerable evidence that Lawrence was a masochist, as a result of the abuse, according to psychologist John E. Mack,* who believed there was a possible connection between his penchant for masochism, and the childhood beating he received frequently from his mother. There is also strong speculation that when Lawrence was captured by the Ottoman military during the First World War, he was beaten and sexually abused. This would have merely added salt to the wounds that were representative of his grievous and submissive tendencies. All of this behaviour was solely the *stimulus* that prompted his abiogenetic propensities.

**John E. Mack was an American psychiatrist, writer and professor and the head of the department of psychiatry at Harvard Medical School.*

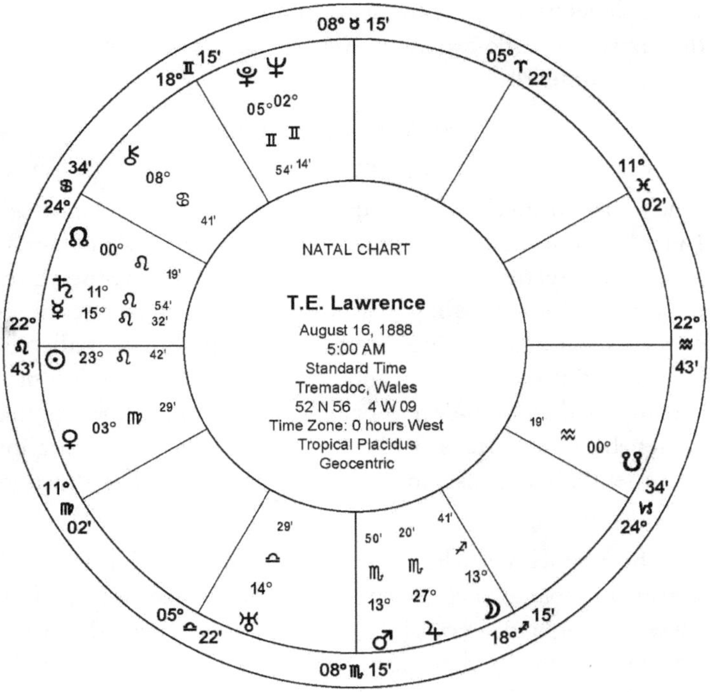

The Natal Chart

In this splay-type chart Pluto is intensely pronounced (see relevant chart below).

Most prominently, Pluto converges with its mythical brother Neptune to form a close conjunction – both of which oppose Jupiter from the fourth house. Pluto also opposes the Moon, which may have accounted for some of the abuse Lawrence encountered as a child from his mother. Moreover, Pluto makes a tight square to a detrimental Venus in its fall. Considering that squares create impasses in energy flow, a Venus-Pluto square would be the main catalyst for his conception of asexuality. Neptune and Pluto are also elevated in the natal chart – synchronized in the MC-ruled tenth house. Mars also opposes the MC.

These planetary configurations would have been responsible for the sexual abuse he experienced at the hands of all his tormentors (Neptune/Pluto).

Provocative Degrees

According to William Lilly two degrees of Gemini (Neptune's natal degree) is afflicted; hence it is pitted (blemished). Thus, Neptune's afflicted degree, with its opposition to Jupiter, posed as a 'negative influence', and would have further perverted the effects of a powerfully-placed Pluto. Further, at twenty-seven degrees of Scorpio, Jupiter's degree is pitted. Essentially, the Neptune-Pluto conjunction and Neptune's opposition to Jupiter is considered to be *nebulous* complete with undercurrents that are tenebrous by nature. This particular planetary configuration was essentially the instrument for Lawrence's professed acts of masochism.

The Midheaven (MC) lies at eight degrees of Taurus, which is also deficient, hence an azimene degree, according to Lilly. Therefore, eight degrees of Taurus on the MC would have increased the already detrimental effects of Venus in Virgo. Venus is of course the natural ruler of Taurus. In effect, Lawrence would not know the meaning of the word *love.*

In Conclusion

The deeper and more intimate feelings that were concealed in the soul of Lawrence of Arabia would have always remained somewhat hazy and obscure throughout his life. This is perhaps the reason why he failed to get really intimate. However, these powerful planetary configurations evident in the natal chart would have nonetheless *reinforced* his overall sense of personal power. This is perhaps the reason why he possessed such an enormous influence over others, especially during the Arab revolt, and throughout the entire First World War. Lawrence of Arabia was essentially a catalyst for transformation of himself and others. Simply, he couldn't afford to be intimate.

Bruce Springsteen: Character Analysis

Before I begin, I would like to reiterate that Bruce Springsteen hasn't contracted, or indeed suffers from HIV or AIDS. But I thought it was appropriate, however, to include his astrological profile as a crucial part of my analysis, thus extending the disposition of these unpleasant conditions. One of the reasons I wish to include him as part of analysis is because Springsteen wrote and performed the title song for the 1993 film Philadelphia, which highlighted HIV/AIDS, homosexuality and homophobia. The song was called *On the Streets of Philadelphia.*

The Natal Chart

In this bundle-type chart (see relevant chart) Pluto's position is one of authority. It is also dominant and decisive – enjoying a loose conjunction to Mars (dominance) –and a tight sextile to Mercury (decision). Mercury is, however, the planet of overall communication. Moreover, the bundle pattern often determines an individual who possesses a great deal of drive and determination, and in Springsteen's case this is no exception.

The characteristic of decisiveness exists solely because Pluto tenants a medical zone, hence the third house. Traditionally, the third house is the house of communication and is ruled by Mercury. In this bundle chart, the third house is considered to be exceptionally creative. As previously spoken, Mars and Pluto are in masterly Leo, and both planets are in sextile formation to insightful, idealistic and a very creative Neptune. In the chart, Neptune tenants the natural home of Leo, hence the skilful and gifted fifth house. In essence, this ingenious capability offers Springsteen a form of guided protection, especially from any impending physical illness and disease. This is because 'honing creativity' constrains the potential for the onset of illness and disease.

Apart from having a long history of depression, which can perhaps be attributed to Pluto's square to Venus, and its half-

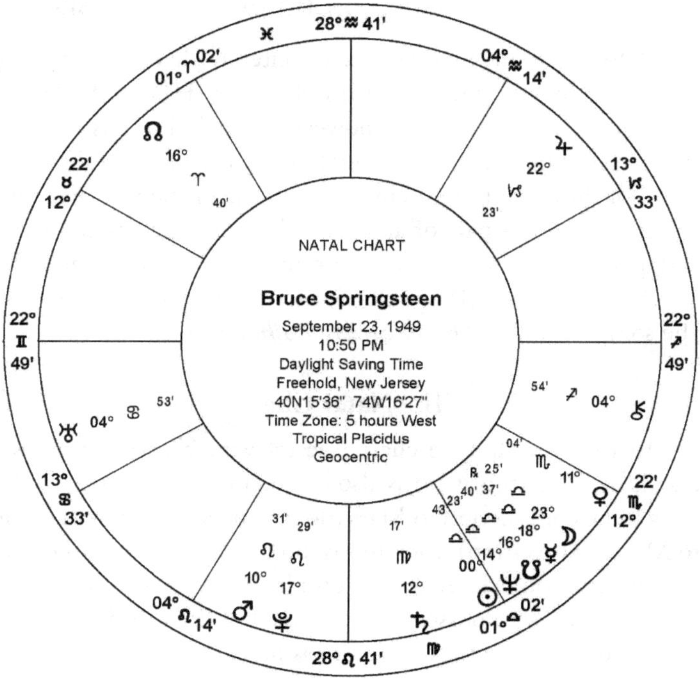

square to the Sun, and with Saturn virtually unaspected aside from a sextile to Venus, Springsteen continues to remain extremely healthy in a physical capacity. He is also youthful (Venus) in mind (Mercury) and in spirit (Neptune). The third house is indeed the focal point of the entire chart because of its medical implications. Pluto assembles alongside a dynamic Mars. Both planets tenant the consolidating sign of Leo in a wide and applying conjunction. This combination not only adds strength to the third house, but it applies a sense of courage and commitment. Pluto sextiles the Ascendant and squares its polarity planet Venus, which is detrimental in Scorpio – adding more ingenuity to the third house.

Objectivity

In addition, all of this powerful Pluto planetary interplay symbolizes that there is also a strong sense of justice present in the life of Bruce Springsteen. This attribute is especially symbolic of the square from Pluto to its polarity planet Venus, partly because the anaretic Sun in justice-orientated Libra assembles at the midpoint of this polarized aspect.

Springsteen is simply an influential Libra, which is emphasized by the Sun at zero degrees of Libra (anaretic). An anaretic Sun in Libra would embody all of the airs and graces associated with this judicial sign. However, an anaretic Sun would consider injustice to be an expression of sheer tastelessness. The anaretic Sun forms part of the powerful Libra stellium – comprised of Neptune, Mercury and the Moon, which are all in sextile formation to Pluto. It is perhaps best said that Neptune's sextile to Mars and Pluto is symbolic of Springsteen's musical abilities. Therefore, in the eyes of Bruce Springsteen, this ingrained planetary characteristic would pose as a greater opportunity to "set the record straight" through song.

Moreover, Pluto's square to Venus (the natural ruler of Libra) highlights that Springsteen would *denounce* bigotry and homophobia, which he is often ridiculed for in the press[10]. Reprisals and repercussions are counteractions that are often associated with the challenging nature of the square.

An Exceptional Musical Talent

Aside from other attributes in the natal chart, it is fair to say that this Mars-Pluto conjunction has been the driving cornerstone for Springsteen's musical career. This is because both planets form a sextile to a conjunct Neptune (music) and Mercury (writing). Interestingly, Mercury and Neptune are a natural polarity – making this an extremely powerful configuration. In addition, Mercury and Neptune oppose the directional North Node in Aries, which adds further weight to Mars as the ruler of Aries. The North Node from the collective eleventh house is besieged between its opposition to Mercury and Neptune. In essence, there is not much room for manoeuvre. This means that Springsteen has little or no option but to proceed upon his

Nodal path. In effect, he is driven upon his Nodal path, and he is very much a 'people person'.

Melodies

Neptune (sympathetic) and Mercury (erudite) are at the center of the Libra stellium, therefore these planets determine the style of music he prefers to perform. Springsteen's songs are often a combination of *studious* stories tinged with *melodic* themes. Furthermore, some of Springsteen's songs are *distinguished* as being notable rock anthems, such as his legendary anthem *Born to Run*. However, in the case of the title song from the film Philadelphia, Springsteen's social interaction (Venus) with the people of this ancient city, which is displayed in the official video of a particular movie song, is therefore a testament to a profound story told in music; and one that upheld his career.

When Springsteen was offered the opportunity to sing the title song for the 1993 film Philadelphia, it was a golden opportunity to express his natural compassion (Neptune) and understanding towards a frequently deemed repulsive subject (HIV/AIDS) – one that often remains in the shadows (Pluto). As previously explained, the fact that Bruce Springsteen recorded and performed the title song for a film about HIV/AIDS is the reason I chose to exhibit this particular case study.

Concatenation

The planetary configurations in his natal chart determine that Bruce Springsteen was most definitely the right man for this particular job in hand. His performance was indeed an enormous influence and a guiding light, which was necessary for the successful production of this influential movie. Therefore, it is fair to say that no one could have written and performed a more befitting song for this meaningful and influential blockbuster movie.

Lastly, it is fair to say that Pluto's sextile to Neptune with Saturn on the midpoint implies that Springsteen's musical abilities are indeed a congenital factor. This is an attribute that he had already honed in previous incarnation, or indeed in the spirit world. However, with the condition of Neptune in the chart, the latter would seem to apply.

Pancreatic Cancer: Steve Jobs

Pancreatic cancer is a disease in which malignant (cancerous) cells form in the tissues of the pancreas. Virgo is the sign, and Pluto is the planet that is most concerned with the pancreas. The primary reason why Pluto is associated with the pancreas is because it is a glandular organ that produces chemical hormones.

In much greater detail however, the pancreas is a small gland located behind the stomach and in front of the spine. Thus, the pancreas produces digestive juices and hormones that regulate blood sugar. According the *The World Health Organisation* (WHO) pancreatic cancer is on the increase. Official statistics record that this disease has risen 30% in the last five years, primarily because of the high levels of diabetes and pancreatitis. Pancreatic cancer however can be difficult to diagnose in the early stages of the disease.

The entrepreneur and business magnate Steve Jobs was a special case indeed. This is because he suffered from a rare and unusual form of pancreatic cancer, known as a neuroendocrine tumor, or an islet cell carcinoma.[11] Let us learn about the onset of this condition from his natal chart.

The Natal Chart

In this splash-type natal chart, Pluto's position is perhaps tenuous and possibly negligible. Thus, its debilitated position is very much 'open for debate'. This is because different systems will calculate a slightly different degree, thus altering its location and orientation in the chart, which is this particular instance, is important. However, its position on a cuspal point has very much determined the style in which Jobs preferred

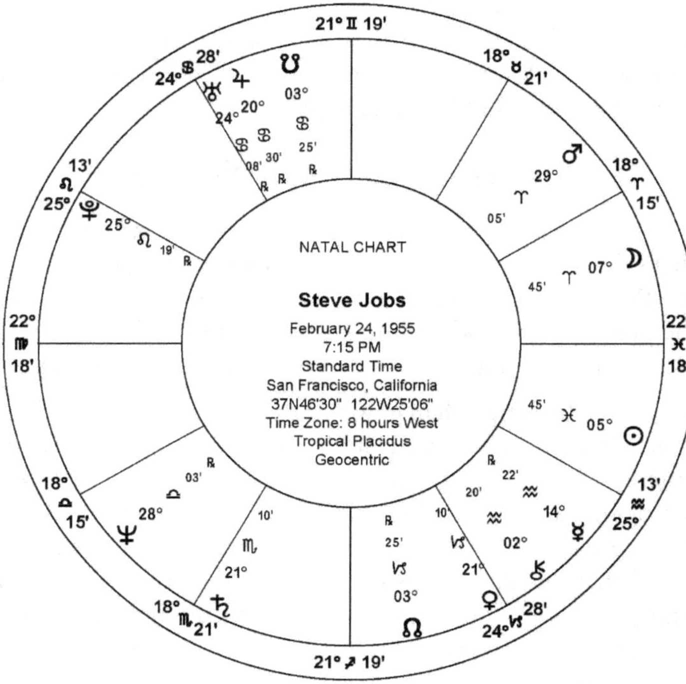

to make use of and employ his unbridled power – power that would benefit the evolution of the collective soul – as well as his own.

Karma

The splash chart pattern often determines an individual who possesses a wealth of life experience spawned within a magnitude of immense karma, simply because the planets are literally *splashed* everywhere around the chart. Loosely speaking, the planets may well signify *ripples* in the chart. This is to say that Steve Jobs had a multitude of issues to address and therefore balance upon the Earth plane. In effect, the splash configuration represents a particular pattern that is often symbolic of tremendous obstacles upon the life path.

So, using the Placidus house system Pluto can be viewed positioned on the eleventh/twelfth house cusp* – wherefore Pluto is *cocooned* by the congenital and synthetic characteristics of both the eleventh and twelfth houses. Ordinarily, this planetary position creates an environment where there would always be a division where one's circumstances are concerned. Hence, this Plutonian situation would manifest as an inner conflict suggesting how to best utilize one's power. This uncertainty was always very evident, especially when Jobs took to the podium to announce the latest breakthrough in Apple Mac technology. Thus, his voice lacked drive; and instead it aired a melodic sense of de-energized inconsistency.

Division: From this impugning position, Pluto creates a dichotomy of uncertainty, and therefore it raises some very important questions concerning his balance of power. For example, from exactly what position does the power that drives the natal chart emanate? Moreover, what, if any, are the other major influences that impact upon Pluto? With all of this in mind, we have to ask a further question. Does Pluto's position denote Steve Jobs as the private man few knew (twelfth house), or Steve Jobs as the man inside of the machine (eleventh house)?

Embryonic Divisions

Firstly, let us examine 'the man inside of the machine', theory – governed by Pluto and Leo's partial influence of the eleventh house. From its 'half back' eleventh house influence, Pluto wields enormous power and authority from this house of invention, ambition, liberty and regulation. This would seem to coincide, because at the height of his success, Steve Jobs was most definitely the leading pioneer of the *Apple Mac* organization.

Thus, his *earned* success was also fuelled, in part, by the relatively close conjunction between Jupiter and Uranus positioned in the tenth house. This technologically advanced conjunction also falls on the midpoint of the sextile between Pluto and the MC. This comparable configuration was responsible, in part, for his remarkable inventions, and his astounding technological breakthroughs. Interestingly, Uranus (invention) is positioned on the cusp of the eleventh house using Placidus houses once again. This cuspal position increases the significance of the planet of technology in the chart, because, for one, the eleventh house is Uranus's natural domain. With all these planets frequenting the cuspal points in his chart we are looking at an individual who lives close to the edge.

We may now turn our attention to another possibility and examine the private man few knew – taking into account Pluto's partial influence over the twelfth house of privacy and secrets of the subconscious mind. Strikingly, there is a sextile present between Pluto and Neptune (exclusion) with the Ascendant on the midpoint of the sextile. Ordinarily, this would cause him to look further within himself, and analyse (Virgo) his subconscious potential (Neptune). If Pluto does, however, wield its complete power over the twelfth, his inspiration and idealism would be driven by a need for contemplation. This would mean that Jobs would have had to subconsciously ask the divine power for permission to bring his instrumental ideas into the realm of physicality. It would also mean that his subconscious concealed a profound secret (see conclusion).

Susceptibility

Speaking from a purely medical perspective, the sextile from Pluto on the cusp of the twelfth house to the natural ruler of the twelfth house, Neptune, positioned in the second house of personal self-worth and consonance would impede the body's ability to *restrain* illness and disease making him susceptible to all kinds of afflictions. This is because this particular sextile is enervated by the abundant influence of wishy-washy Neptune. However, Jobs would have had plenty of time to contemplate his precarious situation.

When Steve Jobs was diagnosed with pancreatic cancer, he was forced to ponder his life, which he did in absolute privacy (twelfth house). This was in accordance to reports in the local media. It was also reported that Jobs was, on occasion, prone to depression, which aside from the gloomy effects of Saturn, can often be associated with the twelfth house, especially when Mars tenants this deep watery domain.

Brief Conclusion to the Man in the Machine/Privacy

Steve Jobs was without doubt the 'leading brain' behind *Apple Mac*. Therefore, he was most likely *drawing* his remarkable and inventive power from an eleventh house positioned Pluto. But when he was later diagnosed with pancreatic cancer, he was most likely drawing on Pluto's obscured power, solely from the twelfth house – purely for self-analysis. Cancer has been designated as a 'lonely disease', and the twelfth house is concerned with both loneliness and chronic cancer in medical astrology.

Wielding such a powerful and sub-muted division of power in the natal chart; Pluto's partitioned influence did no doubt assist in the orchestration of the pancreatic cancer. Essentially, it was the catalyst. Interestingly, if a human being were to lay flat out on their back over the Ascendant/Descendant polarity, the position of Pluto in the chart would designate more or less the position of the pancreas in the body.

* Planets that are situated on cusps are similar in strength and value to planets that are deemed as intercepted. Using progressions however, outer planets on cuspal points are more noticeable when they *shift* position throughout the course of the life.

Further Cosmic Shortfalls and Ill Health

According to William Lilly 25 degrees of Leo (Pluto's sign ruler) is void and concealed. Basically, what this means is that Pluto's power and influence becomes seriously weakened and obscured as a result of this imperfect and fractured degree. However, and speaking in medical terms, this nugatory degree characterises a disposed frailty, especially around the area of the pancreas, and surrounding tissues. Furthermore, a deficiency in the pancreas is indicated by Mercury's applying square to Saturn; and Mercury tenants the domain that Leo naturally rules over, hence the fifth house. Saturn, however, is accidentally placed in Scorpio, the sign that Pluto naturally rules. Thus, there is a kind of *projected* mutual reception at work here.

Pluto's 'vulnerability factor' is heightened further by the Sun's position in the sixth house of health; and tenants Neptune's sign of Pisces and of course the twelfth house. In a natural chart, the sixth house is ruled by Virgo/Mercury, which co-rules the pancreas. The Sun of course is the natural ruler of Leo (Pluto's accidental sign); and apart from a wide trine to Neptune (the natural ruler of the twelfth house), the Sun remains virtually unaspected. This would mean that Steve Jobs marches to the beat of his own drum complete with a sense of having a unique personal rhythm in life. There can also be a strong desire to work solo, and to be in charge, or at the very least, to operate from a leadership position.

Once again, and speaking from a purely medical perspective, a virtually *unaspected* Sun in Neptune's sign means that Jobs has virtually no immune defences that will help to safeguard the body and help to fight off the prospect of illness and disease. Thus, the Sun tenants the sign that is the natural cusp of the twelfth house, Pisces. This combination will nullify the Sun's paregoric and analgesic rays. All of these pointers are intimations indicating the strong possibility for ill health. The further potential for ill health is highlighted by Pluto's association with Neptune – Neptune being the planet that *magnetizes* dis-eases such as cancer.

Additional Pointers

The Ascendant is also lame at 22 degrees of Virgo according to Lilly – incapacitated by its lowly position. Therefore, the Ascendant *enervates* the chart further. Pluto also squares Saturn and semi-sextiles Uranus; and as we have already established, Uranus conjoins Jupiter; and Jupiter is exalted in Cancer. In medical astrology, Jupiter symbolizes tumors alongside Pluto. Therefore, Jupiter's expansive influence from its dignified sign position would systematically cause the tumor (cancerous cells) to multiply.

The 'multiplying effect' would also be initiated by Jupiter's close connection to Uranus, the planet that is semi-sextile to Pluto. Metaphorically speaking however, Jupiter is directly connected to Pluto because of its conjunction with Uranus. So, in some anomalous sense Jupiter does have an influence over Pluto. At the time of death, it was reported that the tumor had *mushroomed*. Anaretic Mars [29 degrees] sits on the cusp of the eighth house of death and opposes Neptune in close degree. This configuration would also weaken the body's response to fight off the effects of the tumor, causing it to slowly balloon.

Congenital/Karmic Intervention

Perhaps more strikingly, there is an exact Yod configuration (finger of God) in the chart between Venus, Saturn and the MC. Venus and Saturn are in sextile formation; and Venus and Saturn are both quincunx (adjustment) to the MC at the apex of the Yod – lying at twenty-one degrees, respectively. Twenty-one degrees is a degree of awareness. With the addition of the Yod, Saturn's tenancy of Scorpio and its connection to Pluto via a square are 'karmic markers' thereby highlighting the cancer as a congenital disorder. In my opinion, the Yod was placed in his chart in order to remind Jobs that he had undergone something similar in a past life. If he had tuned in via his powerfully placed Pluto, and his Neptune-ruled Sun, he would have realized that the Yod posed as this 'latent image', thus imaging the past.

In essence, God was pointing an evolutionary finger at him. Thus, it was divinely *anticipated* that he would remember, especially through his powerful Pluto and twelfth house connections. This being the case, he would make the necessary adjustments in order to avoid a similar pattern of indisposition from transpiring once again. Jobs was however a natural sceptic, and aside from other conditions in his chart, this was most likely a further result of such a dissented Pluto.

However, with all of the additional deficiencies and frictional alignments present in the natal chart, it did seem almost inevitable that Steve Jobs was going to be diagnosed with some form of illness in the here and now; and in this case, it was pancreatic cancer.

Diagnosis/Prognosis

Steve Jobs was diagnosed with a rare form of pancreatic cancer in June 2003. However, he allegedly delayed the surgery to remove the tumor for approximately nine months. According to reports in the popular media, during this interim period, Jobs attempted to treat his cancer with homeopathic remedies. He even placed himself on a special diet. Could such a delay in conventional treatment have exacerbated his prognosis, and facilitated his ultimate death? The assertion pertaining to the fact that Jobs decided to temporally abstain from mainstream medical treatment after his diagnosis remains *unconfirmed*; however, it was later *reaffirmed* by those who were closest to him.

Steve Jobs had a form of pancreatic cancer called a neuroendocrine tumor. Apparently, this type of carcinoma is not as lethal as the most common types of pancreatic cancer, an adenocarcinoma. Neuroendocrine tumors grow more slowly than adenocarcinomas. "That means patients do not necessarily have to rush to attain treatment, said Julie Fleshman", who is the president and the chief executive officer of the Pancreatic Cancer Action Network in Manhattan Beach, California. This is an organization that advocates for pancreatic cancer research, as well as patient and family support.

According to Fleshman, "If surgery is an option for an adenocarcinoma, the patient is usually in the surgical room the next day. However, for a neuroendocrine tumor, the length of time before you have to make decision about your treatment is not as quick as someone whose been diagnosed with an adenocarcinoma. It could be normal that someone would wait some time before they decide to have surgery". Steve Jobs' alleged decision to delay his treatment may not have been as ill-advised at all, as some have claimed.

Further to this, and according to Dr. Maged Rizk, a gastroenterologist at Cleveland Clinic, who told WebMD in a recent interview: "I don't think waiting nine months for surgery was a bad decision. If it is limited disease, especially if it is an islet-cell tumor (neuroendocrine) and the cells are [typical of early cancer], and as long as you don't have symptoms, you can sit on it a while".[12]

Divine Conciliation

When Steve Jobs decided to opt for natural treatments as a way of containing the cancer, unbeknown to him perhaps, he was conversing with his divine internal influence (his soul). This is clearly shown by the seraphic sextile between Neptune and Pluto in his chart – with the Ascendant laying on the midpoint of this saintly aspect. In effect, this configuration symbolized a 'direct line to God'. Had he possessed more conviction in matters of faith, he would have injected light into his body; and thus his immune system would have reacted, and set about destroying the tumor. We all possess the ability to hone 'natural immunity', it just requires a deeper understanding of its existence.

Let us now examine the diagnosis chart (see below) in order to ascertain whether the decision made by Steve Jobs to delay conventional medical treatment was in fact the correct one for him.

The Decumbiture Chart

Primary significators in the decumbiture chart (diagnosis) are Neptune at 13 degrees of Aquarius, which is conjunct Mars at 14 degrees of Aquarius. Traditionally speaking, this conjunction is representative as being tremendously *idealistic*. However,

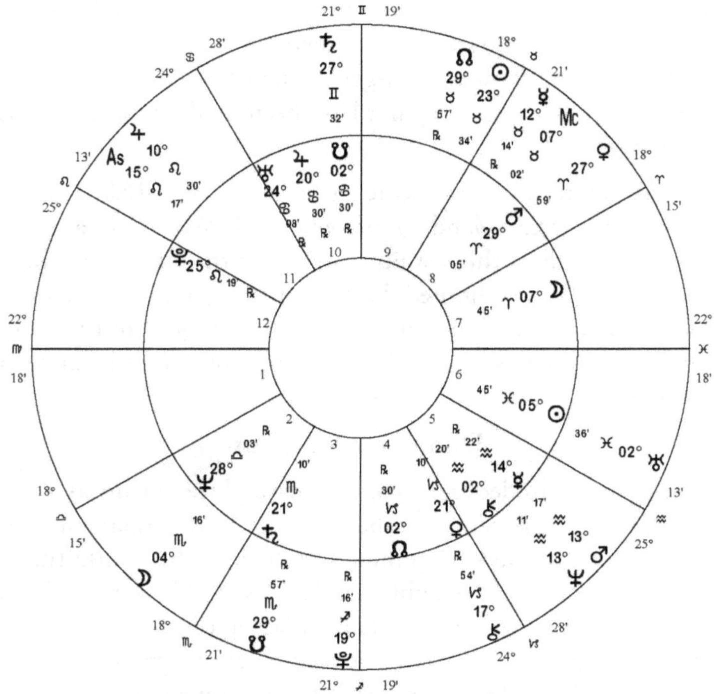

Inner Wheel: Steve Jobs Natal chart
Outer Wheel Steve Jobs Diagnosis Chart: May 15, 2003, 12:00 PM; San Francisco, CA; Placidus Houses, Mean Node

and speaking in a medical capacity, the effects of this transit conjunction would significantly block the flow of energy around the body. Furthermore, the natural flow of energy indicative to this chart would be hindered further by the transit Mars and Neptune's square to Saturn in the natal chart. In most cases, this would indicate the potential for illness and disease, and in this case it would fractionalize the onset of pancreatic cancer.

In addition, the Mars/Neptune conjunction *besieges* Mercury in the natal chart. Although this 'cosmic blockade' would have the potential to heighten awareness, it would nevertheless cause a *deceleration* in the body's natural healing process. As a result, the detrimental effects of the pancreatic cancer became compounded. Therefore, the body goes into systematic meltdown.

Disclosure

Looking further into the intricate workings of the decumbiture chart, we notice Pluto resides at 19 degrees of Sagittarius, and opposes Saturn at 27 degrees of Gemini. Transit Pluto and Saturn both square the Ascendant and Saturn conjoins the MC, with Pluto at the point of opposition. Generally speaking, this mutable configuration would *disclose* the existence of cancer; and in this case it was the presence of the tumor. Furthermore, this shifting planetary/angle configuration would slowly exacerbate the condition to the point of 'no return', primarily because of the square connected to the Ascendant.

A further important significator is the Moon located at 25 degrees of Scorpio, which has formed a quincunx to Saturn at 27 degrees of Gemini. Furthermore, the transiting Moon exactly squares Pluto in the natal chart. Ordinarily, these difficult configurations would seriously expose the location of the cancer. They would also indicate that an adjustment needs to occur on the life path in order to subdue the effects of the cancer – altering the soul's directional path. Configurations of this magnitude are meant to instill in the subconscious 'heightened awareness'.

Finally, the transiting Nodal polarity sees the North Node at 29 degrees of Taurus, and the South Node at 29 degrees of Scorpio, which are both anaretic. The transit Sun is conjunct the North Node. The transit North Node and the Sun are square to Pluto in the natal chart, and the South Node and the transit Moon conjoin Saturn and square Pluto. These are all further extremities pointing to disclosure.

Conclusion

These awkward configurations in the diagnosis/decumbiture

chart, which all act as primary significators, clearly distinguish the cancer as being congenital. Furthermore, the diagnosis/decumbiture chart calls to attention the cancer as being terminal. The primary significant indicator for this concluding factor is without doubt the Mars-Neptune conjunction, which squares natal Saturn. In addition to this, the diagnosis/decumbiture chart typifies that Jobs *would* consider alternative therapy and concluding treatments. Aside from the alternate influence of the Mars-Neptune conjunction, the penchant towards homeopathy is determined solely by the effects of the transiting Nodal polarity.

Cyclical Sequences

A repeating pattern of energy is emerging from the cuspal position of Pluto in the natal chart, which is symbolized further by the square between Pluto and Saturn. Remembering the law of attraction here, it all means that Steve Jobs has not yet *diffused* the cycle of 'inherent complications'. Thus, it seems that Jobs has failed to strengthen his ability to counteract disease, which is inherent in us all. Ideally, Saturn's position in Scorpio should have strengthened his immune system, but due to its square to Pluto sitting on the cusp of the twelfth house, it rendered the opposite effect, thus weakening it somewhat. Therefore, his immune system (Saturn/Pluto) was unable to fight of the effects of the tumor.

In essence, the cyclical sequences of congenital disease equates to a lingering and the karmic dark night of the soul. Notwithstanding, Steve Jobs had been fully versed to this cycle of despair before his incarnation.[13] Fear however was always a key element in his life; and with Saturn in Scorpio his fear ran deep.

The Dichotomy of Evolutionary Karma

There are two important questions that remain unanswered here. Firstly, why was Jobs diagnosed with a slower growing type of pancreatic cancer? Moreover, why did he seek alternative measures in the hope of defeating it? Perhaps we will never really know the answer to both these questions. However, this karmic division may be a further indication to the challenging effects of the powerful square between Saturn and Pluto. Thus, in my opinion it was given as a way to project his soul from the karma of darkness that was evident in previous incarnations. Ideally, this dichotomy of evolutionary ideals would propel the soul towards the light of hope. However, as with the nature of any square, it would need considerable attention and the toil of soul exertion to be overcome. An alternate hypothesis would be to suggest that in a previous existence an evolutionary seed had to be set firmly and deeply in his soul – one that would initiate a wholly new cycle of development (Pluto).

With all of this in mind, it remains solely my belief that when planets frequent cuspal points, the planet involved has the potential to initiate entirely new growth, because it has been infused with the major influences of two house systems. Moreover, if Jobs choses to return to incarnation in the distant future, after balancing the initial setbacks of the past, he may very well succeed in this ultimate quest to attain enlightenment. Furthermore, he may finally break this cyclical rhythm of internal despair that is highlighted by Pluto's position on the cusp of the twelfth house, and the karmic disposition that has led to the onset of repetitive disease, determined the Pluto's square to Saturn.

In the meantime, however, I sincerely hope that his soul acquires peace and spiritual enlightenment, whatever sphere it resides!

Bowel Cancer

Bowel cancer, also known as colorectal cancer, is a form of cancer that affects the colon (large bowel) and rectum (back passage). However, in conventional Pluto style, colon cancer usually grows very slowly over a period of up to ten years. This occurs before it spreads to other parts of the body, such as the stomach, the liver and the kidneys.

Farrah Fawcett

Farrah Fawcett was an American actress of stage and screen, a model and an artist. A five-time Emmy Award nominee and six-time Golden Globe Award nominee, Fawcett rose to international stardom when she starred as private investigator Jill Munroe in the first season of the television series Charlie's Angels. Farrah Fawcett died on June 25th, 2009, from unforeseen complications associated with anal cancer. Her death has always been considered by her Hollywood associates as a tragic end to a glittering and illustrious career.

The Natal Chart

In this locomotive-type chart (see relevant chart) Pluto is incontrovertibly pronounced. Thus, the planet of transformation heads up a series of powerful and oblique oppositions along with Saturn from its second house tenure – to its natural domain – the eighth house. Medically speaking, these planetary oppositions have the potential to generate impediments that further polarize the second-eighth house polarity. In effect, the second-eighth house polarity has become impenetrable like solid concrete, so that anything that sits under the surface will simply fester and deteriorate. Essentially, what this means is there is absolutely no room for manoeuvre within these twin domains. Moreover, these difficult and tense oppositions, particularly the one from Mars to Saturn and Pluto act as the catalyst for Fawcett's colonic complications. The eighth house is however the natural domain for the colon.

Physical Functions

The colon is colloquially called the large intestine and is essentially a water-based organ. Primarily, this is because the colon absorbs water, salt and other nutrients before they are discarded as waste. Once the water has been removed the remaining waste material is then stored before being removed by defecation via the anus.

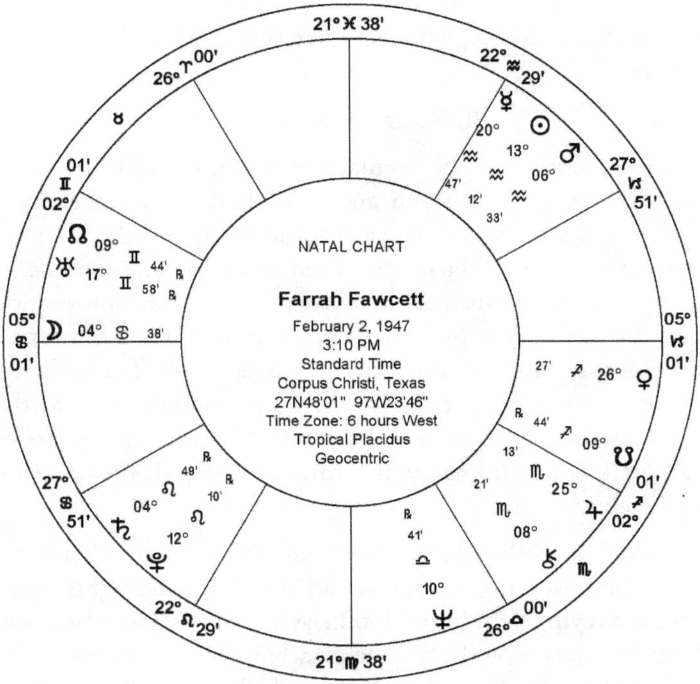

The anus is essentially a colonic conduit (opening) at the base of the colon. The purpose of the anus is to allow the body's detritus to pass safely through, which is comprised largely of fluid-based waste. If the waste solidifies through dehydration for example, it is referred to as inspissation. Inspissation means that the waste fails to pass through the anus. Thus, the lining of the anus can become infected with malignant (cancerous) cells as a result of inspissation. Therefore, the passing of the body's waste, which is a spontaneous bodily function, becomes almost impossible to achieve, which can be excruciatingly painful at the best of times.

Unfortunately, and because of that rigid second-eighth house polarity this was the case for Farrah Fawcett. Moreover, internal bleeding (Mars) in the colon can also occur as a result of bowel and anal cancer, which in Farrah Fawcett's case, was a common occurrence, which only exacerbated her dire situation further.

Planetary Significators

Pluto opposes a detrimental Sun in Aquarius (the life force) and Mars (pain). The Sun and Mars both tenant the eighth house of death; and, as we have already ascertained, this is Pluto's natural home. Mars, considered to be the ancient ruler of Scorpio, is traditionally domiciled in the eighth house. However, because of the Sun's tight opposition to Pluto – from its detrimental station in Aquarius – coupled by the Sun's afflicted degree (see paragraph entitled Infectious Conditions for further information)), Fawcett incarnated with what can only be termed as a 'dark Sun'. Ordinarily, this casts a gloomy shadow over the entire chart.

The Sun is the natural source of light that illuminates the chart. In most cases, the Sun would 'transform' the eighth house, thus conveying light into this otherwise unlit and jet-black zone. Equally, Mars would also energize both the transformational and medical attributes associated with the eighth house. However, because of Pluto's opposition to both these planets, and not forgetting that Pluto rules the eighth house naturally, a reversal of energy has taken place. As a result, a veil of unfathomable darkness has been cast over the eighth house, thus creating a blockage of energy in the body's zone of elimination. In addition, Pluto's accidental rulership of the second house, which is naturally ruled by Venus, *accentuates* the law of attraction (see Congenital Successions for further information).

Bowel cancer is frequently referred to as a 'dark and sinister disease'. In the case of Farrah Fawcett, the karmic seeds of this terrible infirmity have most definitely been set in the eighth house. However, because the eighth house is naturally twin-ruled by Mars and Pluto, think of this zone as being representative of the anus – with Mars representing the left buttock

– and Pluto the right. Unfortunately, because of Pluto's opposition to Mars, Pluto simply *anthropomorphizes* the habituated influence of the red planet.

Intensified Energy

Further, a Pluto-Sun-Mars opposition would ordinarily symbolize a powerful driving force in the chart. Hence, it would denote a configuration that systematically increases the external (Sun/Mars) and internal (Pluto) energy levels of the individual concerned. It was frequently remarked upon by Fawcett's friends and colleagues that she always processed an abundance of energy. Certainly, this elevation of vitality was clearly evident throughout all of her acting roles. She was ecstatic. Notwithstanding, Fawcett may have burnt herself out on more than one occasion because she thought she had more energy than she actually did. Mars's opposition to contractual Saturn would indeed impose fatigue. Depleting her energy levels in this way would no doubt cause her body to become susceptible to illness and disease.

The energy that is released by a Sun-Mars-Pluto opposition must be *honed;* otherwise, it can be calamitous. One could always say however that Saturn's close presence would balance it all out, but Saturn would exemplify the problem. Therefore, speaking from a medical perspective, oppositions of this magnitude emanating from such powerful domains can be symbolic to an unfortunate and unrefined mechanism, that contributes to the onset of illness and disease, which can afflict the throat, kidneys, and of course the colon. Moreover, oppositions of this dimension can equally be responsible for the onset of blood disorders.

The Infectious Conditions of the Dark Sun

When residing at 13 degrees of Aquarius, the Sun is said to project a 'forbidding influence'. according to William Lilly. Further, the Sun's influence is epitomized by the unyielding darkness encompassing the eighth house. Neptune (Pluto's mythical brother) at 10 degrees of Libra tenants the fourth house of the grave, and trines both the Sun and Mars. According to Lilly, 10 degrees of Libra is a dark and unfathomable degree[14]. Unfortunately, an undermined Neptune alters the tranquil effects of the trine somewhat – transforming it into a more inimical influence. In addition, Jupiter in Scorpio (Pluto's rulership sign) squares Mercury; and Mercury is also positioned in the eighth house. Jupiter's square to Mercury would simply metastasize the colonic cancer.

Karmic Providence:

Overall, this hive of planetary energy points to impending difficulties surrounding the areas of the body that concern the process of elimination in the chart. In addition, this planetary activity elicits the sexual organs of the body. It was often reported in the media by those who knew her intimately that Fawcett often placed much emphasis on sex before love in her life. This may have accounted to the fact why her solar plexus and base chakra was severely *unbalanced* – adjudged by the imbalance of the second-eighth house polarity.

Farrah Fawcett died at the age of 62, just shortly after her second Saturn return. At the time of the estimated diagnosis transit Saturn was besieged between its natal position and Pluto – opposing the Sun and Mars. Transit Saturn made a sextile to Neptune (cancer). In essence, this sextile merely posed as an opportunity for the cancer to proliferate, especially when transit Saturn opposed Mercury near to her death.

Moreover, transit Pluto (bowel) opposed the Moon and the Ascendant and made a quincunx (the death aspect) to Neptune – announcing that death was imminent – in this case it was just a whisper away (Neptune). Overall, these planetary pointers signified a karmic destiny, pointing to a cycle of recapitulation.

Congenital Successions

Fawcett's cancer was most likely congenital, and it was sustained via circumstances that were wholly synthetic by design, hence the presence of blocked energy. Further, it is fair to speculate that Fawcett suffered from something similar in a past life; therefore, the current effects of the cancer would be *cyclical.* Pluto's wide conjunction to Saturn (karma) in the natal chart, coupled by Pluto's opposition to the Sun, were essentially the deciding factors outlining this cycle of karmic repetition.

If there was no resolve to these health issues in past lives, then the cycle repeats (perpetuity). Unresolved karma in the here and now is a part of Pluto's many hidden assurances. Repeating cycles are also concerned with the law of attraction, which is overseen by Venus, which is Pluto's polarity planet.

When the Roman centurions engaged in battle they recited a prolific affirmation: "what we do in life echoes throughout eternity". This expression is very Plutonian! What they failed to take into consideration, however, is for all of their killing and maiming, their abominable actions would, after their death, place them in the dark realms of the spirit world, which are reflected in the realm of Pluto.

Absolution

Despite the presence of Fawcett's dark Sun, it was widely believed that she was indeed a good and kindly soul. Perhaps then, at the time of her death, transit Pluto's quincunx to Neptune would have helped her make the adjustment back to the spirit world. Once there, she would have no doubt *shone* like a true angel – working for God, as opposed to Charlie – the main but absent character from the TV series Charlie's Angels. Her character portrayal of Jill Munroe was perhaps her most famous role. The Neptune-Pluto quincunx would have no doubt given her the opportunity to finally escape the dark night of the soul that is deeply reflected and ingrained in her natal chart.

Unfortunately, the life of Farrah Fawcett was most definitely cut short by a debilitating and karmic disease. Thus, her life symbolized a very 'short season' in the transformational and generational realm of Pluto. Maybe now she will finally be given a prolific opportunity to rise out of the ashes of her earlier lives. I wish her soul every success whatever spiritual sphere she resides in.

Hyperhidrosis

Hyperhidrosis is a common condition in which a person sweats excessively, and in excess of that required for the successful regulation of body temperature. Although it can be regarded as a physical burden, hyperhidrosis can deplete the quality of life from a physical, emotional and social perspective. It has been named by some as the 'silent and lonely handicap'. These are qualities that very much characterized in Pluto's realm of authority.

David Hasselhoff (AKA 'the Hoff')

David Hasselhoff is an American actor, singer, producer and businessman, who set a Guinness World Record for the most watched man on TV. On June 26th 2002, Hasselhoff checked in to the Betty Ford Clinic for alcohol-related problems. During his time in the clinic, he was often seen sweating excessively. After seeing a physician, he was told he suffers from hyperhidrosis.

The Natal Chart

In this bundle-type chart (see relevant chart) Pluto is in a very prominent and an extremely influential position. In the chart, Pluto, which is frequently referred to as the God of the Underworld, is surrounded by a hive of potentially 'disposed' planetary activity – highlighting it as a very shady influence. As Pluto appears at the base of this combined planetary activity aside Mercury, and with Uranus at the tip of this cosmic elevation, it could very well be deemed as a planet that resides in the underworld. The effect of this will be significant.

In addition, a dignified Mars, that would naturally personify

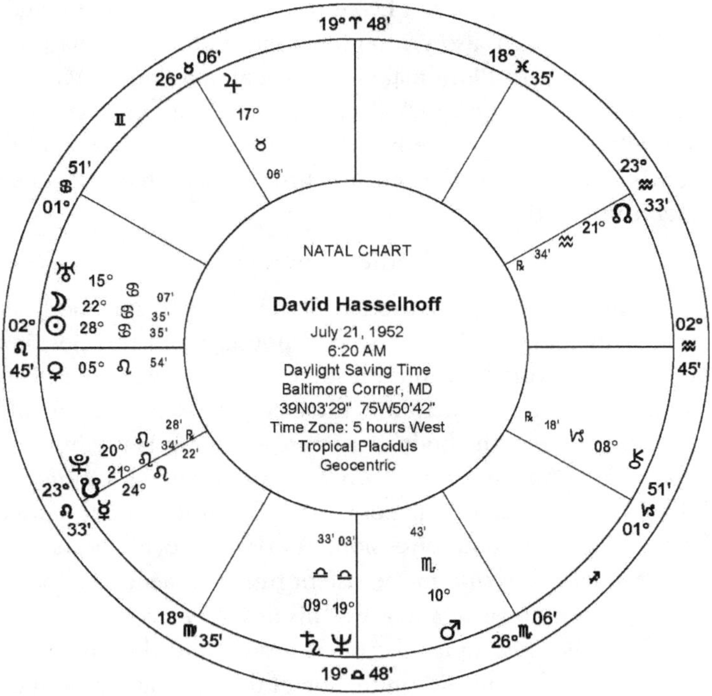

the 'heat factor' within the body, opposes Jupiter. Traditionally, Jupiter is symbolized as the planet of excess and overindulgence, so the body's ability to overheat will simply go into overdrive because of this opposition. Mars is fixed at ten degrees of Scorpio (Pluto's rulership sign) and is a pitted (lame) degree according to William Lilly. Pluto is, however, anchored to this opposition via a square to Jupiter; therefore Pluto's potential for activating the sweat glands would border on *excessive* and *intense.*

Catalyst

The 'lame effect' that is embedded within the degree of Mars, coupled by the red planet's occupation of Scorpio (Pluto's rulership sign), and its opposition to Jupiter is the primary catalyst in the natal chart for the onset of hyperhidrosis. In addition, Pluto tenants the sign of Leo; and Leo is the sign that is naturally ruled by the Sun, which also symbolizes heat in the chart. As previously determined, Pluto makes a tight conjunction to Mercury, which symbolizes the 'quicksilver effect'. This powerful conjunction will also increase the body's ability to sweat more rapidly, especially in view of the medical first house, which has been *superheated* by the Sun's rulership sign.

Predicaments

Using the Placidus house system, Pluto and Mercury both lay close to the cusp of the first/second house. From this position, both would naturally relinquish some of their power potentially causing paranoia. Furthermore, these default occurrences would ordinarily weaken the body's structure – leaving Hasselhoff vulnerable and prone to a miscellany of fixations and obsessions. Is it likely that Hasselhoff's hyperhidrosis is connected to a buried fixation, or even some obsession? According to his peers Hasselhoff has an obsession for persistent freedom; hence he doesn't like to be tied down in any way. This obsessive desire may emanate from the close square between Uranus and the MC in his chart. Because Uranus sits on the top of this planetary mountain in the natal chart, the effect of the square resonates through the stellium, and thus it comes to rest on the base of the Pluto-Mercury conjunction.

Further, Planets residing on the cusp of a house emit some of the qualities that are attached to anaretic degrees; these are planets that reside at 29 or 0 degrees respectively. So, from this cuspal position, Pluto is faced with a potential crisis of where its authority and its power are brought into question. Thus, should the planet of transformation make the first house his permanent home? Or alternatively, is Pluto going to hone his power from the second in light of its conjunction to Mercury?

Karma

I suspect that Hasselhoff's health problems are in fact

karmic by nature. In the natal chart however, the Sun and its natural polarity planet Uranus tenant the twelfth house of karma, which are configured in a very wide conjunction. Therefore, this reticent silhouette of planetary superpowers will haul to the surface a myriad of explicit self-centered emotions that are consistent with being immeasurable, defiant and ineffable. I use the word reticent because the twelfth house is essentially a vast and fathomless ocean; and when planets appear to be drowning in it, their energies become diffident.

If we were to examine the psychological profile of this analogy, it would suggest that in a previous incarnation Hasselhoff experienced some kind of trauma, hence a bolt from the blue (Uranus), which was life changing by its very design. As a result, it may mean that he is still being persecuted in some way, which the cause may not be easy to identify (twelfth house). Perhaps, he permanently feels a sense loss (Pluto); and he may be plagued by the notion of apprehension (the Sun). Combined with the planetary stellium, these feelings ultimately cause his sweat glands to go into overdrive.

In addition, all of these conceivable notions parallel Neptune's opposition to the MC, and its square to the Sun and Uranus. Neptune is of course the natural ruler of the twelfth, and the accidental ruler of the eighth house, which is Pluto's natural domain. This is further evidence as to why Hasselhoff cannot identify the source of his ultimate concerns.

A Compulsion for Chemical Stimulants

It has been widely reported in the media many times that David Hasselhoff has battled a lifetime of alcohol addiction – Neptune's compulsion to vanquish the mystification surrounding the twelfth house. Perhaps his sweating disorder is supplemented by all the additional fluids and semi-poisonous toxins he regularly floods his body with. This is a notion that is also conceivable with Neptune's tenure of the medical third house.

Hasselhoff's alcohol addiction may also be karmic, because Saturn, the Lord of Karma, also tenants the third house and opposes the MC. Further evidence that strengthens this hypothesis is Saturn's rulership sign of Capricorn is the accidental ruler of the sixth house (health), which of course is the polarity of the twelfth house.

David Hasselhoff's alcohol addiction is perhaps another reason why Pluto forms a sextile to Neptune – reflecting the natural karma of this particular disorder. Neptune is often perceived as the 'personalized karmic mirror'; and in this case Pluto will simply intensify the magnetic reflection of the mirror.

Furthermore, Neptune's sextile to Pluto represents the catalyst for intensified glamour. Hasselhoff has always deemed as one of Hollywood's 'sex symbols'. This notion came to the forefront when he played Mitch Buchannon in the popular American TV series Baywatch.

However, it is fair to point out that in such a warm climate he would naturally *perspire.*

Anhidrosis

Anhidrosis is a condition where perspiration is diminished or is absent. It is a disorder that increases sensitivity to heat due to an inability to cool down. It can cause such things as dizziness, muscles weakness and a rapid heartbeat. Anhidrosis is a relatively rare condition with only 20,000 cases worldwide being reported each year.

HRH Prince Andrew: The Duke of York

In November 2019, in an interview, and with regard to underage sexual assault allegations, Prince Andrew told the interviewer * that he "very rarely sweats". Ordinarily, this is a condition known as anhidrosis. However, because of all the speculation and the insinuations surrounding this interview, it has compelled me to examine the natal chart of HRH Prince

Andrew, in order to determine whether or not he *realistically* suffers from this underlying and extremely rare condition.

The Natal Chart

In this locomotive-type chart (see relevant chart) Pluto is decidedly prominent and powerful. In which case, the planet of transfiguration is instrumental in its pursuit to *transform* the natal chart into the ultimate 'master of disguise', which has always been Prince Andrew's trademark. As a point of reference however, locomotive charts often represent individuals who think that life is just one big adventure. Therefore, this particular cosmic ornamentation sets the precedent for Prince Andrew's often controversial lifestyle.

Pluto, the planet of power, and an exoteric dark spirit that represents that which lies beneath the surface tenants the second house in the natal chart and opposes the anaretic Sun at zero degrees. The Sun lays on the cusp of the eighth house using the Placidus house system. This potentially oblique and underhanded opposition determines that above all else he craves power that will ultimately serve his own sense of impartiality and justification. However, because of Pluto's tricky connection to Neptune via a mutable/fixed sextile, many in the media would argue that his sense of power is often tinged with deception, slyness and trickery. This is partly true because the sextile is an aspect that is both experimental and exploratory in nature.

Moreover, the second-eighth house polarity is concerned with the sensual (second house) and lustful (eighth house) act of sex. However, the youthful Venus overall influence that is concerned with the second house, and coupled by the wider implications of the Sun-Pluto opposition is perhaps the reason why Andrew is 'alleged' to have had sex with underage teenage girls. Furthermore, the natural rulers of both these houses, Venus and Mars, are in very close proximity to each other in the natal chart, which would personify this allegation further. In addition, a further underscoring implication

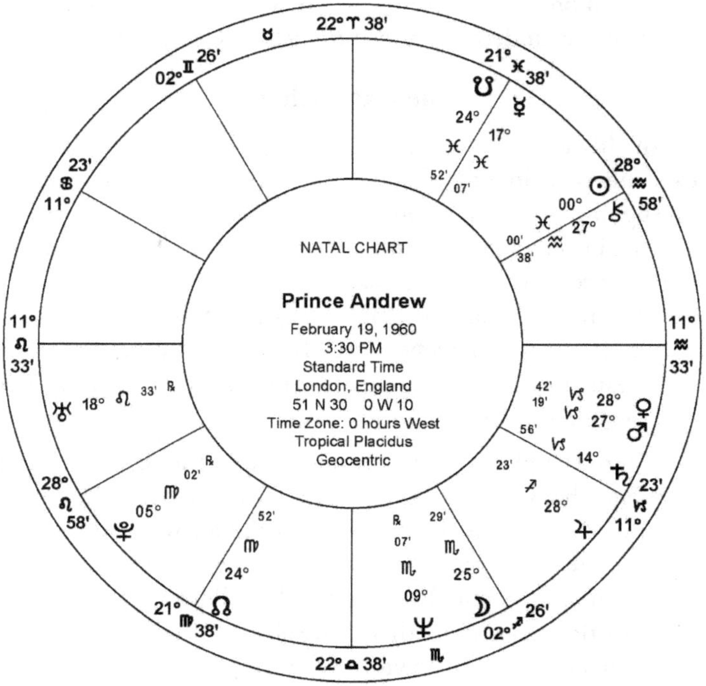

that we can firmly say that is also connected to the allegations may well lay deep in the realm of Pluto, which in this case tenants the sign of Virgo, which represents the adolescent virgin. Thus, Virgo is associated with purity, pubescence and adolescence; and it is the natural ruler of the sixth house. The sixth house in this case is where Venus and Mars apply *cement* to their bountiful and copious relationship. In essence, sex would always play a role on Prince Andrew's state visits, hence his busman's holidays.

Contravening Deficiencies

nI the natal chart, Pluto lies quite *comfortably* at five degrees of Virgo, which is a sensitive point. I say comfortably because according to William Lilly five degrees of Virgo is a dark and deficient degree, which, at the traditional level of influence, the dark very much suits Pluto. The psychology of this would determine that Pluto is continually shrouded by darkness in this chart, and because of its wide combustion to the Sun via the opposition; it is therefore a planet that is rarely discerned as being in the *light*.

With Pluto permanently shrouded by a dark mist means that Prince Andrew would give very little away, especially with regards to his movements and his secretive activities. Pluto also makes a disassociated trine to an expansive Jupiter. From a medical perspective, this configuration alone is likely to increase the prospect of 'defective sweat glands', which of course is the condition known as anhidrosis.

Further significators that would indicate the prospect of defective sweat glands are Pluto's sextile to Neptune, and Neptune's fixed square to the Ascendant. Defective sweat glands are often a sign of underlying guilt, which would in this case be concerned with Neptune's square to the Ascendant. Furthermore, Neptune's degree is deficient [pitted] according to Lilly. Unfortunately, this shady combination, which involves a darkly-placed Pluto, contravenes all of the above characteristics. Therefore, it also casts doubt over Andrew's claim that he actually suffers from the condition of anhidrosis.

An Alternate Hypothesis

Pluto's disassociated trine to Jupiter (expansion) with Neptune at the midpoint of this configuration, coupled by the sextile from Neptune to Pluto could actually work to *exacerbate* the natural function of the sweat glands – rather than contract them. Furthermore, Venus's conjunction to Mars, with Mars representing heat is a further significator that points to the prospect of excessive sweating. In this case, excessive sweating would therefore be evident during the act of sex, as determined by this close conjunction.

Hyperhidrosis

Considering reports in the media to the contrary, especially those surrounding the Jeffrey Epstein investigation, in which Prince Andrew is strongly affiliated, it is more likely that Prince Andrew suffers from excessive sweating (hyperhidrosis). * Ordinarily, a Neptune square to the Ascendant, especially one that is influenced by a darkly-placed Pluto has a tendency to *oscillate* towards deception and duplicity.

Heated Nobility

There is one particular sign of the zodiac that is mostly evident within the royal family, and to which Prince Andrew is a prominent member, and the Queen's favourite son. This sign is a kind of royal parsonage. The sign of course is regal Leo. Leo is the sign on Prince Andrew's Ascendant. Leo of course is ruled by the Sun (heat). The Sun tenants Pluto's natural domain, the eighth house.

Here, this naturally cold and dark domain would become superheated – reaching boiling point. This is because the energy from Pluto would intensify the heat of the Sun via the opposition. Heat paralysis, which is a condition in itself, would occur, especially during the act of sex, which is contrived by Pluto and the eighth house. Medically speaking, heat paralysis and heat exhaustion will always be factors when the Sun tenants Pluto's natural domain. It is a fair assumption to suggest that Prince Andrew 'burns himself out'.

Moreover, the entire chart can be representative of a boiling cauldron. This is because the Sun tenants the water sign of Pisces – fire heats water – and the Sun's sign of Leo rises on the Ascendant. These are all further indicators pointing to Prince Andrew's impaired sweat glands, which are more likely to be the result of hyperhidrosis.

Conclusion

In November 2019, amid a flurry of accusations, Prince

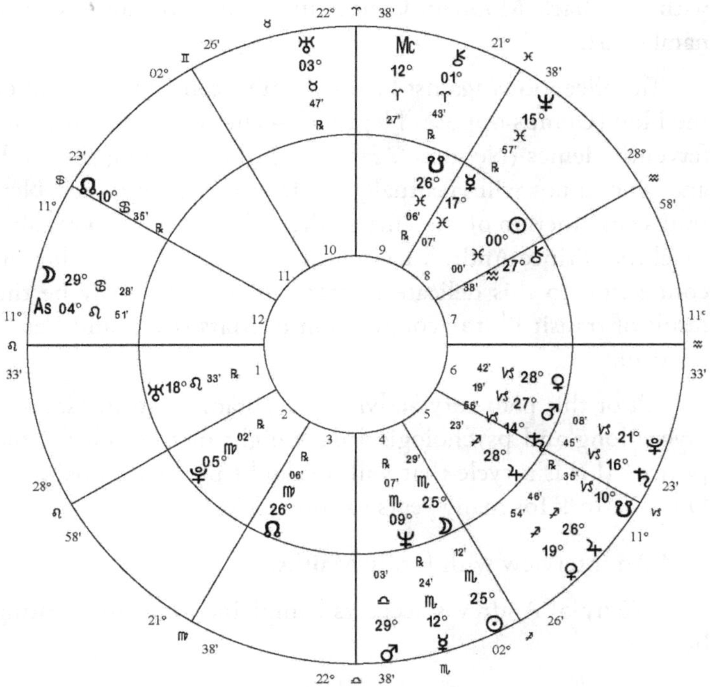

Inner Wheel: Prince Andrew Natal Chart
Outer Wheel: Inrerview; November 17, 2019, 9:00 PM; London UK; Placidus Houses, Mean Node

Andrew was instructed by his peers to step down from his royal duties. Ironically, this monumental embarrassment occurred for the Prince at the time of his second Saturn return in the sixth house of work and other work-related activities.

Other significant factors that contributed heavily towards his downfall are transit Saturn and Pluto squared to the MC, with Saturn opposing the Black Moon, transit Neptune conjunct Mercury in the eighth house, and transit Uranus opposing Neptune. Over the years many have insinuated that his royal highness is the 'black sheep' of the family. Assuming this notion is correct, this dark persona may have something to do with the Black Moon in Cancer in the twelfth house of the natal chart.

The allegations against Prince Andrew came literally out of the blue (Uranus opposes Neptune) – allegations to which he fervently denies (Neptune). However, who is telling the truth and who is not will eventually be determined by transit Neptune's conjunction of Mercury in the eighth house. Regrettably, I feel that Prince Andrew has a lot more sweating to endure in connection to this delicate matter, which will mostly be the result of transit Pluto's conjunction to Mars (heat) and Venus (justice).

All of this planetary activity is a testament to the start of a very long and psychological dark night of the soul for the prince. This is a cycle that will no doubt persecute HRH the Duke of York for many years to come, I fear.

* An interview with Emily Maitlis.

* Many of Andrew's accusers complained of him sweating heavily.

Crohn's Disease

Crohn's disease is a chronic bowel condition that causes severe inflammation of the digestive tract, and seriously affects the overall quality of life. In some cases, Crohn's disease can be fatal. However, it is important to point out that all diseases that afflict the colon are in effect pointing towards a major transformation (Pluto) that the bowel (emotional brain) is therefore undergoing.

Shannen Doherty

Shannen Maria Doherty is an American actress, producer, and television director. She is perhaps best known for her role as Brenda Walsh in the TV show *Beverley Hills 90210*. In 2015, Doherty was diagnosed with breast cancer, which at the time was believed to be in remission. However, in 2019 the cancer returned, and according to the latest reports she is now battling stage 4 of breast cancer, which is still the case to date.

However, since her early childhood, she has been suffering from Crohn's disease.[15] Perhaps, the toxic and debilitating effects of the Crohn's disease in her body, which have been evident for so long, are partly responsible for the onset of the breast cancer? In order to determine this, let us now examine the natal chart in an attempt to discover the triggers for the Crohn's disease.

The Natal Chart

In this locomotive-type chart (see relevant chart), Pluto's position, which is rising on the Ascendant, represents the embodiment of both personalized and evolutionary transformation. Essentially, these are the attributes that are necessary to her psychological and physical well-being. Medically speaking, Doherty's well-being can be balanced and therefore maintained through on-going service to others. Primarily, this characteristic is exhibited by the Virgo archetype; the sign that Pluto tenants, and the sign ruling her Ascendant. Thus, doing service for humankind would benefit her life enormously, and in all manner of ways. This selfless act would also help her to find peace and achieve parity in her life, which has most likely been lacking because of the presence of the Crohn's disease. The need for *equality* in all ways is highlighted by the powerful Libra-ruled first house. Her need for peace is in fact an indispensable and an incumbent component – required for all souls born under the sign of Aries.

Prime Characteristics

Uranus and the Black Moon both tenant the first house. As previously determined, balance and harmony are essential attributes that Doherty must *ideally* acquire in the here and now to prevent any possibility of illness and disease. However, because of the karmic Black Moon's position in the personally-orientat-

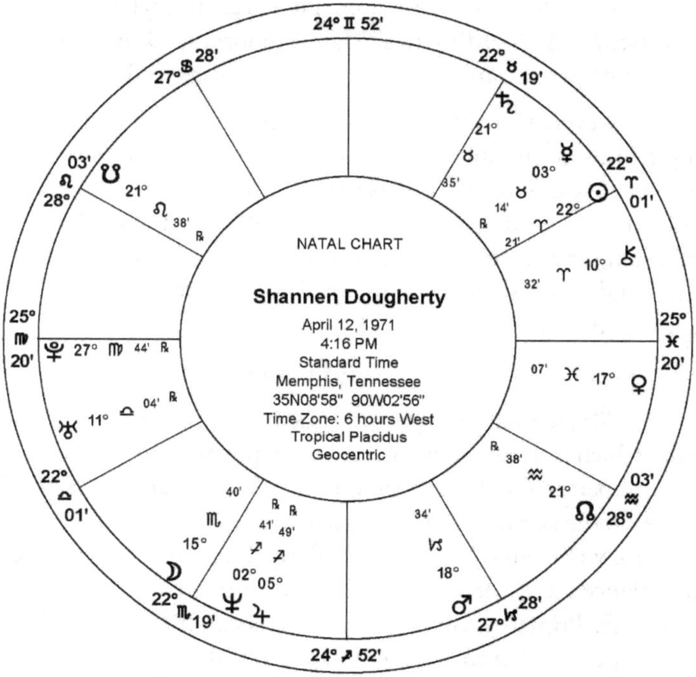

is formed. Ultimately, this Grand Trine is essentially the 'driving force' in the chart, with Pluto acting as the main power unit for it.

Moreover, Pluto's disassociate sextile to Neptune – Neptune being indicative to the film and TV profession provides a sense of flair to her many incentive and motivational roles. Thus, in both her movie and acting positions Doherty has managed to *captivate* her audiences across the world with her powerful and expressive performances. Perhaps then, her penchant for acting is in fact her chosen way that ultimately allows her to perform service to others subconsciously. If so, this self-expression is a trait displayed by the Virgo Ascendant, which is powered by Pluto, and further expressed by Pluto's sextile to Neptune.

ed first house, harmony is an attribute that she simply *failed* to secure in past lives – even though she craved for it – a fact that is projected by the Libra ruled first house. A failure to reignite peace in her life this is perhaps the main reason why Shannen Doherty was afflicted by such a serious health condition so early in her life. Thus, this enervating bowel disorder is displayed largely by the disassociated and wide conjunction between the Black Moon and Pluto. The Black Moon is symbolic to the conditions of a past life, and Pluto, in this case, represents the failure to achieve transformation thereby creating an imbalance within the second brain [bowel].

Virgo is the sign closely associated with the digestive system, by which the colon plays a major role; and Pluto is rising in the first house. From this powerful position it is crucial that the planet's internal resonance (energy) is discerned and defined in a clear and precise manner, hence its energy should not be snared in any way. If it is not, there can be *lingering* problems that are mostly associated with past life health concerns. More often than not, Pluto *craves* power, especially from this position in the first house, and so close to the Ascendant. However, if Pluto's power is manipulated in any way illness and disease are likely to become issues that *terminate* the flow of energy around the natal chart.

Steering the Karmic Journey

In this life Shannen Doherty chooses to climb the career ladder; and this is especially so within the film and TV industry. Thus, she did it with such grit and determination. Perhaps, however, she put her career before her overall health? Deep down (Pluto) she is the only person who can truly answer this. Doherty's personal sense of navigation within the media circus can be contributed solely to the conjunction between the Ascendant and Pluto and its wide trine to exalted Mars in Capricorn (career), which is exalted (career). This is coupled further by Mars's trine to Saturn and placed all together a Grand Trine

Misdirection

According to Louise Hay, Crohn's disease is the result of "building up a resistance to change". Unfortunately, some of her fellow actors have accused Doherty of being a 'manipulator', and furthermore a 'pathological liar', who is 'strongly resistant to change'. She has even been accused of instigating cruelty towards others. Doherty has however gained a reputation in the media for bad behaviour, which dominated her public image for many years. In 1993, Doherty had a restraining order served on her by Max Factor, to whom she was previously engaged. This restraining order alleged that Doherty had directed 'physical violence and constant threats' towards him.[16]

Assuming this information is correct, these aggressive and duplex infractions are consistent with Pluto's square to the MC in Gemini – further to its conjunction with the Ascendant. There is no doubt that Doherty possesses a dark side to her personality. This is further emphasized by the Ascendant-Pluto-Black Moon conjunction. In addition, the wide opposition from Venus to the Ascendant feeds her pent-up antagonism (Pluto) and her fiery aggression (Mars). However, with Venus exalted in Pisces, and Mars exalted in Capricorn and both in sextile to each other, her anger is often tempered with compassion.

However, with Mars, the natural ruler of her Sun sign, in square to Uranus from the first house, this natural form of understanding is always going to be a tall order to achieve. Perhaps, the saving grace is that Venus is the accidental ruler of the first house.

Doherty's temperament however, which has been fashioned by Pluto rising in the chart and with the Moon in Pluto's sign – a reality that was fabricated solely by her troubled childhood, is also likely to be the cause of the breast cancer. In addition, it is quite likely that her repressed anger that emanates from her childhood, and which is exhibited by the Mars square to the Ascendant and Pluto, is the sole cause of the Crohn's disease.

Resolution

The Moon's opposition to Saturn (karma) in the natal chart suggests that Doherty has incurred something similar in a previous life. Crohn's disease is often a physical mechanism for the eventual onset of cancer. However, if we examine the natal chart from a wholly new perspective, Pluto's close conjunction to the Ascendant and Black Moon would suggest that in order for her to break the karmic cycle of disease, and therefore move on with her life in a more healthy way, she must try to dissolve the internal anger that has brought about alienation and misfortune in her life on more than one occasion. Thus, Doherty can only achieve the necessary balance via her Libran psyche by seeking the answers from within her heart, through service to herself (meditation), and through continual service to others (enlightenment).

Final Significators Pointing to Crohn's Disease

The Moon, which oversees our childhood and adolescence tenants the sign of Scorpio (Pluto's sign rulership), opposes planet Saturn in the natal chart. This combination is primarily a natural polarity [polarized]. Moreover, Pluto's close conjunction to the Ascendant and the Black Moon, with Pluto essentially *besieged*, combine as 'frictional alignments', which make up the principal catalysts for the onset of Crohn's disease.

In addition, the Moon-Saturn opposition would also prove to be the primary catalyst for the onset of breast cancer in 2015. Perhaps also, the transit of Saturn in Scorpio beginning in 2012 through to 2015 became the trigger, especially when transit Saturn conjoined the natal Moon in 2013, and thus opposed its natal position. This would have been a very tense and fearful transit.

Furthermore, Neptune's domicile transit of Pisces in the sixth house of health, which squared Jupiter (expansion) and the MC (direction) in the natal chart, was the primary catalyst – marking the return of the breast cancer in 2019.

Conclusion

In my estimation, the primary significator for Crohn's disease is definitely Pluto rising on the Ascendant – fuelled by their combined square to the MC. This configuration would also indicate that the disease is congenital (Pluto) – compounded by synthetic conditions, such as indignation and displeasure.

This is also compounded by reports in the media stating that Shannen Doherty prefers to live life in her own influential, manipulating and immovable style – refusing to accept order and responsibility in her life. Therefore, Pluto rising on her Ascendant would orchestrate these physical and psychological complications.

Further, it was reported by her co-stars on the set of Beverley Hills 90210 that she would not conform to the 'on set' rules and regulations. She was repeatedly late for rehearsals, which is an omission of such a wide Neptune-Pluto sextile.

Further Karmic Nuances

In the natal chart, there is a tight quincunx between Neptune and Mercury. On the one hand, the quincunx highlights her predilection for poor timekeeping, which requires a prompt adjustment. On the other hand, the quincunx symbolizes that an adjustment must be made that will allow her to hone her thought patterns via empathy and concern for others – from the confines of reckless irresponsibility (Neptune/third) – towards the conformity of trustworthiness (Mercury/eighth). It is from this position in the eighth house (Pluto's natural domain) that Mercury, the planet of communication, symbolizes an instinctive urge to *develop* the transformational platform from which the objective mind operates and transmutes towards the realm of the subconscious mind (for more information about this see further on).

It was also alleged by her on-set colleagues that 'she would often resort to violence and animosity when she failed to get her own way'. This could be attributed to the South Node in Leo –

powered by her Sun (the planetary ruler of Leo). The Sun also makes a wide quincunx to the Ascendant. Here, the required adjustment signifies a release of all the karmic characteristics (South Node) that were evident in past lives, such as a powerful and dominant ego. Ideally, these adjustments must happen so that soul transformation can take place (Pluto on the Ascendant).

Equilibrium of the soul must also be obtained in the here and now. This is exhibited via the North Node in the fifth house; coupled by its planetary ruler Uranus in the first house tenanting impartial Libra. Once an innate balance has been successfully achieved, it is virtually assured that the Crohn's disease will be eliminated from her body once and for all.

Intuitive Restoration and Guidance

Aside from the obvious health issues, the main focus of Doherty's natal chart determines that she is 'psychically aware' that balance is something that is required in her life. Perhaps then, and as a result of this internal echo, Doherty agreed to play a significant acting role as Heather Duke in the 1988 production of *Heathers*. Medicinally speaking, heather (the shrub), is said to create balance especially in the digestive tract (Virgo) and the elimination (Pluto) areas of the body. Heather also prevents diarrhoea (Pluto), especially when it is consumed as a calming tea – mixed with other herbs.[17]

Perhaps then, and by agreeing to act the role of Heather in Heathers, it would *psychologically* enhance her wellbeing; and thus become a trigger in order to restore the necessary balance in her life. This would surely assist in detaching her soul from the on-going experiences that take place during her frequent psychological visits to the zone of her chart, hence the first house, which symbolizes the dark night of the soul (Pluto).

Acute Radiation Syndrome

Acute radiation syndrome [sickness] is caused by exposure to a high dose of radiation, which may be the result of a nuclear attack, or from a failure within a nuclear facility. Symptoms include nausea, vomiting, diarrhoea, and a significant drop in the blood cell counts. Conventional treatment includes decontamination (Pluto), supportive care (Venus, Pluto's polarity planet), and the management of symptoms (Neptune).[18]

Marie Curie

Maria Salomea Sklodowska was born in Poland and was a naturalized French physicist and a chemist who conducted pioneering research on radioactivity. Later she married Pierre Curie and became known as Marie Sklodowska Curie. She was the first woman to win the Nobel Prize; and the only woman to win the Nobel Prize twice. But more importantly, she was the only woman to win the Nobel Prize in two different scientific fields. She died on July 4th, 1934, due to aplastic anemia contracted from exposure to radiation.

The Natal Chart

In this very commanding locomotive-type chart (see relevant chart), Pluto and its zodiac symbolizations [Scorpio] are all connected in a very distinct and powerful way. Furthermore, Pluto's power is exemplified because it intersects a dominant kite formation in the natal chart. This kite configuration will *accentuate* Pluto's transformational characteristics, meaning that Curie was forever searching for safer ways to isolate radioactive isotopes, which was the main theme of her work. Most notably, Pluto is residing at 15 degrees of Taurus and conjoins the IC. According to William Lilly, 15 degrees of Taurus is a *fortunate* degree. Moreover, the MC at 18 degrees of Scorpio (Pluto's rulership sign) is also a fortunate degree. Pluto of course opposes the MC.

This stellar combination of advantageous zodiac degrees is perhaps the reason why she achieved her many breakthroughs in the field of science. However, Curie was considered to be relatively young when she died at 66 years of age. Maybe it was because she was always circumnavigating so near to the grave (IC) with her volatile and dangerous work (Pluto). It must be said, however, that such an early death of this magnitude is so out of character with this chart. Essentially, the natal chart symbolizes 'long life', especially as Saturn (maturity) is so close to the MC – with generational Pluto opposing this elevated angle of destiny. Thus, in most cases, a powerfully placed Pluto in the chart can invariably signify a long and illustrious life.[19]

Uppermost Significators

Pluto opposes the Sun, with the Sun occupying Pluto's rulership sign of Scorpio. The Sun is also elevated in the chart, hence at the highest point. This substantial configuration is characteristic of powerful and life-altering connotations. Therefore, when applying patience and determination via the Pluto archetype, a Sun-Pluto opposition has the potential to orchestrate tremendous leaps forward, especially in terms of evolutionary development. For Curie however, evolutionary development came with the discovery of radium. Furthermore, and as we have already determined, the Sun/MC-Pluto opposition is *compounded* by the presence of nearby Saturn, which is loosely conjunct the MC.

According to William Lilly, Saturn at 25 degrees of Scorpio is a degree that denotes great femininity; and this degree will be embodied by Saturn's elevation [highest point] in the chart. Thus, twenty-five degrees of Scorpio will help to soften Saturn's turbulent effects, so to speak. Therefore, when applying the application of hard work, Saturn is most likely the planet that was responsible for Curie winning the Nobel Prize – distinguishing her as the first woman to do so. This would have been an amazing achievement, because at that time it was very much a world where masculinity ruled.

Moreover, Saturn's separating square to Jupiter, combined with its exact conjunction to Venus (Venus being naturally feminine) would also contribute to Curie acquiring this notable accolade. Utilizing the application of hard work, patience and con-

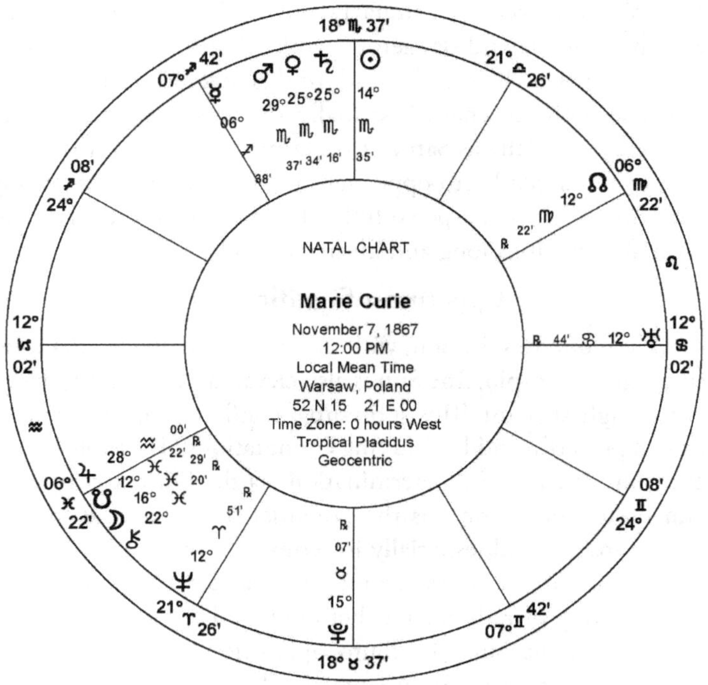

centration, Saturn does reward those it considers as its worthy students, especially in later life.

Evolutionary Significators

Jupiter tenants Aquarius in an intercepted first house, using the Placidus house system. Thus, intercepted houses and planets represent problems with gifts in their hands. Jupiter's interception in Aquarius signifies that, with the application of insight and perception; coupled by a personal need to bolster one's personal beliefs, anything is achievable. This is especially relevant when ideas come to the forefront – ideas that are gleaned at a much higher level of scientific understanding (Aquarius).

Scientific breakthroughs are also the theme of Uranus, which lies on the cusp of the sixth/seventh houses, and exactly opposes the Ascendant. Uranus is of course the natural ruler of the first house intercepted Aquarius (collective). Marie Curie's breakthroughs were after all for the good of the entire collective. Uranus is exactly opposing Curie's Ascendant; and Uranus tenants Cancer. Aside from the obvious scientific connotations, this cosmic amalgamation *highlights* a very turbulent and overwhelming childhood, and one that no doubt prompted her into discovering her unerring scientific vocation in life.

Upheaval

Curie's childhood was distinctly *unsettled* because it was reported in the media at the time that her family squandered their fortunes (Jupiter square Saturn). They were involved in patriotic involvements concerning Polish uprisings (Uranus) – aimed at restoring Poland's independence. This condemned the subsequent generation (Pluto), which included Maria Curie, and her elder siblings, to a difficult family life, and one in which she needed to overcome in order to get ahead in life. Uranus in the seventh house would also attach the 'need to be noticed' label. Thus, Uranus in the seventh house can make quite a dramatic entrance into an unknowing world.

Interceptions (Hidden Potential)

Using the Placidus house system, the primary theme of this Aquarius/Leo/Jupiter interception symbolizes the unique potential tethered into Curie's soul decision to return to incarnation, in order to develop these significant scientific breakthroughs. One of which was to develop the theory of radioactivity (Uranus/Pluto), and to discover the elements of polonium (Uranus) and radium (Pluto). She also developed a successful technique (Jupiter/Aquarius) that would isolate radioactive isotopes. It is also fair to suggest that Curie was the right person for the job at hand, which was most complimentary of the interceptions.

Notwithstanding, Uranus is afflicted in the natal chart at 12 degrees of Cancer, which according to William Lilly is lame [azimene]. Ordinarily, this will narrow the natural characteristics of Uranus; however, the trine to the Sun/MC conjunction from Uranus, and its sextile to Pluto offsets the affliction somewhat. Thus, these soft aspects will provide the planet of scientific development with a stronger hand that furnishes Curie with much greater insight.

Good Fortune

Curie was also blessed with the presence of a Minor Grand Trine in her chart. The presence of a Grand Trine would therefore pose as the 'secondary driving force' that would drive her further forward into accomplishing her amazing achievements. Essentially, this Minor Grand Trine is very influential because Pluto intersects it with its opposition to the Sun and MC. This would further energize the trine – giving it additional power.

This paradisiacal and euphonious configuration provides additional weight to a nonetheless already weighty chart – reflecting the enormous potential contained within it. Furthermore, there are no frictional aspects to the Moon, which lies at the western elevation of the Grand Trine. Traditionally speaking, the lack of hard aspects would weaken the Moon's influence somewhat; but its gradation is heightened by the Moon's clement sextile to Pluto. In addition, this is a very creative and sympathetic Moon because of its close proximity to the Grand Trine – characterizing utmost awareness and sensitivity.

Misfortune

A source of potential misfortune however is denoted by the anaretic Mars at 29 degrees of Scorpio, with its tight square to Jupiter. Although this means the hand of God would often join her side against her unchosen enemy, she would often lose the battle, as a result of her long-term efforts. However, in her case, Curie's unchosen enemy was radiation poisoning. Unfortunately, and as a result of this flawed square, her liver (Jupiter) became fallible, and was therefore susceptible to absorbing the deadly effects of the radiation that was evident in all of her experiments. This increased her susceptibility to contracting this fatal illness, most notably radiation poisoning. Neptune's quincunx to the Sun also has a hand in this.

At some point in her life she developed near-blindness, which was the direct result of cataracts. The presence of cataracts can be attributed to Mars's disassociated conjunction to Mercury (eyes), which is detrimental in Sagittarius. The mere fact that Curie didn't experience complete blindness due to Mercury's wide conjunction to Mars. Two degrees closer and it would have been a different story entirely.

Conclusion: A Life of Development/Disorder

Marie Curie would have been totally aware of the fundamental purpose of her life that was clearly spoken in a very intuitive way by her natal chart. Therefore, she would have unwittingly *sacrificed* her life in the realm of physical incarnation for the sake of raising 'collective awareness' within the realm of science. Furthermore, she did all of this in the name of scientific innovation, which was determined by her Leo/Aquarius/Jupiter interception. Esoterically speaking, however, Jupiter does often indicate the soul's 'final journey' upon the Earth plane, especially when the planet of direction is intercepted.

Evolutionary Strength and Honour

It is often remarked upon that Pluto goes where 'angels fear to tread'. Spiritually speaking, Curie was fully aware what she was 'getting herself into' before her soul agreed to take on this challenging task in physicality. Nonetheless however, her death from acute radiation syndrome (poisoning) was deemed as purely synthetic – brought about by circumstances that were beyond her control. Medically speaking, acute radiation syndrome is very indicative to the unfortunate and the perhaps the 'unlucky nature' of that tense opposition aspect in the chart – between the

Sun and MC and of course Pluto.

Marie Curie had in fact stepped off the wheel of incarnation a long time ago. Therefore, she had returned to the Earth world at a time when radium had not long been discovered, and plutonium was in the making. The purpose of her incarnation was to raise awareness, and thus *advance* the scientific community with her brilliant mind and amazing insight. In effect, she did successfully raise awareness towards the dangers posed by these subatomic elements that mankind *continues* to be remissible and play God with. Whilst she was alive, however, Curie was living through a permanent very dark night of the soul.

Cosmic Consummation

Similar to the plight of the mythical Phoenix, it would be fair to surmise however that Maria Salomea Sklodowska has successfully risen from the *radioactive* ashes of her earlier life. Furthermore, her soul has been fully cleansed by the supernal light – deeply representative of the Sun/MC/Pluto interconnection. Her work on radioactivity would have naturally raised the vibration of the opposition.

Truly, she is perhaps on her final journey towards the spiritual realm of the Godhead, as she traverses the breath-taking and stupendous spheres that are the ethereal foundations of the supernal spirit world. The Jupiter interception may possibly indicate that Curie is working on a cure for radiation sickness that will be imparted to the Earth world at the time when its collective inhabitants (Aquarius) are ready to receive it safely. In my meditations I was informed that Curie is now working alongside the soul that was previously known as Albert Einstein.

Psychological Ramifications

Moving on, and in order to finalize the personalized case studies, I would like to touch upon the subject matter that gives rise to the concept of 'psychological ramifications'. These psychological ramifications are responsible for inaugurating a wide range of mental health problems. In addition, psychological ramifications can lead to the onset of physical illness and disease and are very much considered to be Pluto characteristics. In the natal chart, Pluto often retains a 'psychological imprint', which exhibits all the hallmarks of its underworld idiosyncrasies, thus concealing them deep within the psyche. Psychological ramifications are, however, reminiscent to the dark night of the soul.

Moreover, these psychological imprints reminiscent of the Pluto archetype can have long and lasting effects upon the psyche, which are clearly displayed in the mannerisms and the personality of the individual. An example would be prolonged and persistent anger.

Furthermore, a classic example that best describes the psychological imprint of Pluto is burnt toast. When toast is burnt there is often an invisible but distinguishing residue that tends to linger for quite some time after the event. You know it's there, but you cannot pinpoint it. This strong residue will continue to linger in the nasal passages. Conveniently, Pluto and its rulership sign of Scorpio rules over the nasal passages.

Pluto and a World of Celebrities:

Citing a precise and perhaps recent example of Pluto's psychological imprint was exquisitely displayed by the American actor Joaquin Phoenix, who portrayed Joker in the 2019 movie. Joker represented a shady and umbrageous character, which was based upon the DC comic's character of the same name. Even though Joker was made into a blockbuster feature film, it nevertheless defines these masterful Pluto impressions in a way that can only be described as *comprehensible.*

This film was a very dark and psychological depiction, and one that characterized sublime immorality denoting characteristics that are firmly attached to the underworld. It was however a brilliantly acted film, which was all down to the precision and timing of Phoenix himself. He 'literally' absorbed himself and became Joker. Some would argue that it was his best film to date. According to *Film Weekly*, 'Phoenix played the role *magnificently*, because he was hand-picked for the role; and he was a natural, giving a masterful performance'. Perhaps, then, it comes as no surprise that these powerful Pluto characteristics are reflected in the natal chart of this fine actor.

Conceptual Developments

Speaking in a recent interview, Joaquin Phoenix revealed that he 'developed a psychological disorder after losing weight for the role as Joker'. Furthermore, he became obsessed (Pluto) with his new weight. Phoenix shed a whopping 52 pounds for the role, and this transformation did take its toll, he revealed that it became a "serious disorder for him".

But in light of the physical and psychological challenges of losing so much weight, Phoenix said that "it was necessary for him to have a delicate frame as it helped carry out the iconic comic book villain's movements and mannerisms". He also said, "But I think the interesting thing for me is what I had expected and anticipated with the weight loss was the feelings of dissatisfaction, hunger, and a certain kind of vulnerability". He went on to say, "What I didn't anticipate was this feeling relating to a kind of fluidity that I felt physically, which, at times made me feel psychologically sick, and completely out of sorts".

The interviews are a classic example of Pluto leaving a psychological imprint in the psyche of Joaquin Phoenix after he had been swathed by Pluto's dark temperament – imprints that can have long-lasting and traumatic effects. Phoenix is however a Scorpio with notable aspects such as Pluto tenanting the first house and opposing the Moon.

However, emotions that *transmuted* into sheer psychological paranoia, as portrayed in Joker were perhaps all-in-all nothing too outlandish or unfamiliar to him, because heightened sensitivities such as those that emanate from the Pluto realm of consciousness are also reminiscent to a Moon-Pluto opposition.

Furthermore, with Pluto in the first house of his natal chart, his perceived feelings of 'fluidity', which he spoke about, should be nothing too invasive.

Joaquin Phoenix: Character Analysis

In this bucket-type chart (see relevant chart), Pluto opposes the Moon – fractionating the chart. This spilt in cosmic consciousness provides a certain gradation to the bucket pattern – indicating that the bottom half of the chart represents a physical bowl that holds Phoenix's deep and fiery emotions – and the top half represents a spiritual cap that houses his supple power and gritty determination. Generally speaking, the bucket pattern determines an individual that possesses tremendous inner strength. This is coupled by a definite drive towards a certain objective. However, bucket chart types can often be single-minded and uncompromising.

A Cosmic Dichotomy

The Moon-Pluto opposition represents a planetary configuration that has been, on more than one occasion, *popularized* as a Hades (Devil's) Moon[20], therefore making it a 'life-testing' affiliation. Aside from making him somewhat reserved, the Moon-Pluto opposition would account for the fact that Phoenix has experienced a great deal of loss in his life. This would include the death of his brother River Phoenix in 1993, from an overdose of drugs (for more information about River Phoenix refer to my previous book *Discovering Faith in Neptune's Ocean of Dreams*).

Pluto reposes at seven degrees of Libra; and tenants the first house. From this lowly position Pluto represents a bottomless well of sensitivity coupled by deep emotional needs, especially in view of its opposition to the Moon. Furthermore, and according to William Lilly, seven degrees of Libra is a deep and pitted degree. As a result of all of this, Phoenix may well have, and perhaps still finds it difficult, to come to terms with his unfathomable, chasmic and powerful emotions, which are clearly displayed in equal and precise measures throughout all of his movies. Moreover, his deeper and much wider emotions were clearly evident in his role as the overemotional, deceitful and psychotic Commodus in Ridley Scott's production of *Gladiator*. Interestingly, Ridley Scott has his Moon placed in Scorpio, which conjoins Phoenix's Sun. This is perhaps one reason why he was selected to play the part of this particular Roman Emperor.

By the same token Pluto is in mutual reception with its polarity planet Venus. This configuration would ordinarily provide him with in-depth skills, such as an innate adaptability to social and public surroundings despite the fact they are not natural inclinations indicative to such a reserved personality.

Psychological Undercurrents

Further, in the natal chart of Joaquin Phoenix, the Sun lies at four degrees of Scorpio (Pluto's rulership sign); which according to Lilly, four degrees of Scorpio is a masculine degree. This mesomorphic and robust Scorpio degree may well have added to Phoenix's instinctive desire to *emulate* psychologically disturbed individuals. Furthermore, with a closely-conjunct position of Venus and Mars to the Sun, by which the Sun is in quincunx formation to the Moon, this cosmic backdrop of luminaries and personal planets completes a precise and veritable ambience of emotionally-charged undercurrents – offering a powerful requirement for adjustment in the chart. In essence, Phoenix has the potential to act out any role he chooses to do so.

The Priceless Quality of Effortlessness

Joaquin Phoenix seems to find it 'relatively easy' to *mould* his persona into playing characters that are psychologically compromised so to speak, especially characters that are clearly neurotic in nature. In the natal chart, this idiosyncrasy can be attributed

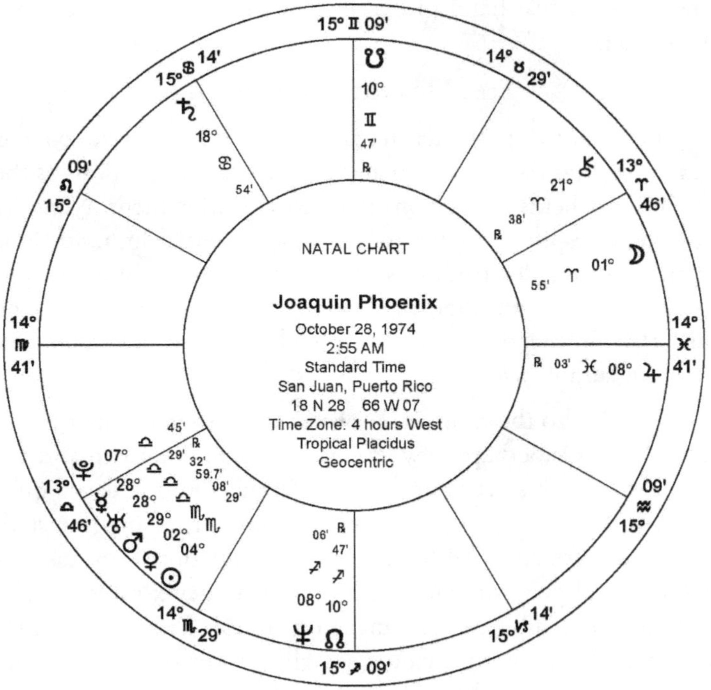

to the close conjunction of Mars to the unpredictable and often volatile Uranus. In addition, Uranus is exactly conjunct communicative Mercury, which both lay at twenty-eight degrees of Libra – completing a mental overlay that provides Phoenix with a very temperamental and impulsive disposition – but one that is *guarded* at the same time.

Furthermore, and according to Lilly, twenty-eight degrees of Libra is a deep and pitted degree. Ordinarily, this particular degree would characterize extreme anxiety. Coincidentally, anxiety is a component that is evident in all of his roles. Interestingly, Joker was an adapted role that clearly demonstrated the principal element of anxiety most prolifically. Moreover, Jupiter (jollity) opposes the Ascendant; therefore, it is not a coincidence that Phoenix was hand-picked to play the exuberant but deceptive Joker.

Free Flowing Adjustment

Overall, this particular natal chart is representative to a cosmic soup that contains deep and unfathomable emotions as the main ingredients – emotions that require adjustment. Nonetheless, and despite the presence of these potential imperfections, a chart of this description is often the true mark of a fine and perpetual actor. Further, the chart also signifies a free-flowing and rhythmic signature that is upheld by a very adaptable, conforming and fluidic Pluto.

This is also the chart of an obsessive personality (first house Pluto). This is perhaps why Phoenix gives one hundred and ten percent to all his acting roles. In addition, Pluto makes a quincunx to Jupiter in dreamy Pisces; and Jupiter tenants the sixth house of work and health matters. Primarily, this all means that with careful planning and organization, Phoenix gives a make-believe but credible performance in every role he chooses to play. All of Phoenix's performances are glitzed not only by a make-believe psychological profile, but they are intensified and thus tempered with a timeless enormity of quintessential spirit.

Standing Alone

Some of Phoenix's fellow actors have stressed on many an occasion that although he is sociable, he is nevertheless a 'loner'. His portrayal of psychologically compromised characters may add further weight to this notion. Saturn is elevated at the top of the chart; and aside from making a very wide sextile to the Ascendant; Saturn is relatively *unaspected*, especially by major aspects. Generally speaking, this means that the planet of upstanding and responsibility stands firmly alone. Furthermore, Saturn lies at eighteen degrees of Cancer; and according to Lilly, eighteen degrees of Cancer is a void, desolate degree. Joaquin Phoenix has often made reference to the fact that at certain times in his life he has felt 'worthless, inconsequential, and he stands alone'. Perhaps this statement is why some have referred to him as a loner? But perhaps Phoenix lacks true heartfelt self-esteem? This may be partly due to his afflicted Pluto in the sign of social standing, Libra.

The notion of the loner or lone wolf, however, could be deemed as yet another side to the characters he portrays most brilliantly. Some would no doubt say that Joaquin Phoenix is a psychological enigma. Others would no doubt accuse him of being power mad. Phoenix does like his own way apparently, especially when he is on set. Pluto is most definitely an enigma. Thus, in the first house, the planet does seek to, more than anything else, acquire personal power; no matter of the cost to itself and others.

Conclusion: The Brilliant Mind behind the Lonely Enigma

Principally, the exact conjunction between Mercury (the mind) and Uranus (the brilliant enigma) is the cutting force behind the man who has been deemed both the gifted mind and the outcast that represents the enigma (Uranus). Perhaps, Phoenix has been stamped with this label because of the lonership that is determined by the Black Moon, which tenants Aquarius (Uranus's rulership sign). In essence, his 'lonely appearing persona' is likely to have been fashioned from the depths of evolution (Pluto in the first house). In other words, Phoenix may well have been ostracized (Uranus and Aquarius) for his radical beliefs and his creative abilities throughout many of his previous lives. It certainly would seem that way.

The fact that he may well have been ostracized may also be representative to the psychological and emotional burden that he *clearly* carries around with him in the here and now. Perhaps being ostracized can be deemed as a modern-day disease? Thus, this emotional burden is best portrayed by the Black Moon (emotion) in the fifth house, and in a trine to Pluto (psychological) in the first house. A trine means that the solution to this problem is actually easier that he thinks.

Although a solution to this 'evolutionary downfall' may have already been sought in a psychological capacity, which is more or less representative to the minor Grand Trine between the Black Moon, the South Node and Pluto, it nevertheless completes a monumental picture, and one that defines the meaning of magniloquence. In other words, he has been given another exceptional chance to express his evolutionary abilities, as someone who can *adapt* to any shoe he wishes to step into.

Duality and Celebrity Status

Joaquin Phoenix's notoriety and rise to fame is perhaps best displayed by Neptune's close conjunction to the North Node, and the twin opposition to the MC. However, eight degrees of Sagittarius, the degree with which Neptune tenants is lame [azimene], according to William Lilly. This gives rise to Phoenix's notoriety. The South Node in Gemini also indicates a brilliant mind. Thus, this is a mind that has been integrated into his delicate but nonetheless powerful persona, which has been born throughout the course of evolution – stipulated by Pluto's trine to the South Node.

Infatuation

Jupiter is still regarded as being dignified in Pisces, because Jupiter is the ancient ruler of this sign. However, Jupiter's exact square to Neptune means that Phoenix can literally *absorb* both the dualistic (Neptune) and sublime (Jupiter) characteristics of any chosen personality he is emulating, and particularly those of a psychotic nature. With Pluto in the first house, the downside to all of this, however, would be that it would become easy for Phoenix to be obsessed and overwhelmed by the character he has ultimately mastered. That being the case, this particular characteristic was clearly demonstrated when he took on the role as Joker. Infatuation, hence obsession, is a major part of Pluto's psychological code of distinction – something that needs to be honed. Obsession and in particular the condition known as Obsessive Compulsive Disorder (OCD) are a particular type of mental illness. Understandably, these conditions can be deemed as serious and perhaps threatening to the unacquainted. They would also be deemed as threatening to those who retain a sensitive personality, especially if they go unrecognized and are left unchecked. Look at the consequences of the character Joker. It has been suggested, however, by some in the medical profession that Phoenix suffers from both of these disorders.

This being the case, there are pointers in the natal chart involving Neptune and Pluto that suggest this hypothesis is correct. However, Phoenix also has the ability to rise above the illusion (Neptune) of it all, especially the characters he has adapted for a time in his acting roles. Thus, similar to his ancient namesake he can become the mythical Phoenix – diffusing the stigma that has cast him in Hollywood as the lonely enigma.

True Courage

Truly, Joaquin Phoenix is a remarkable actor, and I suspect we haven't seen the best from him yet. In fairness, it must also be said that it is far from easy playing the roles he chooses to enact. Instead, his characters are a noteworthy tribute to his incredibly intense expertise. There is a saying 'Pluto treads where angels fear to go'. Thus, it takes courage, especially the psychological kind, to follow a particular path, which he chooses to do. Maybe in time, and through his approaching maturity, he will receive his deserved Saturn rewards.

Having said that, when Pluto frequents the first house there will always be an element of ridicule, envy and even jealousy present in his life. This is most likely the result of what he has achieved. However, having Pluto positioned in the first house may well mean that Phoenix has incarnated to relinquish the 'ultimate stain of envy', which continues to discolor his personality in the here and now. Maybe this evolutionary stain is in fact representative of a psychological illness he endured in the forgotten realms of a past incarnation.

Thus, this karmic blemish that is strongly indicated by the South Node conjunct the MC in Gemini (psychological) represents his ongoing evolutionary dark night of the soul. All of this is portrayed further by his bottommost Sun – a major component of the sensitive Scorpio stellium.

Tragic World Events

Not only does medical astrology determine the health of a human being, but it can also determine the overall health of the Earth. Standing on its rocky surface, the Earth is representative of a physical form; and operates in very much the same way as the human body does – with neuro-impulses and responses. However, evident upon its mountainous surface are some very powerful and prolific markers that take on the appearance of reposing tumours. Hence, these compelling signposts are volcanoes. When the Earth is under stress, these tumours become inflamed. This is similar to a physical tumour that has turned malignant. Thus, when volcanoes become active, it is often because the Earth is experiencing a period of poor and impoverished health.

Volcanoes fall under the jurisdiction of Pluto. Because of the planet's long-lasting (evolutionary) effects, Pluto is deemed as a very important planet in medical astrology. Likewise, Pluto is responsible for the 'gradual onset', and the 'lingering aftereffects' that are associated with many forms of illness and disease.

The Whakaari White Island Volcano Eruption

On the 9th of December 2019 at 14:11 PM, the volcano that incorporates Whakaari/White Island in New Zealand's Bay of Plenty erupted. There were 47 people on the island. At the time of writing this analysis eight people were confirmed dead, eight were missing and presumed dead, whilst a further 28 suffered serious injuries, 23 of which were critical. Considering the fatalities involved, this eruption has been classified as a major catastrophe. The culprit however was most definitely Pluto.

Significators

In this interactive chart for Auckland, New Zealand (see below) *, there are powerful significators that characterize the whole of New Zealand as being susceptible to volcanic eruptions, and seismic activity. Further, Pluto (ruling volcanoes) tenants the sign of Taurus (the sign of Father Earth*); and Pluto squares Venus, the planet that naturally rules Taurus. Venus is also Pluto's natural polarity planet. Venus resides at six degrees of Leo, and is pitted according to William Lilly, and Venus is also retrograde. The afflicted degree coupled by the retrograde motion of Venus imparts additional tension to the already volatile square between Venus and Pluto. Further, and because of these factors, the square declines in its attempt to mastermind any ingenuity that is naturally attached to the Venus attribute of imperturbability. In addition, the square also fails to bring about the Venus art of restoration – balancing the juxtaposing and challenging nature of the square – bringing stability to the whole of New Zealand.

Meanwhile, Pluto conjuncts Uranus, the planet that rules earthquakes and seismic disturbances; and Uranus lays at seven degrees of Taurus, which is a lame degree [azimene], according to Lilly. As a point of reference, afflicted degrees are quoted from William Lilly's *Christian Astrology* (page 116) Furthermore, Saturn conjuncts the Black Moon in Taurus. Overall, all of this celestial activity represents a fraught and eruptive combination of planetary volatility. There is also a significant Yod in the chart with the Ascendant at the apex – receiving quincunxes from Saturn and Neptune, which are of course in sextile formation.

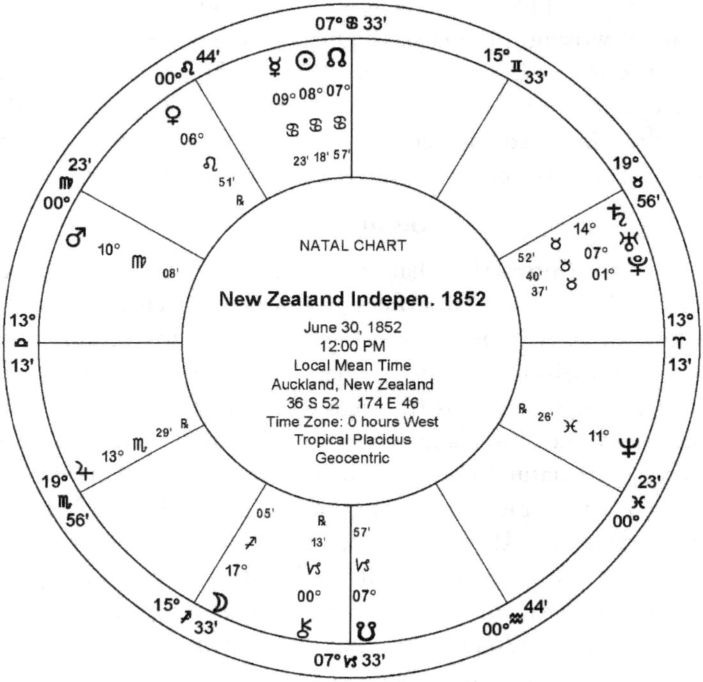

However, coupled with the powerful influences of Saturn and Uranus close by, the Yod's power is intensified. Thus, all of this volatile planetary activity determines that New Zealand is always at risk of a sudden catastrophe; and one that it must always adjust too. In effect, these kinds of disasters, particularly the ones that epitomize death and destruction on a grand scale, will always appal and horrify the watching eyes of the world.

Adaptation

The Auckland chart is essentially a medical [decumbiture] chart, mostly because of the troublesome nature of the quincunxes. * With that said, the influence of the Yod in the New Zealand chart presses home the need for a continual adjustment and awareness within the eyes of the nation itself. This is an adjustment that will always require a much-balanced approach, which is determined further by the Libra-ruled Ascendant. In essence, the people of New Zealand need to be constantly on their guard. New Zealand is, however, a nation that 'keeps its head' under pressure. This structured form of awareness must always be administered towards the protection of its citizens – permanent (Saturn) or temporary (Pluto). The attributes of adjustment and awareness were demonstrated recently during the Covid-19 crisis. New Zealand was one of very few countries to bring the virus under control very quickly. The people responded exceptionally well.

The Malodour of Death

Moving further on, Mars opposes Neptune in the chart, and Mars's degree, which is 10 degrees of Virgo, is dark and void, according to Lilly. This increases the negative potential of this malefic planet. Mars signifies heat; its opposition to a domicile Neptune in Pisces stipulates that water vapour from the erupting volcano is always *superheated*. Most likely, this would cause the skin (Saturn) of the visitors on the island at the time of the eruption to have been burnt (Mars) beyond recognition. It was reported in the local media that many of the visitors had had their skin 'incinerated' from their bodies. Further fatalities were the result of poisoning (Neptune) from volcanic gas. Some were crushed by falling rocks (Saturn) being propelled from the crater of the volcano.

Faults in the Earth's Crust (Over New Zealand)

This stellium of planetary interplay, especially those planets that tenant the sign of the Earth (Taurus) in this interactive chart determines that New Zealand is a 'powerhouse' of volcanic activity. The presence of Uranus and Pluto in the chart indicates that this volcanic activity is ready to be discharged at any time, which was the case on the 9th of December 2019. In the event chart, (see below), transit Pluto is aligned with transit Saturn, as they prepare for their monumental and much spoken about conjunction in 2020. This powerful conjunction *reflects* the closeness and combined influence of these powerhouse planets in the Auckland chart.

Transit Saturn and Pluto square the natal Ascendant. Essentially, this would have been the 'active trigger' for this latest eruption – previously occurring in 2000. Fortunately, transit Saturn and Pluto are trine to Saturn in the Auckland chart. This means that any eruption at this time would be relatively short-lived. The implications however would be long-lasting. An additional catalyst for this sudden volcanic eruption was transit Uranus besieged between its natal position and natal Pluto. Transit Uranus was also square Venus in the Auckland chart. Ordinarily, this imbalance would have created disparity on the island at the time. Furthermore, it would have been some time before any rescue attempt was made to extricate the survivors.

At the time of the volcanic eruption transit Mars in Scorpio was exactly conjunct Jupiter, and it was opposing Saturn in the Auckland chart. Mars is essentially the *trigger* that fires the smoking gun. This particular volcano, however, was indeed representative of a smoking gun. Shortly before the eruption, White Island was declared as 'potentially hazardous' by the authorities, but with the opposition of Mars to Saturn, it may also have been a case of reckless responsibility. Further, the question that arises is what were tourists doing on the island in the first place? Perhaps we will never know the answer to this question. Perhaps also, New Zealand experienced a severe lapse in concentration at this time.

In the meantime, it is important to note that these unfortunate souls were labelled as 'selfie tourists' (Neptune) by the worldwide media.

Further Triggers

At the time of the eruption the transit Moon (a further trigger) was positioned right over Uranus in the chart – having previously moved over Pluto. Furthermore, the Moon was also conjunct the Black Moon and square Mars in the Auckland chart.

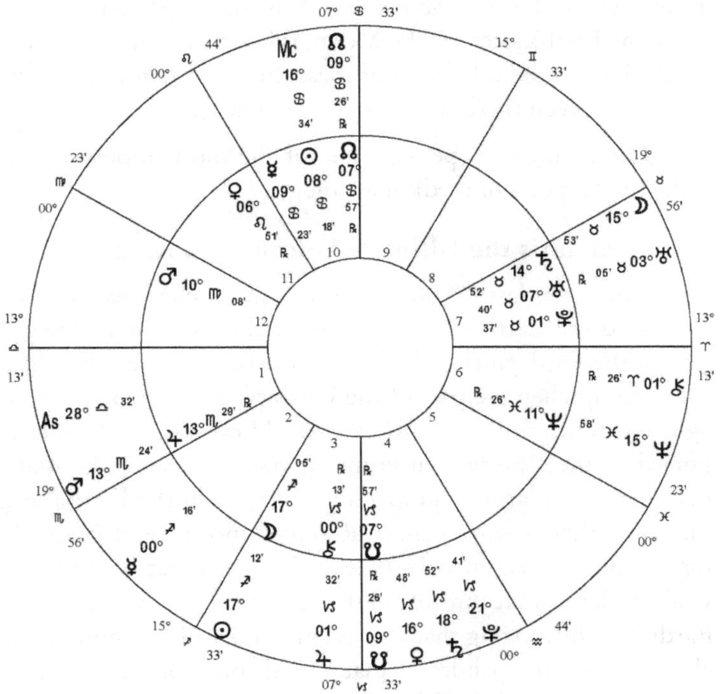

Inner Wheel: New Zealand Natal Chart
Outer Wheel: Whaakaari/White Island Eruption; December 9, 2019, 2:11 PM NZDT;
White Island, New Zealand, 37S31, 177E11; Placidus Houses, Mean Nodes

This lunar influence would seem to indicate that the beating karmic heart of New Zealand will be emotionally compromised for many years to come, as a result of this terrible tragedy. However, its heart will remain attentive; and it will always remain 'on guard'.

* This is the significant point of latitude for this interactive chart, and it should not be mistaken for other charts cast for Auckland.

* Despite popular consensus regarding the Earth being feminine, hence Mother Earth, the Earth is in fact masculine. This is

according to The *Akashic Records*. This makes perfect sense because the Earth's satellite, the Moon, is feminine. Likewise, there would have to be a balance of masculine and feminine energy present between these cosmic bodies of energy.

* Quincunxes are perhaps one of the most important and influential aspects in medical astrology.

Atlantis the Ultimate Volcanic Continent

Within the last 70,000 years volcanoes have become congenital to the Earth plane. They have always been an integral part of the Earth since as far back as the time of Atlantis, which was a comprehensive part of the Earth plane over 65,000 years ago, according to the *Akashic Records*. However, it is further reported in the *Akashic* that erupting volcanoes sunk the island continent of Atlantis – propelling it deep into the Earth's magma core. That is why there is absolutely no trace of it remaining today. The reason Atlantis was destroyed was because of a viral pandemic that threatened the rest of the inhabitants on the Earth. It is interesting that the recent Saturn-Pluto conjunction also symbolized a pandemic that would compromise the whole of our collective way of life. Not to mention the damage to the Earth plane.

Today, volcanic eruptions are mostly caused by environmental conditions and negative vibrations that are wholly synthetic by nature.

Evolutionary Conclusion

Speaking in the broadest of evolutionary expressions, Pluto is 'in theory' helping to *restore* the overall health of the Earth. I say in theory because it all depends on our actions over the next decade as to whether Pluto's influence will be beneficial. If we continue on our present course, then Pluto's influence will no doubt be unspeakable and distressing.

Currently, the Earth appears to be dying – due mostly to the effects of climate change, violence, wars, pollution and disease. Thus, climate change and violence are triggering natural disasters; and natural disasters will increase further after the Saturn/Pluto conjunction that takes place throughout 2020. I feel that 2023 could very well be a challenging year for humankind. However, many, including myself, believe the Earth is being *cleansed*, and therefore *reborn*. Therefore, it would be appropriate to say that the Earth is entering a 'season for ashes'. This notion will become particularly relevant when Pluto enters Aquarius, and then Pisces sometime after that.

Major changes in the Earth will be accelerated once Pluto enters Aquarius in 2024 – following the Jupiter-Saturn conjunction at zero degrees Aquarius at the end of 2020. At that point Pluto will be square to Taurus (the Earth's sign). This planetary transition takes place during the latter stages of Uranus's transit of Taurus – Uranus being the natural ruler of Aquarius.

The scientists continue to inform us that the Earth's magma core is cooling. This would seem to coincide with Pluto helping to restore the health of the Earth, because Pluto is naturally a 'cooling planet'. Furthermore, if the Earth's core is cooling, Pluto's volcanoes will eventually be neutralized. According to the *Akashic Records*, the Earth should have a temporal climate of 24 degrees, apart from at the equator, which is always warmer. This moderate temperature of 24 degrees should also affect the North and South magnetic poles. The magnetic poles froze during the last major ice age, roughly 11,700 years ago. This was considered to be an Earth cataclysm. This evolutionary cycle that occurred via an evolutionary default is now dissipating.

The Warming Effect: A Brief Illustration

Global warming is occurring. This is an elemental fact. However, global warming is definitely not occurring in the way the world's scientists and climatologists perceive it – a cataclysmic methodology that has 'gripped' the collective heart of mankind. Those who are able to *download* information from the *Akashic Re-*

cords will be more than aware that the Earth is attempting to restore itself to the temperate climate that has always been a distinguishing factor throughout the course of classical evolution. This moderate global temperature was approximately 24 degrees Celsius, expect for at the equator.

Throughout our current level of evolution, ice shelves are breaking from the main ice shelves of Antarctica and Greenland. Glaciers are continuing to thaw and disappear as a result of *evolutionary warming*. Colossal lumps of ice in the form of icebergs are continually reported as breaking away from these floating ice shelves, and the ice will eventually melt away as a result – increasing sea levels. Meanwhile, these itinerant ice shelfs are accelerating climate change. However, as alarming as this notion may seem, this is further evidence that Pluto is restoring the health of the Earth, because Pluto has its rulership over icebergs, and the Earth should not be covered in all this ice. For example, and according to the *Akashic Records*, what is referred to as Antarctica was once called Lemuria. Lemuria was a continent, subtropical in nature. There are many hypotheses however that Lemuria was situated somewhere in the Indian Ocean. Lemuria was ruled over by Pluto's mythical brother Neptune; and represented a physical hub for the Earth's delicate biosphere.

Transformation: Scientists are gravely concerned that the sea levels will continue to exceed current levels as a result of this evolutionary 'thaw'. These facts are in fact true. However, throughout the course of future evolution, which will be more spiritual in nature, the waters will begin to recede. These events will be similar in design to the narrative of Noah and the Ark, which is very Neptunian.

Simply put, Pluto replenishes. Pluto upgrades. In time, the Earth will be transformed with the assistance of the Pluto archetype, as indeed the planet of transformation has done on several occasions throughout past evolution. Thus, Pluto is at the heart of evolution.

Pluto's Healing Techniques:

The Innocent Prestige of the Subconscious Mind

"The Divine Spirit is omnipresent all around me and guides me at every step."

For more information visit: www.self-help and self-development.com

The subconscious mind is similar to that of an innocent child – a child that has not been steeped in unintelligence and unenlightenment. Thus, the subconscious mind takes measures based solely on its desires and emotions – ignoring everything else in its peripheral vision. It wants the things it wants right away, and without waiting, and with disregard to any social norms. The souls of children are essentially pure and innocuous, until they become conditioned and corrupted by the negative vibrations of the Earth plane. Initially, it is around five years of age when the 'extended' dark night of the soul begins – giving rise to Earth plane conditioning – normally in the form of conventional schooling. While a child is innocent, so to speak, it needs to explore the depths of the subconscious mind. This will help it through the later years when Pluto becomes a power to be reckoned with.

Mythology: The evolutionary seeds that ultimately *germinate* the dark night of the soul are firmly set during the years of adolescence, and therefore they develop further throughout middle life. According to mythology, Pluto (Hades), wanted to remain in a childlike state of consciousness. He desired this more than anything else. Maybe this is one reason why he abducted so many children. Perhaps, this is where the earliest notion of paedophilia first began? Today, paedophilia is connected primarily to Neptune, Pluto's mythical brother.

The Vital Life Force: Every human being possesses an established mechanism, which is situated within the heart of the psyche. This mechanism holds the potential to *fracture* the negative sequence of events that are associated with the dark night of the soul. This innate potential is generally recognized around the time of the second Saturn return, and the beginning of the third Saturn cycle. This evolutionary point in time symbolizes the location at which point the heart of the subconscious mind is beginning the process of being spiritually *purged*. Likewise, this period also represents the extremity when the spiritual Phoenix (the soul) rises out of the ashes of its earlier life, and thus soul healing begins. Furthermore, it is the subconscious mind that assists us in our undertaking, and the overcoming of the distressing events concerned with the dark night of the soul.

Impede or Blaze: Interestingly, an intercepted or combust Pluto will proceed to take measures in this very same way – assisting us through the dark night. Therefore, the evolutionary purpose of an intercepted or combust Pluto in the natal chart is for this planet to be given the opportunity to rise out of the ashes of containment – ashes that are a representation of the unconscious state [house] in which Pluto tenants – moving into the supernal light of consciousness. Thus, an intercepted or combust Pluto *absolves* the subconscious mind of the tenebrous effects associated with the dark night of the soul.

Healing: Coupled with the supple and evolutionary propensities of Pluto, we hold within us all the necessary power to heal ourselves, especially from the effects of illness and disease. This also signifies the natural healing potential that is facilitated by a much-sanctified subconscious mind. Normally, this process represents the point in our evolution when Pluto's 'darkened vibrations' have been successfully honed and mastered; and thus, brought into the light. In essence, Pluto's vibration has been successfully *raised.* Ultimately, Pluto's occupation of the natal chart represents our capability to connect to, and to avail oneself of, the subconscious mind that reflects the deeper recesses of the psyche. Frictional aspects to Pluto in the natal chart imply that the connection to the subconscious mind is powerful, and its positive appliance is well within our grasp.

Aspects: It will take time to 'filter out' the impurities that are placed in the psyche by those so-called hard aspects from Pluto. These evolutionary impurities, which are created by environmental and psychological conditions, will, in the fullness of time, prevent our understanding to the essential capacity that dwells within the subconscious mind. Working constructively with Saturn (time) however will help us to eradicate these contaminants.

Meanwhile, hard aspects from Pluto to the luminaries or to Jupiter are particularly effective when it comes to self-healing; and to purging the depths of the subconscious mind. Essentially, these aspects symbolize 'healing aspects'.

Once again, I must stress that self-healing is largely accomplished through stillness and mindfulness, which is always at the heart of the sub-conscious mind. Thus, self-healing functions purely in harmonious conjunction with the positive effects that emanate from the evolutionary depths of the subconscious mind, characteristics like perception and soul awareness.

The Power of Forgiveness

As we have already established, in the Pluto powered natal chart Pluto provides us with an immeasurable capacity to *forgive* ourselves and indeed others. Stillness and mindfulness are both excellent and useful tools that will help us to acquire this heartfelt and evolutionary characteristic. However, for a great many souls, forgiveness, which is a spiritual characteristic, is not easy to successfully accomplish. It is important to emphasize that before we can forgive others, we must learn to forgive ourselves.

Forgiveness is a particular type of knowledge that must be felt purely from the heart center (soul). Dispassionate natal aspects such as the trine and the quintile, especially from the Sun or Venus to Pluto provide hope, which will, through the course of evolutionary time, allow us to achieve forgiveness (heartfelt love). Alternatively, Pluto interceptions and combustions are difficult to balance; and therefore their qualities must be understood and accepted in a much greater capacity before the individual can successfully attain forgiveness.

Meanwhile, in this context, both congenital and synthetic illnesses and diseases are brought about by an unforgiving and resentful objective mind, which in turn creates a broken heart.

Indemnity: Forgiveness is 'essentially beneficial' for the heart center; for it keeps the heart healthy and in good working order. In addition, forgiveness is also beneficial for the brain. Thus, the brain functions much better, thereby increasing intellect. So, when an individual has embraced the power of forgiveness, amazing things happen.

A study from the Journal of Behavioural Medicine associated forgiveness to lowering heart rates, it lowers blood pressure and stress release. A further study from the University of Tennessee and the University of Wisconsin attributed forgiveness to fewer medically diagnosed chronic conditions, and fewer physical symptoms from illness and disease.[21]

Pluto Healing Techniques: Deep Tissue Cleansing (Detoxification)

Deep tissue cleansing, which is also characterized in the Pluto realm of consciousness, represents overall body and soul detoxification. Furthermore, deep tissue cleansing creates anti-aging properties in the body. Thus, deep tissue cleansing is a supple transition that regenerates the body. It absolves the body of contaminants and toxins, and restores it to its unique and powerful design, which is overseen by Pluto in an evolutionary capacity. Deep tissue cleansing eradicates the body's external needs – pointing towards addictions. In essence, deep tissue cleansing transforms the mind, body and the soul into a higher frequency, which resonates at a higher psychological and evolutionary [spiritual] capacity.

Functioning: Deep tissue cleansing is a remarkable process because it labors on a particular evolutionary notion, as well as an incorporeal resonance. Thus, deep tissue cleansing is unique and is unparalleled to that of the mythical Phoenix – ascending from the ashes of its earlier life. Therefore, deep tissue cleansing returns the lipid ratio of the cell membranes to a ratio closer to the one enjoyed by the individual in younger years. In a way, the biological clock is also being backtracked. Deep tissue cleansing revives the cells – restoring them to the same elasticity that they displayed when the body was younger. Essentially, this is Pluto's regeneration process at work!

Likewise, deep tissue cleansing strengthens the antioxidant defences of the body. Furthermore, and as we have already established, it regenerates the natural function of the nerve cells. This occurs through nutritional infusions, and through a thorough cleansing of the bowels from accumulated toxins. Recommended infusion techniques include coffee enemas and antioxidant infusions.

Deep tissue cleansing is particularly effective when Pluto is intercepted in the natal chart. Moreover, it is also effective when Pluto is combust or opposing a luminary in the natal chart. However, deep tissue cleansing is always recommended, no matter how Pluto powers the natal chart. Thus, deep tissue cleansing is a powerful instrument that helps to sidestep the effects of illness and disease.

Final Conclusion (A New Life)

"In that book which is my memory, on the first page is the chapter marking the day which I met you appears the words, here begins a new life".

A Citation from *La Vita Nuova* (The New Life), by Dante Alighieri.

Medically speaking, Pluto heals the body via the elimination of synthetic and unnatural toxins, and especially from the effects of unfettered emotions, which are often congenital by design. In addition, the Pluto archetype presses us to explore the deeper meaning of the human psyche, and of the subconscious mind. These transitional characteristics are necessary for successful healing. At the evolutionary level of consciousness, Pluto embodies and disembodies. Thus, it dissolves form, and binds this disintegrated matter into a wholly new form of matter. Pluto is both the creator and the destroyer. All of these attributes impel the soul towards 'a new life', hence to rise out of the ashes, similar to the mythical Phoenix.

However, these impenetrable changes cannot occur unless there is an internal fixation towards personal and evolutionary transformation present within the spiritual heart (soul). All of these considerations are the basis for eliminating illness and disease from the body – afflictions that – through the course of evolution – become firmly attached to the ethereal soul.

I would now like to conclude this section with a series of Pluto affirmations that have been compiled by my dear friend and spiritual mentor Dovid Strusiner. They have been extracted from his exceptional book *Astrology for Self-Empowerment.* These archetypal affirmations will successfully assist the mind, body and soul in the elimination of illness and disease; thus propelling the individual towards a wholly new regenerated (Pluto), and anchored (Neptune), eternal life:

- I am strong and powerful.
- I destroy only to build more beautiful forms.
- I feel deeply and then I think.
- I face this crisis with courage.
- I speak the truth.
- I am a power for positive change.[22]

Pluto/Scorpio Symbolize Regeneration

Chart Data:

- Event chart, Coronation of William the Conquer UK chart, 25th December 1066, 12:00 Noon, Westminster, London, UK, Placidus Houses, Mean Node.
- Natal chart for Charles Darwin, 12th February 1809, 03:00 AM, Shrewsbury, UK, Placidus Houses, Mean Node. (Chart source *Astrotheme*).
- Natal chart for Gia Carangi, 29th January 1960, 22:10 PM, Philadelphia (PA), USA, Placidus Houses, Mean Node. (Chart source *Astrotheme*).
- Natal chart for Rock Hudson, 17th November 1925, 02:15 AM, Winnetka (IL), USA, Placidus Houses, Mean Node. (Chart source *Astrotheme*).
- Death chart for Rock Hudson, 2nd October 1985, 12:30 PM, Beverly Hills (CA), USA, Placidus Houses, Mean Node.
- Natal chart for T.E. Lawrence, 16th August 1888, 05:00 AM, Tremodoc, UK, Placidus Houses, Mean Node. (Chart source *Astrotheme*).
- Natal chart for Bruce Springsteen, 23rd September 1949, 22:50 PM, Freehold (NJ), USA, Placidus Houses, Mean Node. (Chart source *Astrotheme*).
- Natal chart for Steve Jobs, 24th February 1955, 19:15 PM, San Francisco (CA), USA, Placidus Houses, Mean Node. (Chart source *Astrotheme*).
- Diagnosis chart for Steve Jobs, 15th May 2003, 12:00 Noon, San Francisco (CA), USA, Placidus Houses, Mean Node.
- Natal chart for Farrah Fawcett, 2nd February 1947, 15:00 PM, Corpus Christi (TX), USA, Placidus Houses, Mean Node. (Chart source *Astrotheme*).

- Natal chart for David Hasselhoff, 17th July 1952, 06:20 AM, Baltimore Corner (MD), USA, Placidus Houses, Mean Node. (Chart source *Astrotheme*).
- Natal chart for Prince Andrew, 19th February 1960, 15:30 PM, London, UK, Placidus Houses, Mean Node. (Chart source *Astrotheme*).
- Event chart for Prince Andrew's interview, 17th November 2019, 21,00 PM, London, UK, Placidus Houses, Mean Node.
- Natal chart for Shannen Doherty, 12th April 1971, 16:16 PM, Memphis (TN), USA, Placidus Houses, Mean Node. (Chart source *Astrotheme*).
- Natal chart for Marie Curie, 7th November 1867, 12:00 PM, Warsaw, Poland, Placidus Houses, Mean Node. (Chart source *Astrotheme*).
- Natal chart for Joaquin Phoenix, 28th October 1974, 02:55 AM, San Juan (Puerto Rico), USA, Placidus Houses, Mean Node.
- Interactive chart for New Zealand, 30th June 1852, 12:00 Noon, Auckland (NZ), Placidus Houses, Mean Node.
- Event chart, Whakaari White Island, 9th December 2019, 14:11 PM NZDT, Placidus Houses, Mean Node.

References:

[1]: *The Astrology Place.*

[2]: Statistics courtesy of *The World Health Organisation* (WHO). Heart problems develop because life has ultimately lost its sweetness.

[3]: Bowel cancer often occurs when the gallbladder is surgically removed, because there is nowhere for the bile to be stored, and therefore it ends up in the colon.

[4]: According to *The World Health Organisation* (WHO) HIV is an inherent gender issue.

[5]: Information source *Wikipedia.*

[6]: *The Hades Moon* by Judy Hall was published in 2007 by *Red Wheel/Weiser* publications.

[7]: Christian Astrology by William Lilly.

[8]: Information source *Wikipedia.*

[9]: Christian Astrology by William Lilly, page 116.

[10]: Reference to comments made in the Times Newspaper (circa 2003).

[11]: Information source *Wikipedia.*

[12]: Information source *Wikipedia.*

[13]: Reference to Steve Jobs: *The Exclusive Biography.*

[14]: Christian Astrology by William Lilly, page 116.

[15]: Information source *Wikipedia.*

[16]: *People Magazine.*

[17]: Information source *Wikipedia.*

[18]: Information source *Wikipedia.*

[19]: Trans-Saturnian planets become very influential in the natal chart at the start of the third Saturn cycle – around the age of 60.

[20]: Reference to the astrologer Judy Hall

[21]: Information source *Wikipedia.*

[22]: Cited from Astrology for Self-Empowerment by Dovid Strusiner, and published by *Llewellyn Worldwide Publishing.*

Appendix

The Psychology of Evolution

"It is not the strongest of the species that survives, nor is it the most intelligent that survives. It is the one that is the most adaptable to change, that lives within the means available, and works co-operatively against common threats."

Charles Darwin

Throughout the natural course of evolution, individuals have generally preferred the power of preservation, rather than the power of transformation. Principally, preservation means to hold on, especially to that, which is familiar in some way. This is why illness and disease have always been common factors upon the Earth. In almost all cases, illness and disease are conditions that are set in motion when the soul refuses to acknowledge its birthright, which is to progress in a psychological and spiritual capacity, while incarnate. According to the Akashic Records, this is the elemental construct for spiritual evolution.

Darwinism however, is the theory of biological evolution — developed by the English naturalist, Charles Darwin. Darwin had a very pronounced position of Pluto in his chart; residing in the visionary sign of Pisces. It was also conjunct a domicile Mercury, and Jupiter in the third house of communication, and squared the Ascendant (see chart). Despite impending criticism of his life's work, Darwin was nevertheless able to communicate his conjectures in an, impulsive, ardent, and confident manner. Thus, he eventually convinced the establishment that his theory of evolution, was in fact an image of real life events.

Pluto, the planet most associated with the natural course of

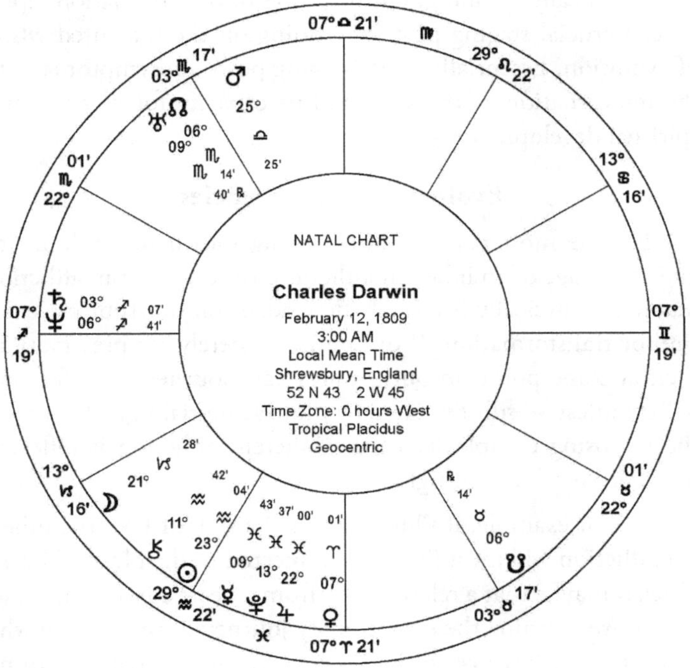

evolution, is often feared, because its psychological element of evolutionary transformation means to progress into unfamiliar territory. Evolutionary Transformation therefore requires courage, and strength of spirit — necessary characteristics for the wellbeing of the individual, and the collective.

Undoubtably, Pluto is a complexly-transformational planet. Thus, the power of evolutionary transformation is an extensive conception; and one which is facilitated and developed through Pluto's psychology of evolution — Pluto's passage through the twelve signs of the zodiac. Furthermore, Pluto's power of transformation represents a psychological image of the future — something salutary to aim for — like the Phoenix that emerged from the ashes of its earlier existence. The Phoenix is an evolutionary representation of Pluto, and its ruling sign, Scorpio.

Karmically speaking, Pluto's power of transformation represents a crucial staging post — residing on the measured wheel of evolution. Essentially, these staging posts are symptomatic to the reincarnation of the soul, and its capacity for physical and spiritual development.

Evolutionary Inherencies

For the most part, a human being incarnates with an ingrained image of an inherent affliction. Exactly how an affliction manifests physically is entirely dependent on our subjective desire for transformation. If our desire is merely for preservation, then at some point on our evolutionary journey, the affliction will manifest — substantiated by Pluto's celestial sign. Therefore, the imposing complexity of the inherent affliction is reflected through Pluto's ruling sign.

So, for example, if Pluto tenants the sign of Leo, the inherent affliction will most likely be connected to the physical heart. Thus, it maybe that a relative died from a heart condition. However, if we examine the evolutionary journey of the relative who died from the heart condition, it may well reveal that little or no soul transformation was actually obtained during their life. It may also reveal that the individual endured the heart condition for many years.

Physical transformation is possible via the other planets and points in the natal chart. However, 'psychological (unsurpassed) transformation' is only achieved through the Pluto archetype, and via its primary cosmic influence, the celestial sign that Pluto tenants in the natal chart. Therefore, unsurpassed transformation accounts for psychological and evolutionary (soul) transformation.

Pluto Iniquity

All throughout history, Pluto's power has been continually corrupted. As a result, mankind has furnished his evolutionary timeframes with mostly rapacious tendencies. Just how extreme the psychological boundaries within these immoral timeframes were, was dependent solely on the disposition of Pluto's celestial sign. Perhaps, one of the most notorious of all the generational timeframes, and which was considered mostly as a dark realm, was the Victorian period. Thus, the Victorian period was very much powered by Pluto, at its most obstructive and fatalistic of influences.

The Victorian period (1837-1901) was symbolized as a dark phase in our collective evolution. Principally, this is because it housed severe eye-watering crimes, such as, violent theft, violent affray, child prostitution, and calculated murder — shadowed by intense darkness. Throughout the Victorian era, Pluto tenanted the signs of Aries (ruled by Mars), Taurus (ruled by Venus) and Gemini (ruled by Mercury). These types of crimes would also coincide with the ruling planetary influences of these signs — operating at the lowest vibration of influence. At the same time, the Victorian period was a low vibrational influence — captured within the historical chronicles of darkness. In effect, Pluto operating from these signs, accompanied by the dominating influences of the Victorian period, created a confluence of darkness and evil — corrupting Pluto's power.

Evolutionary Transformation

Meanwhile, it is important to emphasize, that it is very unlikely that individuals who were born into the Pluto in Aries, Taurus and Gemini generations, prior to the Pluto in Cancer generation of 1914, are still alive today. Therefore, it would be difficult to complete an analysis with regards to Pluto in these signs, particularly at that time. Nor, is it possible to theorize and predict the future outlook and conditions that will be associated with these same generational soul groups — proceeding the Pluto in Pisces generation, which culminates in 2067. Thus, we can only speculate as to the effects of these futuristic sojourns of Pluto.

During these early periods in history, there were of course remarkable individuals, who strived towards unsurpassed transformation. For example, from the Pluto in Gemini generation, came someone who transformed the lives of so many during the second World War. He was Nicholas Winton. Winton was born just before the advent of Pluto's transit of Cancer. His greatest achievement was to supervise the rescue of 669 children, most of them Jewish, from Czechoslovakia, on the eve of the second world war — an operation that was later referred to as the Czech Kindertransport. He also found homes for them, and arranged for their safe passage to Britain.[1]

In this natural chart (birthtime unknown), Pluto's mythical brother Neptune tenants the sign of nurturing Cancer, and opposes Uranus. In this case, the opposition means to liberate (Uranus/Neptune) the children (Cancer), under duress caused by the opposition. Pluto of course was in Gemini, and trines determined Mars in the humanitarian sign of Aquarius — recapitulating the emphasis of the Uranus-Neptune opposition. Gemini is naturally ruled by Mercury (communication), and Pluto is transformation. Winton successfully communicated his intent (Mercury) to the British authorities, in order to establish a new life (Pluto), for these children. Mercury is also conjunct Pluto in the chart. Thus, Winton possessed great power, which he used to influence the masses.

In my opinion, this was a truly remarkable accomplishment, which denotes psychological and evolutionary transformation. Nicholas Winton will no doubt be remembered in the Pluto archives, which records great achievements — symbolizing individual and collective transformation.

The Evolution of the Dark Night

The evolution of the dark night is a metaphor for a prolonged period of intense cruelty. Therefore, the Pluto-Aries-Taurus-Gemini generations that influenced all of civilization prior to 1914, are considered by many evolutionists to be the epochs,

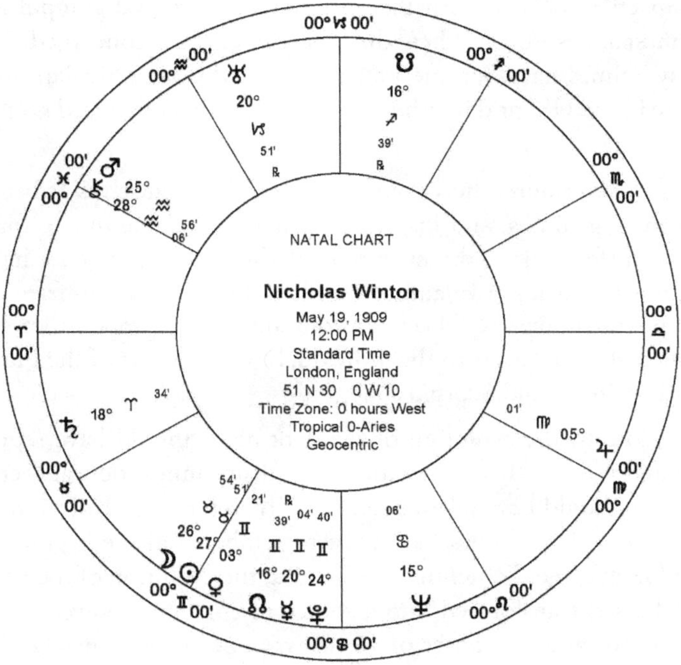

which marked the beginning of 'the evolution of the dark night.' Perhaps then, the evolution of the dark night symbolized the ultimate preservation of evolution? Characteristically, the evolution of the dark night symbolized the beginning of the Victorian period, which was also a manipulative, warlike, and sexual-orientated epoch — packed full of Pluto duplexities and ambivalences.

Meantime, if memory serves, the evolutionary astrologer Jeffrey Wolf Green, remarked on something similar in one of his lectures, that took place in Cleveland, Ohio, in 2014. He remarked on the darkness surrounding this particular Pluto era. In every aspect of Victorian society, soul transformation was a far cry from the truth. This was Pluto plying its power at its lowest quality. In many ways, we are all still experiencing the negative impacts associated with this pitiless, obsessive and compulsive timespan, especially where the nature of crime is concerned. Today, crimes have become more intense. This is particularly the case in the UK, and in other parts of the Pluto-influenced societies of the world.

Furthermore, those souls who consider themselves as being creative geniuses, and inspired visionaries, and the intellectuals of transformation, the evolution of the dark night must have seemed as being a calamitous and environmentally unfriendly blip, cast upon the wheel of evolution. These propensities are particularly relevant to the individuals who are part of the Pluto in Leo-Virgo and Scorpio soul groups.

Ideally, the evolution of the dark night should have represented a time when inspirational idealism, innovation and creativity should have taken precedent. Therefore, the evolution of the dark night should have been remembered as the beginning of the 'age of enlightenment.'[2] Instead, the evolution of the dark night was transformed into a source of corrupted power, especially towards the onset of world war one. Unfortunately, the individuals who lost their lives during the conflict of wars were mostly denied the opportunity for evolutionary transformation.

Initially, the oscillating backwash emanating from this destructive era is only now beginning to dissipate. During these latter stages of this dark epoch, the prospect of environmental and social catastrophes, financial meltdowns, coupled with medically-induced tragedies are likely to be severe. Strange as it may seem, these afflictions are necessary for global transformation. For example, the recent Covid-19 pandemic symbolized the beginning of an essential period of Pluto (purging) transformation — setting apart the start of widespread unification — within the cooperative and corporate powers of the world. The Covid-19 pandemic took hold during Pluto's final passage through Capricorn. Therefore, during Pluto's late transit of Capricorn, we may begin to witness a raft of other violent disturbances, all vying for power and control.

Meanwhile, Pluto's lengthy tenure of Capricorn has generated a transformational turning point — directing us slowly away from the long dark night.

Unsurpassed Evolutionary Transformation

Whatever Pluto soul group, each of us we belong to, it is not too late to transform the very essence of the dark night, before we all enter into the concluding chapter — namely the ultimate endgame for humankind. This takes effect from 2067. However, from 2024, Pluto begins its humanitarian, philanthropic and consolidating passage through Aquarius, so we, as a collective, can begin to heal.

From its Capricorn station however, Pluto has decimated the financial economies of so many countries worldwide. However, had greed not have been such a prolific influence, Pluto in Capricorn would have transformed the corporate economies of the world; and into something more substantially-favourable for all concerned. Furthermore, Pluto's transit of Capricorn would have provided the citizens of the world with liveable wages for all the working. For the retired however, there would be beneficial state pensions — increasing in value every year — in line with other costs and inflation. In addition, there would be free health care for all. These are all fundamental transformations associated with the Pluto archetype. Unfortunately, many countries have currently capped increases in pensions, and all because of the influence of corporate greed, and the Covid pandemic.

Meanwhile, if this current predicament of greed preservation continues, and reaches Pluto's entry into Aries in 2067, humankind will be faced with global catastrophe. At this point, the Earth will no longer support the infrastructure of humankind; hence a continuation of progression upon the evolutionary wheel of development. This information is recorded in the

Akashic Records (see Footnote)

In order to avoid the prospect of a Pluto cataclysm, we need to begin embracing our spiritual roots. This is achieved by remembering who we really are at the source, hence the heart seed. Embracing our spiritual roots is achieved through stillness and contemplation, hence meditation. Advocating the use of meditation is perhaps the ultimate Pluto soul transformation. The illusion associated with time acceleration occurs because human beings are no longer still.[3]

Furthermore, we really need to start repairing the Earth by enveloping it with love and light, through heartfelt visualization, and group meditations. These are Pluto collective soul transformations. Alternatively, if we chose to continue on our current path, complete with all of our catastrophic propensities, a Pluto-type cataclysm, such as simultaneous Volcano eruptions is inevitable.

Footnote

According to Wikipedia, the Akashic Records are a compendium of all universal events, thought, words, emotions and intent, which has occurred in the past, present or future, in terms of all life forms and entities, not just human.

I would now like to examine the twelve signs of the zodiac; and their innovatory effects upon the Pluto archetype. Each celestial sign represents a 'baseline characteristic' of Pluto's preservative, transformational and psychological power — powering the natal chart. Furthermore, if we were to look through a cosmic lens; and one that contains the image of Pluto, we would be able to view the natal chart as a psychological conduit, which mastermind's the capability for evolutionary (soul) transformation.

Individually, we can distribute the potential for transformation to the other members of our Pluto soul group — for the purpose of evolutionary propagation. According to the Akashic

Records, the Neptune and Pluto soul groups, reflect the soul groups we belong to in spirit. Furthermore, the celestial signs that both Neptune and Pluto tenant symbolizes the strength (Neptune's sign) and the purpose (Pluto's sign) of the soul, while incarnate.

Yet, how this power is perceived and distributed throughout the natal chart, is determined by the natal aspects to Pluto; and by Pluto transits to the natal planets. The celestial signs merely act as cosmic filters — discharging power accordingly.

From each sign however, Pluto functions primarily as a generational influence, as we shall now discover.

The Pluto in Cancer Generation — 1914 – 1939 (Approximate Dates)

For this particular soul group, the seeds of inherent illness and disease were most likely sown throughout childhood — only to be extended and exhibited throughout later life. Furthermore, the potential for illness and disease is strongly indicated when there are hard aspects from Pluto to other planets in the natal chart, particularly to the Moon and Saturn.

The way in which an infirmity sprouts, grows and develops so to speak, is solely dependent on the method in which the individual choses to traverse the natural course of their evolutionary pathway. If the individual wanders through life blindly, then the onset of illness and disease is assured. This notion, is of course relevant to all of the soul groups. However, for this group, the presence of inherent anxiety, especially in early life, has no doubt left its mark, in the form of a psychological blemish — imprinted on their otherwise sensitive personalities. Throughout life this psychological scar has slowly become discoloured — leading to the outbreak of illness and disease. It has also left them feeling defensive and insecure.

Furthermore, it is almost certain that this defensive and mostly insecure generation experienced an intensely difficult childhood. The Pluto in Cancer soul group require unending amounts of love and reassurance, above and beyond the other evolutionary groups. However, their parents would have found it difficult to honor these commitments, probably because they too, were busy negotiating ways to survive the conflict of war.

Individually, those from the Pluto in Cancer group may have experienced the loss of a parent in early life, particularly to the ravaging of war. But whatever the reasoning behind their inherent anxiety, this group continues to shoulder a great psychological weight — almost as if it is a natural part of their inherent programming. The Pluto in Cancer generation have become united in their grief. Thus, they have become united with each other. Figuratively speaking, they invented the term 'unified collective.'

Moreover, the Pluto in Cancer soul group have an inbuilt inclination towards the preservation of innocence, recollection and sentimentality. Therefore, this particular soul group are the masters of revisiting the past. Psychologically speaking, they frequently revisit the past to try to reason with it. This is a potentially dangerous endeavour; and that is why they have become particularly prone to dementia — surpassing all of the other Pluto soul groups.

The Pluto in Cancer generation represent a watertight embodiment of souls. Thus, they have traversed the path of life in a manner that can only be described as circumspect and discreet — assembling security and stability as their principle objectives. Nothing will deter them from their aims, and their aspirations, which is mostly to build a better future, especially for their loved ones.

If they can naturally eliminate insecurity from their lives, the Pluto in Cancer generation will fundamentally become a less defensive soul group. Most of the time this in-depth generation likes nothing more than to nurture, and care for their fellow human beings — considering them to be all a part of the collective bosom of humankind.

The Pluto in Cancer generation possesses both powerful maternal and paternal instincts, which have been extracted from the collective excrement that symbolizes upheaval. Furthermore, the Pluto in Cancer generation are in possession of powerful instincts, which are intuitively guided by their souls. They are in fact, the quintessential ambassadors for Pluto-orientated transformation.

Pluto Preservation

As we have already discussed, the Pluto in Cancer generation are perhaps the most vulnerable to illness and disease. The disease cancer is a particularly prevalent condition that affects this soul group, especially in the breast, stomach, prostate and the colon. Psychologically speaking, these types of cancers occur because this group tend to evade personal adjustment, and evolutionary conversion, hence transformation — preferring instead to preserve their rigid ideals.

Furthermore, this group have somehow placed a psychological barrier around them, which is often immovable; similar to the protective shell of the crab, only more intensified in density. Essentially, it is this immovable psychological barrier that is the construct for dementia and Parkinson's — conditions that are particularly widespread within this Pluto group.

The overall manifestation of dementia became evermore noticeable during Pluto's sojourn of Capricorn. Therefore, transiting Pluto made an opposition to its natal position in the charts of the Pluto in Cancer generation. This single planetary configuration was most likely the catalyst for dementia, Parkinson's, and of course cancer. Other factors were responsible, such as a square or quincunx from transit Pluto to Mercury, Saturn or Neptune.

Through my many years of research into the Pluto mechanisms of this soul group, I discovered that approximately ninety percent, and in particularly those, who had been placed in care homes, because of dementia, have undergone some form of upheaval in their childhood. Essentially, dementia represents psychological death and memory loss; hence the preservation of ideals. In other words, they have built a totally resistant barrier towards unsurpassed transformation. Unfortunately, a large percentage of the Pluto in Cancer generation have found it increasingly difficult to adapt to life in the twenty-first century. Dementia is not contagious. However, it will appear to be contagious when there has been a distinct lack of progression in the individual lives of this soul group.

Regrettably, the only way this group is likely to achieve positive soul transformation as an overall collective, is when they are literally coerced into it.

Pluto Transformation

Ideally, in order to avoid the prospect of inherent illness and disease, the Pluto in Cancer generation must embrace soul transformation — without the presence of unyielding and underlying fear. Ultimately, they must strive towards the rebirth of the soul by fusing the emotional bodies (solar plexus), with the soul, through the regenerative powers of stillness and meditation. In essence, they must learn to nurture the fragilities that are present within their souls, especially those souls who have been acutely compromised by the preservation of upheaval.

The Pluto in Leo Generation — 1939 – 1957 (Approximate Dates)

The Pluto in Leo generation can be referred to as a magnificent soul group of divaricating proportions. This is because their radiating personalities have the potential to expand, and touch even the most distant of souls — releasing them from the likes of anguish and misery. Above all else, this Pluto group have the collective potential to heal the core of the Pluto in Cancer generation. Meanwhile, the Pluto in Leo generation are essentially the cosmic children. To be more precise however, they are known in the Pluto realm of consciousness as the children of evolution. Thus, they have embraced the potential to transform the lives of others. This evolutionary certainty has been extracted from the relevant files in the Akashic Records.

One of the primary tasks connected to this particular group, is to transform and nurture their own childlike souls. This will help them refashion the collective veil that represents the other Pluto soul groups. This means that they are capable of infusing other soul groups with creative innovation, which will be consolidated during Pluto's transit of Virgo. A powerful and psychological transformation, involving this group, would have occurred during the traumatic events of the second World War — 1939-1945. According to my research into this soul group, many children who were liberated from the hands of the Nazis, were themselves members of the Pluto in Leo generation. Reflecting further on this notion, a large percentage from the Pluto soul group became immersed in all of the suffering, which was caused by the Second World War. Therefore, they are not averse to the obstructive trappings associated with inherent illness and disease — initiated during adolescence. Individually, the potential is emphasized by hard aspects from Pluto in the natal chart, particularly to the Sun, and Saturn.

Exactly how illness and disease manifests, and takes on physical and psychological form, is solely dependent upon the exploitations of the Pluto in Leo individual. So, for example, inborn stubbornness, and inbred tension, caused by overwork, can be their curse. Thus, this group has a collective tendency towards working their fingers to the bone so to speak. This is precipitated by the psychological scars of having nothing — reflected by such undertakings as food rationing during the second world war.

Cardiovascular problems have invariably become an overwhelming issue for this group, especially during the times when they perceive life has indeed lost it sweetness, or creativity. A loss of sweetness or creativity would be an extremely difficult concept for the members of this group to comprehend; because the Pluto in Leo soul needs constant and meaningful love, and admiration. It is love, and creativity more than anything else, that transforms these souls into greater individual and collective human beings.

Although the Pluto in Leo soul views the potential threat to the health as serious, he or she will nonetheless take it in their stride. However, the innovative sign of Leo has the potential to successfully merge with the Pluto archetype in an auspicious way — creating a confluence of advantageous energy — with the regenerative powers of Pluto. This combination of positive energy is absolutely essential for maintaining good health, and soul transformation. This is because Pluto's sojourn through Leo held the potential to reawaken the spiritual heart, which in turn regenerates the physical heart. Functioning together in this way, this group represent a source of necessary evolutionary and spiritual development, for other groups to commend.

In addition, those souls who form a crucial part of the Pluto in Leo generation are essentially born leaders. However, despite this positive notion, they are often persecuted by personal doubts and anxieties, which they perceive as irritations. Negative improprieties can impair the overall health of their life force energies, causing heartbreak, and other health problems.

The Pluto in Leo generation are also susceptible to spinal (back) problems, particularly in later life, and particularly when they have overworked themselves. This impending circumstance can also occur when a lack of moral and psychological support is lacking in their lives. Spinal discomfort can also occur when the Pluto in Leo soul refuses to support others; for example, because they have become immersed in self-pride.

Pluto Preservation

Personal doubts and anxieties are also issues, which the members of this group can easily become predisposed to. As a result, these souls often bury their doubts deep within the psyche, which causes damage to both the physical and spiritual heart. Self-doubt can also be the root cause of incurring psychological problems, especially in later life. As I pointed out earlier, inherent afflictions that are not contagious, become psychologically contagious within each Pluto soul group.

So, for the Pluto in Leo soul group, psychological concerns can result in personal limitations throughout life. However, this group, above all others, tend to fight to the bitter end, especially for the causes they consider to be extremely personal in nature. Some would say that this is their stubbornness emerging. However, when they ultimately succeed in their creative endeavours, they will eventually acquire the evolutionary blueprints, that determine a successful route towards the transformation of their individual and collective souls.

Pluto Transformation

Ideally, the Pluto in Leo generation must attempt to fuse the physical heart with the spiritual heart, in order to acquire love in their lives, and to avoid the prospect of inherent illness and disease. However, for the Pluto in Leo generation, it must be love that is totally unconditional, unlike its Sun sign equivalent, which is often dependant. This is deemed as the ultimate amalgamation for this soul group. Thus, to successfully attain personal and evolutionary transformation, is no doubt their greatest reward.

The Pluto in Virgo Generation — 1957 – 1972 (Approximate Dates)

The naturally caring and decorous Pluto in Virgo generation have chosen to incarnate at this difficult time in our collective evolution, to necessitate much-needed service to humankind. For the most part, performing service is for the purpose of 'raising awareness.' However, to best describe the concept of raising awareness, is to compound reason (logic) with perception, in the hope of integrating the physical and spiritual heart.

Ultimately, raising awareness will heal the divisions that exist within the heart of humankind. However, before this Pluto group can orchestrate these admirable measures, they must first heal their own souls, by subsequently increasing their own levels of self-worth. Healing the divide that exists between the physical and the spiritual heart would essentially be considered as unsurpassed transformation. Essentially, this higher evolutionary purpose is the greatest achievement a soul in human form can achieve. Therefore, to the Pluto in Virgo generation, this means ultimate perfection. However, if this subtle enterprise is not achieved, the seeds of inherent illness and disease will be firmly set, especially within the psychological framework of this generational soul group.

Overall, this particular group are prone to mental exhaustion, and anxiety — perhaps more than any other of the Pluto soul groups. Principally, when this happens, they become easily distracted, and cannot focus on their primary objectives, which is service. So, it is absolutely vital that these souls learn to silence the mind, especially through meditation, in order to alleviate these conditions — bringing the opportunity for self-healing. There is an old Arabic proverb, 'silence is golden.' For this group, maintaining this is imperative. They also have the potential to exceed, above the other soul groups, to master Pluto's penchant for psychological transformation.

Functioning with the divine gesture of service, will provide these individuals with an evolutionary overhaul of their souls so to speak. Simply, this is the way they acquire inspiration, and inspiration is the vital ingredient they need to control their inherent attraction towards apprehension and anxiety.

Often, it is not until much later in life that these individuals begin to realize their necessity for self-healing. Psychologically this particularly group naturally suffer from a lack of self-assurance, especially within the first half of their existence — leading up to the second Saturn return. However, when Pluto operates from its Virgo station, the generational effects of this planet are mirrored alongside the overall characteristics of Saturn. This means that, in most cases, Pluto transformation of the Virgo archetype occurs within the second half of life.

Traditionally, Pluto is in its fall in Virgo; and therefore, its transformational effects can become suppressed. The transformation of this soul group will begin in 2008, and through to 2024. From 2008, transit Pluto begins its sojourn of Saturn-ruled Capricorn — culminating in 2024. Throughout this period, Pluto will make a trine to its position in Virgo in the natal charts of this soul group. This trine will contain healing properties, which will essentially release them from their self-doubt. Once this happens, the need for service will become apparent. For these souls, performing service is a congenital notion. So, when these psychologically-connected souls finally accept this inherent challenge, the transformation of their individual souls will be underway. For them, initiating their karmic plan of action is a moment of exaltation. Thus, a smile will break out on their otherwise individual bewildered faces.

Although Virgo is a mutable and gentle sign, Pluto, which is the dominant force in this cosmic equation, is a fixed and powerful planet. Therefore, this particular soul group can become borderline on inflexible. So, in order that the perfect balance is achieved between these two very different cosmic factions, the Pluto in Virgo generation must learn to surrender to the natural order of life — rather than controlling it. Once they achieve this fine balance, the individual members of the Pluto in Virgo soul group become naturally confident and self-assured.

In a psychologically capacity, this group need to be operating at their best, and at all times. For the Pluto in Virgo generation however, the embodiment of psychological perfection is only attained when the soul finds solace and contentment from deep within their individual souls, which are often acquired via performing service to themselves and others. Thus, this is when Pluto and Virgo become the perfect collective alliance.

Pluto Preservation

For the Pluto in Virgo generation, being unable to acquire psychological perfection, is often the precursor for mental disorders, as we have previously determined. In addition, individual physical afflictions can be widespread, which center mostly around the pancreas. Furthermore, gastrointestinal conditions can pose as a problem for these souls, which become psychologically contagious throughout this Pluto soul group.

Currently, psychological illnesses and diseases, such as depression and psychosis are beginning to proliferate. However, most psychological disorders that are prevalent today were starting to be recognized and understood during Pluto's modern transit of Virgo. Thus, the evolutionary transit of Pluto in Virgo, perceived in medical terms, benchmarked a turning point in curative awareness, especially throughout the modern world.

The proliferation of psychological-based illness and disease, is perhaps another reason why these souls were ordained to incarnate at this particular point in evolution. Once they confronted their own issues, perhaps they needed to assist in some way with the elimination of this overall psychological disorder. Individually, this conception would be relevant when natal Pluto occupies the sixth, eighth or twelfth house in the individual natal chart. Momentously, the sojourn of Pluto through Virgo, symbolized the beginning of the modern medical era.

Pluto Transformation

Ideally, and in order to avoid the onset of illness and disease, the Pluto in Virgo generation must transform their innate sense of insecurity, into a deep recognition, and one that bolsters their sense of self-importance and reliance on others. Feeling important, and being needed are their major requirements, which will successfully activate their inner compass — pointing the way towards self-healing. Once they begin to feel secure within themselves, the collective souls that comprise the Pluto in Virgo generation, become incumbent in their individual pursuit towards the service to humankind.

The Pluto in Libra Generation — 1972 – 1984 (Approximate Dates)

For this airy, and exquisite generational soul group, the seeds of illness and disease are continually sown throughout the course of their life. This is because the colon (Pluto) and the kidneys (Libra) are connected. They are also reproductive organs; and therefore, they can be a source for concern — continually reproducing the same dis-ease. Thus, the seeds of debilitation are sown deeply into the center of these organs; particularly when there is a distinct lack of personal or collective justice and harmony evident in the individual lives of this 'joined at the hip' collective. In other words, these people become easily irritated and antagonized, when love is replaced by cruelty. This is because, at the heart level, the Pluto in Libra soul group love everyone and everything. Thus, it is this perceived 'lack of love,' that becomes the catalyst for the onset of illness and disease.

Invariably, these souls cannot identify why injustice develops into an ongoing obsession — blanketing their otherwise fair-minded personalities. For them, injustice is an abstract notion that resides deep within their souls, and therefore it cannot be processed psychologically. Their perception of injustice is, for the most part, due to the condition of hard aspects to Pluto in the natal chart. To these souls, a lack of harmony represents a major injustice, to which the Pluto in Libra generation cannot possibly support, or subscribe to.

Pluto is symbolic of generational core transformation, whereas Libra is the sign of spiritual equilibrium, and the equipoising of physical matter. Thus, this Pluto in Libra consociation is perhaps best suited to the facilitation of the major life-enhancing challenges, which ultimately lead to core transformation; the essential lifeblood of Pluto. This means that the Pluto in Libra generation possess the individual and collective will power to attain soul transformation, by striving to lead the way into bringing the world into perfect balance and harmony. To these souls, this beautiful conception represents the supreme notion of fairness.

Striving to bring the world into perfect balance is a difficult endeavour, at the best of times. However, for the Pluto in Libra soul, it can be hazardous. This is because of an innate incapacity for indecision. Indecisiveness can be their ultimate vexation — an annoying irritation — and an intense indignation. So, as an elaborate air sign, they can often leave decision making for others to execute on their behalf. This is a fair-minded function that they subconsciously view as being necessary, especially for the transformation of their souls. When indeed, it represents nothing more than psychological and physical laziness — something they are accused of on a regular basis.

Notwithstanding, if these souls fail in their quest to transform their souls, because of indecision, this inaction can also become a precursor for the onset of illness and disease. Indecision (ambivalence) is a psychological concept; therefore, illness and disease manifests initially as a psychological concept. As we have previously established, Pluto rules over the colon, and Libra oversees the kidneys. Both of these physical elements are a major part of the abdominal system. Libran imbalance is created primarily in the kidneys. Conditions such as lumbago and especially kidney disorders are common themes, especially when indecision infects the life of the Pluto in Libra soul. Colon, ovary and bladder disorders can also occur as a result of indecision.

Pluto Preservation

The Pluto in Libra soul group must learn to detach them-

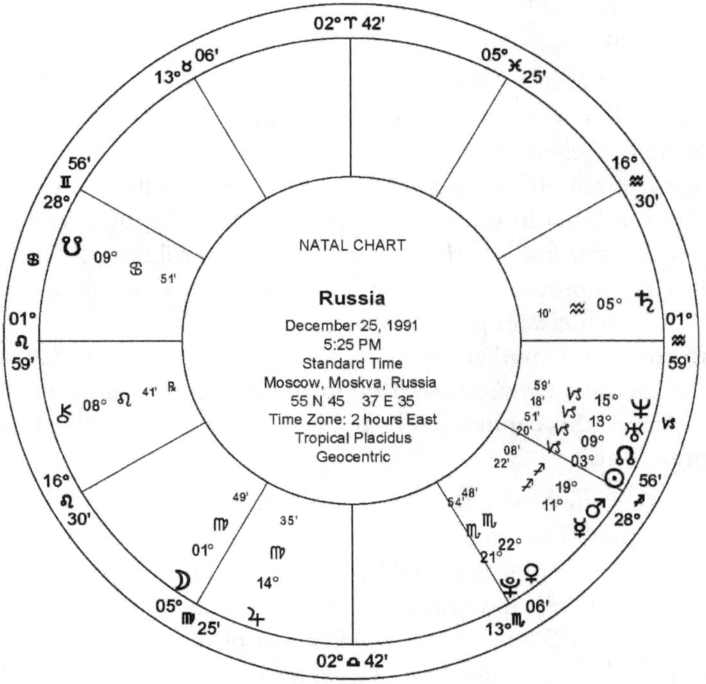

selves from the everyday stresses and strains of life — focusing instead on the everyday joys of life — rather that becoming obsessed by the abstract notion of injustice. However, injustice is a preconceived concept that typifies the seeds of imbalance. Injustice is also a presumption that is incorporated by the absence of truth. However, for this particular soul group, injustice would always prove to be a difficult notion for this collective to resist — even in an ideal world. It is no coincidence however, that they incarnated at a time that signified a mass of global injustices.

One significant example, was the cold war between the USA, and the Soviet Union (the USSR as it was known then). The USA's purpose on this Earth is the police the world (Pluto), and thus restore harmony (Libra). The purpose of the Soviet Union (modern day Russia) is to restore harmony (Libra) amongst its people, after centuries of indecision (Libra) and intense aggression (Pluto).

The Pluto in Libra generation are naturally gifted with an inclination to restore harmony, especially at the global level. This is their inherent ability. As a significance, there are many diplomatic minds on both sides of the USA/Soviet conflict, who have Pluto in Libra in their natal charts. They are the souls who aspire towards finding diplomatic and peaceful solutions; thereby forging improved relations on both sides of this unending conflict, which creates global imbalance. Today, the world is about to enter into another cold war, because of Russia's invasion of the Ukraine. However, with Pluto about to enter humanitarian Aquarius, this conflict can be resolved much more quickly than previously.

To restore balance to the Pluto scales of justice is perhaps a major part of the soul's plan, which has been uniquely designed for this generational assemblage. In addition, striving towards peace, harmony and justice within the confines of these nuclear superpowers (Pluto) is also a major part of their grand plan — instilling peace within the realms of both the individual and collective soul.

Once the Pluto-Libra soul has acquired peace, their internal scales become balanced. Furthermore, the kidneys, and the colon will always remain in perfect harmony with each other. This means that the dialogue between these prolific organs will be nonetheless constant and productive. Talks between these world superpowers however, will need to be conducted with a constantly-productive dialogue, in order to find a resolve. Therefore, I suggest it is left in the capable hands of the Pluto in Libra diplomats.

Pluto Transformation

Not every soul in this group was designated to restore the natural order of the world; especially the disorder caused by global conflicts. Moreover, the fundamental function assigned to the Pluto in Libra individual is to transform their own 'inner conflict' into a genuine, sincere and peaceful accord, which trickles through the soul — an enactment similar to the melodious tones that symbolize the concept of jubilation. So, for the Pluto in Libra soul, jubilation characterizes true harmony, which is the perfect antidote for illness and disease.

The Pluto in Scorpio Generation — 1984 – 1995 (Approximate Dates)

Pluto is Scorpio's ruling planet. Likewise, this is an exceptionally-powerful alliance; because Pluto has developed an immeasurable and intense unanimity with its domiciled and celestial counterpart. Therefore, the fusing of these cosmic elements represents a combination of high-powered forces — making them a formidable strength to be reckoned with. However, hard aspects to Pluto in the natal chart can incapacitate the positive effects of this all-powerful alliance — drawing to attention attitudes and viewpoints that need to be transformed into something entirely new and purposeful — which is the fundamental purpose of evolution. Hard (frictional) aspects, merely impede the positive effects of planetary affiliations.

Pluto in Scorpio is a powerful cosmic alliance, which is capable of strengthening the physical, psychological and spiritual substructures — unique to the individual soul. These substructures represent the elemental cornerstones of life. Evolution, hence developmental progression, is the foundational purpose of the eighth house in the natal chart, which is Pluto and Scorpio's natural domain. Thus, Pluto, Scorpio, and the eighth house, are the most durable and resilient components in the natal chart.

A friend of mine said that "you could drop a nuclear bomb on those who have Pluto in Scorpio and they will no doubt survive."[4] I can see the logic behind this analogy. But realistically, no one would survive the direct impact of a nuclear bomb.

However, with that said, the Pluto in Scorpio generation are an extremely tough and buoyant group of individuals; and they are capable of surviving almost anything that is catapulted their way; particular concerns of a violent and climatic disposition.

The Pluto in Scorpio soul group have incarnated at this point in evolution to extend their powerful collective influence, which is to captivate the need for change and survival. They are also here to provide additional power — powering the evolutionary changes that lie ahead for the whole of humankind — and planet Earth. Therefore, the Pluto in Scorpio generation are perhaps the best equipped group to absorb the harshness of these evolutionary transitions, which according to the Akashic Records begin in 2025. Supposedly, this is when the golden age of enlightenment is ushered in. Therefore, the Pluto is Scorpio soul group symbolize the embodiment of transformation.

However, this powerful soul affiliation are not averse to the dangers associated with physical and psychological afflictions. Therefore, the seeds of illness and disease are invariably planted deep within the individual and collective colon of these individuals.[5] If, at any time however, they consider that life has betrayed them in any way, or they feel that they have failed in their evolutionary tasks, the colon is the organ that is the first to be afflicted — by the imprecation of indisposition.

The prospect of contracting illness and disease, would not however deter them from carrying out their instinctive and evolutionary obligations. This is because the Pluto in Scorpio generation have literally invested their energy into their own individually-tailored life plan. This is to 'set in motion' the seed of transformation into the heart of humankind; in order to highlight a more conscious way of existence. For these souls however, failure is a word that is not in their cosmic vocabulary; because failure, or negligence, are convictions they cannot easily assimilate. So, they do not attempt to do so.

While this is true, there are however a high percentage of

individuals from Pluto-Scorpio group who are especially vulnerable to self-immolation, hence suicide. This represents a specific portion who have Neptune difficultly-aspected in their natal charts — expressly from the Sun, Mars or Saturn. Neptune, is of course, Pluto's mythical brother. So, for them, the concept of self-sacrifice is deeply personal, and it is extremely ingrained. Softer aspects to Neptune, such as a trine from Saturn, or the Sun, would help the individual to develop a more prolific attitude towards death and tragedy, and to a greater extent, more than any of the other Pluto soul groups. Often, they become suicide counsellors, as a result.

Scorpio is a fixed water sign; and Pluto is considered to be a fixed water planet. Therefore, this combination of immovable and iron-willed elements can become firmly anchored in the psyche. Generally, this means that there is no compromise on what they consider as being achievable. Potentially, Pluto in Scorpio represents the perfect synthesis of elements; therefore, Pluto in Scorpio represents the ultimate configuration, especially when attempting to achieve the impossible.

They do however have a blind spot. This 'Achilles heel' is an inbuilt desire to be in total control of everything, and at all times. If, they feel they are not in control, then every measure they undertake becomes a source of disparagement. In some cases, this depreciation becomes detrimental to their overall health.

Prostitution, which is common to the Pluto in Scorpio generation, denotes psychological control over others. Most likely those who have embraced this ancient occupation have experienced deep-set psychological issues, which are mostly brought about by others controlling them. Interestingly, many who make their living in this shady arena of life have Pluto, powerfully-placed in the natal chart.

Pluto Preservation

Sexually transmitted diseases, such as HIV, urinary bladder

infections, and even depression are potentially common factors for the Pluto in Scorpio generation. In fact, the first recognized case of HIV was in 1981 — three years before the start of this Pluto sojourn. During Pluto's transit of Scorpio, HIV and AIDS were dis-eases that were very much in the public eye. Sex is an extremely important factor for these souls. They often consider this particular act to be a form of power and control — increasing the strength of their overall hot-blooded temperament.

Recently, there has been an increase in the use of the drug ketamine; especially for personal gain. According to a recent survey carried out by the World Health Organisation (WHO); the largest group responsible are those in the age group between 25 and 35. This age spectrum is indicative to the Pluto in Scorpio generation. Ketamine is a hallucinogen — providing a sense of self-purpose and sexual euphoria — especially when combined with alcohol. This is particularly prevalent with those who have Neptune badly aspected in their natal charts.

Taking ketamine however, will deceive the anchor-person (reference made earlier to the fixity of this generation), into believing they are increasing their overall control, and their sexual prowess. Ultimately, these are the principle reasons why so many from this group indulge in the use of this powerful drug, which was originally used as a formidable anaesthetic for animals, including horses. The habitual use of ketamine has now become indicative to Pluto's preservation hallmark, especially amongst this group.

Another factor, which is tethered to the Pluto in Scorpio generation, is to raise awareness towards the dangers associated with nuclear power — a deadly and dark consternation symbolized in the subjective realm of Pluto.

Pluto Transformation

Continuing to raise awareness within these particular domains that represent individual and collective annihilation and elimination, the Pluto in Scorpio soul group are capable of conveying light into their own darkened realm of Pluto — neutralizing the prospect of illness and disease. Encompassing the Pluto archetype with light, is symptomatic of evolutionary transformation.

Developing awareness in this way will help the Pluto in Scorpio soul to develop a deeper awareness, concerning the dangers that surround their often-obsessive need for power control, and especially in the arena of their sexual activity. Metaphorically speaking, the one principle piece of their anatomy, which they would most likely boast about, is their 'nuclear-powered' sexual organs. After all, HIV is a form of radiation sickness. Moreover, it is these sensitive organs that are always at risk from external diseases. Transformation in this area is therefore required. Alternatively, look at the sexual organs as being the body's external exhaust; hence a necessary outlet that will channel their powerful energy.

Meanwhile, for this particular generation, who are assisted by the Pluto in Sagittarius and Capricorn generations, their conclusive rise to prominence will be a very slow transition. Therefore, the transformation of this soul group will not begin until the second decade of the twenty-first century. Here, their covert work into altering people's perception towards more spiritual matters will come into effect. In addition, the onset of Covid-19 in 2020 will propel this group into fulfilling their ultimate Pluto mission, which is to raise awareness towards the prospect of global annihilation.

The Pluto in Sagittarius Generation — 1995 – 2008 (Approximate Dates)

For the Pluto in Sagittarius generation, evolutionary transformation is established when the soul is finally liberated from all of its psychological despairs; and when the soul has mastered the importance of responsibility. Once the soul achieves these difficult objectives, the likelihood is, that there will be no more illness and disease in the lives of these spiritually-attuned individuals. The Pluto in Sagittarius group are, in effect, the evolutionary pioneers of the zodiac.

However, if the Pluto in Sagittarius individual perceives that liberty will never be acquired, the seeds of illness and disease will begin to sprout; mostly in the form of depression. Thus, the Pluto in Sagittarius soul group are particularly prone to depression — to a greater extent than all of the other Pluto groups. Sagittarius is the most optimistic sign of the zodiac. Depression however, lies at the polarity of optimism. Once the Pluto in Sagittarius soul succumbs to depression, the arrows, which they fire instinctively, and with a perfect aim, will miss their target. Pluto can function as an intermediary between these two opposing characteristics, so that an equilibrium between the two can be found. Once this occurs, the centaur will develop a much better aim for the arrows to target.

The perception of existing entirely within a psychological and physical bubble of entrapment is perhaps deemed the worst-case scenario for the Pluto in Sagittarius soul group. But this is the nature of depression. In order to avert this crisis, they need to view their existence within a specific field of vision; and one where their three-dimensional compass is operating reliably. This three-dimensional compass is the mechanism that fires their arrows, so it must function at all times.

Subsequently, they need to glimpse their soul's horizon at all times. This is their depth of vision; and their main source, which powers their optimism. Furthermore, they can tap into their ancestral power at any given time, which is hidden deep within themselves. In a sense, this represents their breadth of vision. Furthermore, they can share these intuitive powers amongst themselves in a psychogenic capacity. This is their ESP. The Pluto in Sagittarius soul group are the freethinkers of the cosmos.

They are also the most free-spirited of all the Pluto generational groups. However, they are perhaps the most fragile; therefore, this group are extremely susceptible to a range of mental health disorders.

The only viable way they can overcome the threat of illness and disease is to continually seek inspiration through their wealth of knowledge and evolutionary experience, which they have obtained either in spirit, or in previous incarnations. So, when under the rulership of Sagittarius, Pluto imparts the image of transformation, through Sagittarian's wisdom of understanding, for the purpose of self-development.

Operating from its Sagittarius station, Pluto's otherwise equable persona will change significantly — emerging as rash, hasty, impulsive, and often frivolous in its dealings with other Pluto soul groups — particularly when it involves finance. Pluto is often labelled the Godfather, because, speaking metaphorically, when he summons payment on his long-standing accounts, we must take notice. This is a tendency the Pluto in Sagittarius soul tends to overlook; because Sagittarius can be overly generous and flippant. Thus, financial flippancy was very evident, especially within the banking sector, during the latter half of the 1990s — when Pluto tenanted Sagittarius.

This reckless period of irresponsibility is more in line with Neptune. However, Pluto's sojourn of Sagittarius, marked the beginning of an era where ill-considered and senseless banking came to the forefront in many countries. This was an inadvertent period where banks freely released money without carrying out credit searches. Money was more-or-less given away in the form of loans, credit cards and mortgages to bad debtors, low earners and students — those who are ordinarily considered as high-risk categories — pigeonholed because of financial risk or inexperience. Thus, an impending global financial collapse was inevitable — expected during Pluto's tenure of Saturn ruled Capricorn.

Ironically, from 1995 and through to 2008 marked the period when depression began to proliferate. Although depression has always been around, its modern-day seeds were initially sown during Pluto's sojourn of Scorpio. Furthermore, a recent study conducted by the World Health Organisation (WHO) concluded that those who are most susceptible to the onset of 'monetary depression' were between the ages of 17 and 25. Further studies concluded that the vast majority of students in higher education (Sagittarius) were succumbing to this form of depression, because they were running up colossal and catastrophic bank overdrafts. This was also the time when student grants were abolished in favour of bank loans.

For this particular group, being financially and psychologically damaged is perhaps the worst form of entrapment, because it is inescapable.

Pluto Preservation

Sciatica, which is an underlying and enervating health condition; and is caused primarily by inflammation of the sciatic nerve, is a very painful and debilitating infirmity. Thus, the origins of sciatica are often deeply-ingrained in the body's physical DNA sequencing — congenital patterns that are evolutionary by design. However, speaking in a psychological capacity, sciatica is often a consequence of financial distress, which is equally responsible for the onset of physical entrapment. Thus, sciatica is common amongst the Pluto in Sagittarius generation.

The Pluto in Sagittarius generation are also predisposed to diverticulitis, which is a very debilitating chronic condition, and in this case affects the entire length of the colon. For this generation, the colon is symbolized by the Sagittarian arrow — carried by the mythical centaur of Sagittarius. However, for this Pluto embodiment, diverticulitis is caused, in part, by a dissipation of life's eternal sweetness (optimism).

Meanwhile, all financial concerns contained within the mindsets of this evolutionary grouping, will be finally addressed once Pluto's sojourn of Aquarius begins in 2024. In addition, these apprehensions will be purged once Jupiter (the ruler of Sagittarius) links to Uranus (the ruler of Aquarius) via a sextile in 2022. Thus, the Pluto in Sagittarius generation will be given an opportunity to finally shake off their financial burdens, particularly with those academic students from this group.

Pluto Transformation

Sagittarian idealism, coupled with Pluto's transformation, can be a forerunner for necessary change. Differing and diverse experiences are what drive these souls in their quest for knowledge. Furthermore, when experience is fused with knowledge, evolutionary growth can be achieved. At which point, the Pluto in Sagittarius generation can transform into 'beacons for hope' — a point in which illness and disease are finally eradicated. Ultimately, this marks the evolutionary nature of Pluto's sojourn in freedom loving Sagittarius.

In order to limit and restrain their rash and hasty behaviour, I would suggest courses in mindfulness, and regular sessions in heart-centered stillness. These gentle disciplines are both recommended from preventing and overcoming illness and disease. When stillness (peace) is applied to the psychological mindset and the physical body, the heart becomes free; and is no longer subject to entrapment. Once the heart is free, the scope of these individuals' philosophical beliefs, becomes simply fathomless.

The Pluto in Sagittarius generation are the teachers of life's eternal knowledge. Thus, they are here to pave a new direction for the entire world to follow.

The Pluto in Capricorn Generation — 2008 – 2024 (Approximate Dates)

Because this evolutionary timeline was paralleling the compilation of this book, my analysis of Pluto will extend only to the salient points; thus fusing together these cosmic hierarchies.

For this Pluto group, the seeds of illness and disease are 'karmically sown' when its individuals fail, or refuse to recognize their predestined obligations and responsibilities, which are imprinted upon their souls. Hence, the predestined responsibilities of the Pluto in Capricorn generation are directed towards an indispensable need for accountability. This means that they must always be accountable for their actions. For them karma is swift and apparent — unlike, for example, the Pluto in Pisces generation — who, in most cases, must wait until passing into spirit before karma is applied.

In addition, their predestined responsibilities mean to instil level-headedness within the overall collective influence, at this time of great physical and psychological upheaval, upon the Earth plane. Thus, they are in a sense here to restore a sense of composure amongst the rest of humankind.

Furthermore, the ultimate preservation of new world structures and foundations are also crucial factors of recognition for this group. In other words, they have incarnated to build, restore, and protect the infrastructure for the new world order. A further assignment for them to undertake, is to ensure that the rest of humankind remain in complete control, especially during this period when chaos and upheaval reign supreme. Global turmoil will become paramount during Pluto's final transition of Capricorn, which is representative of the final decan of the sign; hence 20 through to 29 degrees respectively. Moreover, global chaos and uncertainty will be personified when Pluto makes an evolutionary conjunction to Jupiter and Saturn in 2020.

During Pluto's final transition of Capricorn, the world will witness the threat of global annihilation, caused in part by pandemic, power control and systemic globalization. It is therefore the karmic duty of these Pluto-Capricorn souls to bring these concerns to the forefront, so that a long-term solution can be found, and before Pluto's absolute evolutionary transit of Aquarius — beginning in 2024.

Interestingly, when Russia, a country ruled by Capricorn (see chart), invaded Ukraine in 2022, many of the student humanitarian aid workers, and those who were attempting to seek a long-term solution to the crisis, have Pluto in Capricorn. Research also shown that some have Venus in humanitarian Aquarius. Those souls who have Venus in Aquarius in the natal chart will excel, when Pluto enters Aquarius. This is because Venus is at the natural polarity of Pluto.

In effect, the Pluto in Capricorn generation have ingrained in their souls, a moral duty of care and responsibility to themselves and others. They also have a responsibility to the Earth. In effect, they are overseers of the truth, and the abolishers of corruption. They also have the added benefit of time on their side. Psychologically speaking, for the Pluto in Capricorn soul group, they have all the time in the world to put things right.

Pluto Preservation

Pluto's position in Capricorn initializes the onset of illness and disease, via the outer layer (skin) of the colon. Thus, the outer layer of the colon is commonly referred to as the gastrointestinal wall. Diseases in particular that affect the skin of the colon include colitis, gastritis and ileitis.

Depending on the strength and condition of aspects to Pluto in the individual natal chart, the Pluto in Capricorn generation are particularly susceptible to diseases concerning the outer layers of the bone, known as the cortical bone (skin). These include the progressive disease melorheostosis, which seriously inhibits the bone's natural development — preventing the evolutionary transformation of the soul. Stillness and meditation are crucial elements, which these souls need to undertake. Essentially, Pluto in Capricorn is showing us that the skeletal infrastructure of the Earth has also become diseased.

Pluto Transformation

For all of us, further advancements, which result in technological and evolutionary rewards, such as medical breakthroughs, are there for the offering, especially when we consciously agree to raise our current evolutionary awareness. Altering the course of our current direction must become essential, especially when Pluto finally departs Capricorn in 2024. In order to achieve this transformational shift in psychological consciousness, we, as a collective, will have to transfer our collective perspective from the darkness of negative thinking, and towards the light of positive reckoning. Most notably, this is concerned with the transformation of individual and collective awareness.

Evolutionary Transformation

For the moment, the transformation of the Earth, and all of its inhabitants will hopefully begin to move forward — towards an anticipative period of reckoning and serenity. Thus, the notion, and the fallout from illness and disease, should begin to subside the we traverse further and more significantly towards 2067. At that point, everything will become a disturbing, but nonetheless, a distant memory. 2067 is the year that Pluto begins a wholly new evolutionary cycle of the zodiac — beginning in innovative Aries.

The futuristic Pluto generations, namely Aquarius and Pisces, will be able to reposition the cosmic spotlight of optimism and hope, over the current gloomy notion of despair. However, the abolition of illness and disease will only become possible, if the Earth isn't impelled into cataclysm, for a seventh time in its evolution.[6] Thus, as Pluto completes its cycle of the zodiac and moves towards zero degrees of Aries (an anaretic degree)[7], the opportunity for the regeneration of the Earth, and for humankind becomes a realistic (Aries), and evolutionary prospect (Pluto). I, for one, remain hopeful of this necessary and ultimate transformation.

Furthermore, as ignorance and greed are gradually purged from the Earth, primarily by the generational effects of Pluto's sojourn of Aquarius and Pisces, individual and collective unity, enlightenment and awareness begins to increase both exponentially and internally. Moreover, during this forthcoming cyclic era, where the future generations begin to remember their spiritual heritage, and which denotes the cycle of the philosopher's wheel, humankind is being re-awakened to the possibility of telepathy, telekinesis and self-healing. Unfortunately, these spiritual and fundamental characteristics were overlooked, and mostly ignored during the evolutionary period, which was designated as the dark night of the soul.

Let us now briefly examine Pluto's sojourns of Aquarius and Pisces — cultivating their salient points of reference.

Pluto in Aquarius

As we have already ascertained, Pluto is the planet of transformation and regeneration. Aquarius however, is the sign of psychological and spiritual progression, and innovation. Conceivably, this temporary cosmic collaboration has the potential to be advantageous — if absolute transformation is the desired objective for the individual and the collective mindset.

Once Pluto begins its lengthy transit of this sign, life, in all its dissimilarities, will gradually become antiquated. Thus, Pluto's transit of Aquarius characterizes a glorious opportunity for humankind to make some preferred and necessary changes to the collective influence, as well as our own individual lifestyles. In addition, this evolutionary transit symbolizes the dawning of the age of the scientific revolution. Hence, the scientific revolution also distinguishes a prolonged period of observational transformation; meaning that we will have be given a period of time in which we can contemplate the purpose of our existences.

Collectively speaking, we have already experienced a small portion of this approaching transformational epoch — coming to pass in early 2020 — earmarking the beginning of the Covid-19 pandemic. 2020, was the start of the scientific revolution. Thus, the scientific revolution is now very much at the forefront of our existences. For now, until roughly 2043, we will begin to witness a myriad a scientific breakthroughs and major successes; particularly where medicine is concerned. Changes to the law, and social reforms could also be on the cosmic agenda; and there will be an abundance of new ideas, particularly surrounding the colonization of space. Although I doubt whether this will amount to anything tangible. After all, Pluto is attempting to transform our ideas and beliefs away from this notion — concentrating instead on the wellbeing of our Earth — and its inhabitants.

Pluto's penchant for death, and transformation to the spirit world, began to spiral throughout 2020, and 2021, with the Covid-19 pandemic. However, those scientific Aquarian brains, that have become very attached to the scientific revolution created the vaccines, which would inhibit the transmission and deaths associated with Covid-19. Equally, and as with all scientific developments, there are always going to be the 'Aquarian-labelled' conspiracy theorists. We should then, expect a monumental surge in this type of behaviour — distorting the balance of the scientific revolution — when Pluto begins its sojourn of Aquarius in 2024.

Quantum leaps within the scientific community will nevertheless continue, and become a prevalent factor all through Pluto's tenure of Aquarius — providing we hold our 'collective nerve,' so to speak. Pluto's initial entry into Aquarius has the potential to be a problematic and undependable transition, causing further unrest and distrust in the world — until Pluto discovers its grounding — at approximately eight degrees of Aquarius — eight denoting awareness in fixed signs.

Science should however, continue to discover vital cures for some of the world's deadly diseases. I wouldn't be surprised if a cure for HIV and AIDS (Pluto) isn't finally discovered during this time. It all depends on our undivided ability to raise our collective vibration (awareness), as Aquarius demands.

If we can manage to pull off such feats of accomplishment, it would be considered as a monumental achievement, especially within the realm of ecological and biological diversity, which fall under the rulership of Uranus, which is the natural ruler of Aquarius. What is not considered, or even understood by the media, is that deadly diseases not only cause damage to humans, but they also harm the Earth's ecosystem. During Pluto's tenure of Aquarius, we finally have a chance to repair, and further protect the environment.

Humankind will be presented with an opportunity to alleviate disease, once and for all. What an accomplishment that would be; and a timely enterprise for when Pluto commences its journey through the Godly sign of Pisces. Ultimately, Pluto in Pisces marks the final journey — bringing to an end this modern evolutionary cycle, for the planet of transformation and regeneration.

Pluto in Pisces

Pluto transits the sign in which his mythical brother Neptune rules. Previously, when Pluto tenanted Pisces, 1797 through to 1823, it denoted the age of inquisition, and witch trials. Unfortunately, these impudent truths remain forever active in the annals of time. However, these kinds of practices are beginning to proliferate, especially now that Neptune tenants the sign of its rulership.

When Pluto enters Pisces in 2044, humankind will be presented with an illustrious opportunity to forgive — for all those former provocations, cruelties and grievances. Finally, during this transit, the seat of humankind will be able to release the distant memories of all these historical wrongdoings. In essence, this transit will symbolize the dawning of the age of idealism, spiritual regression and higher reasoning. Anyone born during this Pluto cycle, will be collectively known as the Children of Tama. According to the Akashic Records, Tama means 'excessive augmentation.'

Moreover, this fathomless cycle will symbolize an evolutionary period where doubt, fear, pain, suffering, and all of those negative emotions, which have prevented us from progressing as individuals, and as a collective for millennia, can be relinquished forever. However, as always, human beings will be faced with a choice. Either we can move forward in an enlightened and spiritual way, and with the health of the Earth at heart, or we can continue to regress, as we have done so for thousands of years. During Pluto's sojourn of Pisces, humans can spiral further down into more obsessive addictions. Furthermore, human beings can continue to pollute the Earth — increasing the deleterious effects of global warming.

If we choose the latter option, the Earth will be the subject of a cataclysm; at which point, humankind will be eradicated. According to the Akashic Records, this will be the seventh time, and will involve the element of water. Pluto, Pisces, and its ruler, Neptune, are all cosmic components symbolizing the water element. In addition, cataclysm will occur during Pluto's tenure of Pisces, because Pisces ruler, Neptune equates to a seven in numerology; and this will be the seventh time. Alternatively, we can choose another option; and that is to learn to love ourselves, and the natural environment. As always, the choice is ours!

Let us hope that Pluto's tenure of Pisces uplifts our spirits, and stimulates our creative imaginations, and our hopes and wishes.

In Conclusion

If, and this is a very big If, humankind survives its current, and its future challenges, it is inevitable that the Earth will be a very different place around, and certainly long after 2067. This evolutionary amelioration would nevertheless symbolize the natural healing of the Earth, and the Pluto collective world order.

Blessings to you, the Dear Reader

Alan Richards-Wheatcroft

Chart Data:

- Natal Chart for Charles Darwin, 12th February 1809, 3:00 AM, GMT, Shrewsbury, UK, Placidus Houses, Mean Node.
- Natural Chart for Nicholas Winton, May 19th 1909, London, Mean Node.
- Mundane Chart for Russia, 25th December 1991, 17:25 MSK, Moscow, Placidus Houses, Mean Node.

References

[1] Information source Wikipedia.

[2] The age of enlightenment is followed by the golden age of enlightenment, beginning in 2043. This information is in accordance with the Akashic Records.

[3] According to the Akashic Records, the illusion known as the 'acceleration of time theory' initially began in the year 2000. This was the year when the Earth's energy grid was increased to 96 decibels. This increase in energy output was put into place to assist with the major changes that are continuing to occur upon the Earth plane. Since then our traditional concept of time has been transformed somewhat; because time appears to be accelerating.

[4] A reference to the astrologer, John Dawson.

[5] The colon is scientifically deemed as the secondary memory core.

[6] Drawn from the Akashic Records.

[7] Anaretic is a term used for critical degrees. This 29th degree of any sign is deemed as a crisis-orientated point in the chart. Some astrologers have interpreted an anaretic degree as meaning that a point has been reached in mastering an important lesson in the universe, but success has not quite been achieved, as a result.

Communal Interaction

Distinctive Hallmarks of the Venus-Pluto Polarity

"You are part of a complex social network that changes your biology with every interaction, and which your actions can change".

David Eagleman[1]

The Evolutionary Reason (Venus/Pluto)

When someone enters your life for an *evolutionary reason**, it is usually to meet a *need* that you have visibly expressed. Ordinarily, they have come to assist you through a *difficulty*, or to provide you with guidance and support, that will aid you physically, *emotionally* and *spiritually*. They may seem like a good *friend*, and even a blessing, and of course they are. Hence, they are there for a *reason* and nothing more. Then, without any wrongdoing on your part, or even at an inconvenient period, this person will bring the *relationship* to a *conclusion*, hence it may even be considered to be a *death*.

*Note: The words that are marked in Italic are powerful indicators — representative to one or both of these planets.

Sometimes they do *die*. Sometimes they simply walk away. Sometimes they act in a manner that is *unwarranted*; but nevertheless they force you to take a *stand*. What you must realize is that your *psychological* need has been *fulfilled*. Hence, the *desire* has been met, and their work is now *complete*.

Hence, the prayer your *soul* dispatched into the spiritual ether has been answered, and it is therefore time to move on with your life [2]. Moving on with life is deemed as a major *transformation*; and the word *transformation* is the precept to the legend of the *Phoenix* — the mythical bird that rose out of the ashes of its earlier life (very Plutonian).

The Evolutionary Season (Venus/Pluto)

When someone enters your life for an *evolutionary season*, it is mostly because of an *internal need* or expression that you have *expressed* to *share*, *grow* and more importantly to *master* and *assimilate*. Subsequently, they bring you an experience of *peace*, *transformation*, or they simply make you *smile*. On the other hand they may teach you something that you have never *experienced* or even *accomplished* before now. Likewise, they provide you with an unbelievable amount of *joy*. Believe it; it is real, but only for a *season*. [3]

The Evolving Lifetime (Venus/Pluto)

An *evolving lifetime relationship* can bring you *knowledge*, *wisdom* and *enlightenment* that will span throughout the *duration* of *evolution*; and even throughout previous incarnations. These are characteristics that you must build upon and *expand* in order to *strengthen* your *emotional* and *psychological* foundations that will serve you in this *life* and *beyond*. The primary objective here is to accept all that you are given, and learn to *love unconditionally*; and thus *transfer* all that you have learned thus far into all of your other *relationships*, and all other important focal points in life. This represents *transformation* at a higher level of *consciousness*.

There is a saying: 'love is blind but friendship is clairvoyant'. There is never a truer word said with regards to the influence of the Venus/Pluto polarity in the natal chart.

References

[1]: David Eagleman is an American neuroscientist, author and science communicator.

[2]: Prayers, meaning the divine calling or the spiritual invocation are often subconscious requests transmitted by the soul.

[3]: Evolutionary seasons can span from two to five years approximately.

When Pluto is Intercepted

"It is inner stillness that will save and transform the world".
Eckhart Tolle [1]

When Pluto or Scorpio is intercepted in the natal chart (see footnote below), a profound forfeiture of power becomes noticeable in the lives of these individuals. In effect, before the individual returns to the Earth plane and frequents the spirit world, the soul agrees to relinquish its personal power in order to transform the lives of other individuals, which will be advantageous towards their own personal evolution.

This evolutionary transformational process will come into effect once the Pluto-intercepted soul has successfully traversed its childhood years and reached adolescence. Thus, once they have reached the adolescent stage of puberty they subconsciously begin the process of sowing the 'evolutionary seed of transfiguration' — deep within the souls of those they have agreed to assist in physicality. Throughout puberty and midlife, the Pluto intercepted soul carries out this karmic plan mostly within social groups and gatherings. Throughout maturity however, these souls continue to sow the seed of transformation on a more one-to-one basis.

Essentially, this divine process significantly alters the evolutionary path of both the individual and its cosmic clients so to speak. More often than not this extramundane assignment unique to the Pluto intercepted soul has been fashioned in order to assist those who have digressed from their life path —

re-establishing their karmic destiny. Alternatively, it may also be possible that the Pluto-intercepted soul merely adds a sense of balance to another person's life.

Divine Acquiescence: The compliant submissive persona of these souls becomes the vital component that is required in order to *liberate* those less fortunate souls. Particularly, those individuals who are suffering *brutally* at the hands of others; and those who continue to be the unfortunate victims of both damaging and immoral injustice. Equally, the Pluto-intercepted soul believes, that they too, are the victims of some form of karmic injustice. Realistically, what these souls are doing is advancing their power to others, which is then absorbed — giving their recipients a fighting chance to succeed in life. The whole process is performed purely in a *subconscious* manner. This act of Venusian generosity (Venus being the polarity planet of Pluto) will greatly improve the lives of others, especially in a social and inter-loving capacity.

Evolution: Improving the lives of others in this manner is particularly relevant when Pluto tenants Virgo, Scorpio or Pisces in the natal chart. Interestingly, and according to the *Akashic Records*, there will be a final ingress of evolved souls returning to the Earth plane around the year 2050 to assist with the Earth and humankind's final transitional period, as the collective soul reconciles its acceptance of the Aquarian Age. It is therefore a fair assumption to suggest that these souls will have Pluto or Neptune intercepted as part of their natal assemblage.

So, as we have already ascertained, 'giving up one's power' appears to render these individuals *powerless* — having no control over their lives or future — particularly in the years leading up to the second Saturn return.[2] Literally, they appear to be at the mercy of whatever life throws at them. However, these souls wear the shroud of divine protection. Nevertheless, because of this loss of evolutionary power, souls who have Pluto intercepted in their natal charts go through life believing that they are paying back some negative form of karma — bad deeds perhaps that require some exterior pattern of recompense.

Development: The truth is, these people have stepped off the wheel of incarnation long ago, so they are precisely 'out of phase' with the Earth plane, and thus they are no longer compatible, as these souls are highly evolved. However, it is generally at the beginning of the third Saturn cycle that they begin to realize the severity of having little or no power that will ultimately transform their destiny. Therefore, at this point in their evolution a sense of urgency passes over them, as they instinctively begin to reclaim their *unrecognized* power.

Up to the point of the third Saturn cycle beginning directly after the onset of the second Saturn return, * their lives have undergone some much-needed transformation. In essence, these souls are finally clearing the way for their return to Utopia. Giving up their power as a way to transform the lives of others is deemed as the 'final act of service' upon the Earth plane. Therefore, at the start of their third Saturn cycle that they can begin *reclaiming* their power, and they can begin their final transition through physicality. This is also the point in which they often remember their intercepted Pluto, and its deep influence over their soul, and the power which they already possess deep within.

* Saturn's energy becomes more *favourable* after its second return in the natal chart.

The Dark Side

An intercepted Pluto can perhaps be best described as a representation of the dark side, hence a depiction of 'hell on Earth' — evoking evil and immoral injustice that exists upon every run on the wheel of incarnation. However, it is important to point out that the point of darkness in the chart, the zone which intercepted Pluto occupies, represents the place where light has not yet shone. Thus, an intercepted Pluto refers to ignorance (because it has not been recognized), and not evil. Nonetheless, evil has a way of seeking these souls out, which can have a deleterious effect upon their immune systems and overall health. Thus, right up to the final staging post in life, evil will often seek them out in some form or other.

This is why the Pluto-intercepted soul believes they are working through some reluctant form of karma. The key for these souls is to remain in the light at all times, by dispelling the illusion of the darkness. Stillness and meditation are vital components, which will help to keep their souls balanced, and help them to remember the existence of Pluto. The position of Pluto's mythical brother Neptune in the natal chart will assist them with achieving this crucial objective.

Evolutionary Transformation

Essentially, these souls are beacons for hope; and furthermore, they possess the ability to transform the world for generations to come. They have the ability to influence so many who make their acquaintance. Every now and again a deep sense of ingenuity will bestow itself upon these souls, and a light shines in their hearts that they and others can benefit immensely from. Once this divineness occurs, the Pluto-intercepted soul will become ever more motivated and aware of its responsibilities, especially when it comes to motivating the 'transformation of the world order'. At this point, it's almost as if they begin to instinctively remember the purpose of their incarnation. In addition, Pluto-intercepted souls are the cosmic souls who possess a natural intuitive order with the *Akashic Records*, meaning they can extract information at will. In essence, this ability represents the ultimate power of service.

The Divine Homecoming: Deep down within their souls they yearn to see a 'light at the end of the tunnel'. It is reasonable to speculate that even if these souls do not get their rewards in the here and now (physicality); those rewards will be infinitely *greater* in the spirit world. In a sense an intercepted Pluto bears the same fruits as the intercepted Nodes, meaning that these souls can return home to the spirit world whenever they chose to do so — manifesting as an instinctive yearning. They do not have to wait until that arc of energy begins to fade, which is the conventional upshot — characterizing the end of incarnation. However, this notion is only relevant when an individual is still *revolving* around the karmic wheel of incarnation.[3]

Medical Transformation

As we have already ascertained earlier in Part 3, Pluto oversees the colon. Depending on the position of the intercepted Pluto in the natal chart; and the strength of aspects to it, these people invariably suffer from colon-related issues throughout life such as IBS — which is relevant to the point of the third Saturn cycle. Once this point in evolution has been reached the colon, in most cases, begins to regenerate — becoming a focal point of the entire body. Thus, a significant transformation is underway; and one that will transform the lives of these individuals. For this is no ordinary transformation. This marks a transformation of the mental and psychological faculties. The colon is the central plexus positioned within the gut, hence the emotional/psychological brain, and the colon becomes the organ that houses the body's power.

The Final Transformation: When Pluto is intercepted the colon undergoes a massive shift throughout the second period of life. Thus, when the individual begins to reclaim their power, the colon is the point of gathering, meaning that power is housed in this vital organ. Once this occurs the colon acts as a unit of protection for the entire body, ensuring that the body will remain healthy during its final transition in physicality. From that point forward power will be channelled directly from this vital organ — purging the emotions and releasing more of the brain's cerebral capacity. According to the *Akashic Records*, this process is already evident in dolphins. The dolphin uses up to twenty percent of its brain's capacity.

The Author's Final Testament

I have spent a good part of my current incarnation researching the evolutionary and transformative advantages that are attached to the colon. I have also examined the potential benefits of those souls who have an intercepted or a powerfully-placed Pluto present in their natal charts. In addition, I have always had a natural ability to *download* information from the mysterious depths of the *Akashic Records*. According to the astrologer and lecturer Steven Forrest, "those who have Pluto intercepted in their charts have a natural and instinctive inclination towards the *Akashic Records*".

It may therefore come as no surprise to learn that I too have Pluto intercepted in my natal chart (see chart below). I am also a Scorpio, ruled by Pluto. However, for a good part of my life I have been ruled by Mars, which has occurred by default. So, it is fair to say that I have been involved in countless battles and war scenarios without any power to my advantage. I have also suffered from debilitating health problems, mostly involving my colon. For many years I suffered relentlessly from IBS.

Compiling this publication along with my previous book, which concerns Pluto's brother Neptune, is the main reason I volunteered to return to the Earth plane. I too have Pisces/Virgo intercepted. Writing this book has also allowed me to remember the existence of Pluto. Moreover, I no longer suffer from health problems. My colon is now the central network to my spiritual heart — working in synergy — thus defining and conveying messages directly from the spirit world.

My deep admiration goes out to all of the intercepted Pluto souls, who have labored laboriously throughout their lives in order to satisfy some deep inner yearning towards ultimate perfection — viewing perfection within oneself and in others. Perfection, however, on the Earth world is often unachievable; and therefore it is deemed a non sequitur

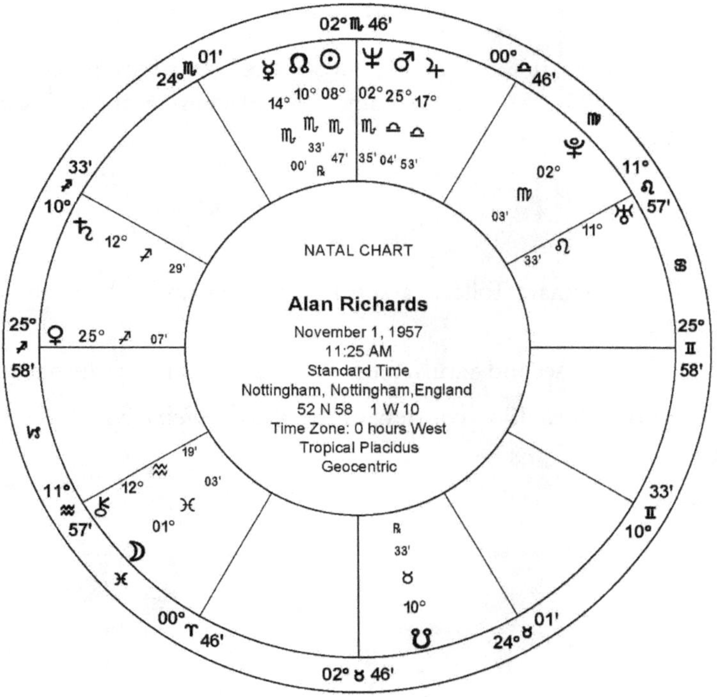

Moreover, my admiration goes out to everyone who simply has a pronounced Pluto in their chart. My heart is with you all, God bless!

Footnote

Interceptions (sequential house cusps) are highly developed houses where the person can influence the environment within, and possibly this is the way the universe compensates for the frustration of an intercepted sign or planet.

Chart Data:

Natal chart for Alan Richards-Wheatcroft, November 1st, 1957, 11:25 AM, Nottingham, UK, Placidus Houses, Mean Node.

References

[1]: Eckhart Tolle is a spiritual teacher and a best-selling author.

[2]: The second Saturn return begins around 58 years of age.

[3]: Information courtesy of the *Akashic Records*.

Index

Other Titles Published by the American Federation of Astrologers (AFA)*

- Aal & Subramanyan/Astrology by Moonlight
- Adams/Understanding Retrogrades
- Addey/Harmonic Anthology
- Adler/Predictive Astrology
- Alexander/Magickal Astrology
- Alexander/Planets in Signs
- Antepara/Aspects: Powerful Keys to Personal Transformation
- Arroyo/Astrology, Karma & Transformation
- Arroyo/Astrology, Psychology and the Four Elements
- Arroyo/Chart Interpretation Handbook
- Arroyo/Experiments & Experiences with Astrology
- Arroyo/Exploring Jupiter
- Arroyo/Person-to-Person Astrology
- Arroyo/Relationships and Life Cycles
- Ashcroft-Nowicki & Norris/The Door Unlocked
- Ashman/How to Survive Mercury Retrograde
- Ashman/Intuition and your Sun Sign
- Ashman/Roadmap to Your Future
- Ashman/Sun Sign Karma
- Ashman/Sun Signs & Past Lives
- Astrolabe/World Ephemeris Midnight 2001-2050

- Astrolabe/World Ephemeris Noon 2001 - 2050
- Avelar & Ribeiro/On the Heavenly Spheres: A Treatise on Traditional Astrology
- Avery/Astrological Aspects
- Avery/The Rising Sign: Your Astrological Mask
- Banzhaf & Theler/Keywords for Astrology
- Barclay/Horary Astrology Rediscovered
- Bell/Midlife is not a Crisis
- Bell/Planetary Threads
- Benjamine/Astrological Lore of all Ages
- Bennett/Astrology: Secrets of the Moon
- Beversdorf/Vedic Secrets to Happiness
- Bills/The Rulership Book
- Bishr (Tr. Holden)/The Introduction to the Science of the Judgments of the Stars
- Blackledge/William Lilly: The Man Who Saw the Future
- Blackwood/12 Faces of the Goddess
- Blackwood/A Lantern in the Dark
- Blake/Vocational Astrology
- Blaschke/Astrology: Language of Life Vol 1, Progressions
- Blaschke/Astrology: Language of Life, Vol 3, Handbook for the Astrologer
- Blaschke/Astrology:Language of Life Vol 2, Sabian Aspect Orbs
- Blaschke/Astrology:Language of Life Vol 4, Relationships
- Blaschke/Astrology:Language of Life Vol 5, Holographic Transits
- Bloch & George/Astrology for Yourself
- Boehrer/Declination: The Other Dimension

- Bogart/Astrology and Meditation
- Bogart/Astrology and Spiritual Awakening
- Bogart/Astrology's Higher Octaves
- Bogart/Planets in Therapy
- Bohannon/North and South Nodes: Guideposts of the Spirit
- Bohannon/Your Solar Return
- Bonatti (Dykes Tr)/Bonatti on Basic Astrology
- Bonatti (Dykes Tr)/Bonatti on Elections
- Bonatti (Dykes Tr)/Bonatti on Horary
- Bonatti (Dykes Tr)/Bonatti on Lots
- Bonatti (Dykes Tr)/Bonatti on Mundane Astrology
- Bonatti (Dykes Tr)/Bonatti on Nativities
- Bonatti (Dykes Tr)/Bonatti's 146 Considerations
- Borstein/The Moon's Nodes
- Bowser/An Introduction to Western Sidereal Astrology 3rd Edition
- Brady/Astrology a place in chaos
- Brady/Brady's Book of Fixed Stars
- Brady/Predictive Astrology
- Brady/Predictive Astrology: The Eagle and the Lark
- Brahy/Confidential Recollections Revealed
- Brittain/Planetary Powers: The Morin Method
- Brown/Cosmic Trends
- Bryan/Houses: A Contemporary Guide
- Bunker/Astrology's Hidden Aspects
- Bunker/Beginner's Guide to Astrology
- Bunker/Quintiles and Tredeciles
- Burk/Astrology: Understanding the Birth Chart

- Burk/Complete Node Book
- Busteed & Wergin/Phases of the Moon - *(OOP – Limited copies available)*
- Cameron/Predictive Planetary Periods: Hindu Dasas
- Campbell/Asteroids Interpreted
- Campbell/Amazing Asteroid Stories
- Campbell/Forensic Astrology: Solving Crimes with Astrology
- Campion/A History of Western Astrology, Vol. I
- Campion/Astrology and Cosmology in the World's Religions
- Campion/Astrology, History and Apocalypse
- Campion/Book of World Horoscopes (2004 updated)
- Campion/The Dawn of Astrology
- Canfield/Brother Pluto Sister Eris
- Canfield/Eris in Signs, Houses, Aspects
- Canfield/Uranus
- Canfield/Yankee Doodle Discord
- Carelli/The 360 Degrees of the Zodiac
- Carter/The Astrological Aspects
- Charubel-Sepharial/The Degrees of Zodiac Symbolized
- Christino/Foreseeing the Future
- Christino/The Best of Al H Morrison
- Christino/What Evangeline Adams Knew
- Circle Books Aspect Finder
- Clark/From the Moment We Met
- Clark/The Family Legacy
- Clark/Vocation
- Clement/Aspect Patterns – *(OOP Limited copies available)*
- Clement/Mapping Your Birthchart– *(OOP Limited copies*

available)

- Clement/Mapping Your Family Relationships– *(OOP Limited copies available)*
- Clement/Mapping Your Sex Life– *(OOP Limited copies available)*
- Clement/Planet-Centered Astrology– *(OOP Limited copies available)*
- Clement/The Astrology of Development– *(OOP Limited copies available)*
- Clifford/Astrologer's Book of Charts
- Clifford/British Entertainers: The Astrological Profiles
- Clifford/Getting to the Heart of Your Chart
- Clifford/Horoscope Snapshots
- Clifford/Solar Arc Directions
- Close/Self-Evident Astrology Book I: Decoding the Solar System
- Clow/Awakening the Planetary Mind
- Clow/Chiron: Rainbow Bridge Between..
- Cochrane, David/Astrology for the 21st Century
- Cochrane, David/The Astrology of Bipolar Disorder: A Scientific Breakthrough
- Cochrane, David/Vibrational Astrology - The Essentials
- Coley/Clavis Astrologiae Eliminata: Key to Whole Art of Astrology
- Coley/Clavis Astrologiae Eliminata: Key to Whole Art of Astrology
- Cornelius/The Moment of Astrology
- Costello/The Astrological Elements: Earth and Air
- Costello/The Astrological Elements: Water & Fire
- Costello/The Astrological Moon

- Costello/The Weiser Guide to Practical Astrology
- Cragin/Astrology on the Cusp
- Cragin/The Astrological Elements
- Cramer/Dictionary of Medical Astrology
- Cramer/How to Give an Astrological Health Reading
- Crane/A Practical Guide to Traditional Astrology
- Crane/Astrological Roots: The Hellenistic Legacy
- Crane/Between Fortune and Providence
- Crowl/The Degrees
- Cunningham/Divination for Beginners
- Cunningham/Healing Pluto Problems
- Cunningham/How to Read Your Astrological Chart
- Curry/Understanding Human Design
- Daath/Medical Astrology
- Darling/Essentials of Medical Astrology
- Darling/Essentials of Medical Astrology
- Darr/Transits
- Davis/Astrolocality Astrology
- Davis/From Here to There: An Astrologer's Guide to Astromapping
- Davis/Horary Astrology
- DeFouw & Svoboda/Light on Relationships
- DeJersey & Taves/Destiny Times Six
- Devlin/Astrology and Past Lives
- Devlin/Astrology and Relationships
- DeVore/Encyclopedia of Astrology
- Dimino & Sherwin/East Joins West
- Discepolo/Transits and Solar Returns

- Discepolo/Transits and Solar Returns
- Doane/30 Years Research
- Doane/Astrology's Wide Influence
- Doane/Blending Astrology, Numerology and Tarot
- Doane/Contest Charts
- Doane/Contest Charts
- Doane/How to Read Cosmodynes
- Doane/How to Read Cosmodynes
- Doane/Modern Horary Astrology
- Doane/Profit by Electional Astrology
- Doane/Secret Symbolism of Tarot
- Doane/Secret Symbolism of Tarot
- Dobyns/Finding the Person in the Horoscope
- Dobyns/Progressions, Directions and Rectification
- Dobyns/The Node Book
- Dominguez/Practical Astrology for Witches and Pagans
- Donath/Approximate Positions of Asteroids 1851 - 2050
- Donath/Asteroids in Midpoints
- Donath/Asteroids in Synastry
- Donath/Asteroids in Synastry
- Donath/Asteroids in the Birth Chart
- Donath/Have We Met Before?
- Donath/Houses: Which and When
- Donath/Minor Aspects Between Natal Planets
- Donath/Patterns of Professions
- Donleavy/The Whirling Winds
- Doser (Dykes(ed))/Financial Significators in Traditional Astrology

- Doser (Dykes(ed))/Professional Significators in Traditional Astrology
- Doser/Astrological Prediction: A Handbook of Techniques
- Dreyer/Healing Signs
- Dreyer/Vedic Astrology
- Dukelow/Coalescent Horoscopes
- Dukelow/Transpluto
- Duncan/Astrology: Transformation & Empowerment
- Duz/A Practical Treatise of Astral Medicine and Therapeutics
- Dykes (ed.)/The Book of the Nine Judges: Traditional Horary Astrology
- Dykes (tr)/Astrology of the World I: The Ptolemaic Inheritance
- Dykes (tr)/Introductions to Astrology: Abu Ma'shar & al-Qabisi
- Dykes (tr)/The Forty Chapters of al-Kindi
- Dykes (tr)/Works of Sahl & Masha'allah
- Dykes (Tr/Ed)/Astrology of the World II: Revolutions and History
- Dykes/Apotelesmatics Book III: On Inceptions
- Dykes/George/Brennan/Traditional Astrology in the 21st Century CD - In Honor of James Holden
- Dykes/Traditional Astrology for Today
- Ebertin/Applied Cosmobiology
- Ebertin/Auxiliary Tables: Calculating Stellar Positions
- Ebertin/Combination of Stellar Influences
- Ebertin/Cosmic Marriage
- Ebertin/Directions: Co-Determinants of Fate
- Ebertin/Fixed Stars and Their Interpretation
- Ebertin/Rapid and Reliable Analysis

- Ebertin/The Annual Diagram:Forecasting Using 45-degree Graphic Ephemeris
- Ebertin/The Contact Cosmogram
- Ebertin/Transits
- Edwards/Astropsychology: A Journey to Yourself
- Edwards/Medical Astrology for Healing
- Einhorn/The Little Book of Saturn
- Eleftheriadis/Horary Astrology: The Practical Way to Learn Your Fate
- Escobar/144 Doors of the Zodiac
- Eshelman/Horoscope Calculation
- Fagan & Firebrace/Primer of Sidereal Astrology
- Falconer/Astrology and Aptitude
- Farley/Astro Mind Maps
- Faugno/Your Fertile Hours
- Finey/The Sacred Dance of Venus and Mars
- Fleuret/Astrological Keywords: A Reference Manual
- Fleuret/Astrological Keywords: A Reference Manual
- Flynn/Astrology and Weight Control: Jupiter/Pluto
- Forrest/Skymates II
- Forrest/Skymates, Revised Edition
- Forrest/The Ascendant
- Forrest/The Book of Air
- Forrest/The Book of Earth
- Forrest/The Book of Fire
- Forrest/The Book of Neptune
- Forrest/The Book of Pluto
- Forrest/The Book of the Moon

- Forrest/The Book of Water
- Forrest/The Changing Sky
- Forrest/The Inner Sky
- Forrest/The Night Speaks
- Forrest/Yesterday's Sky: Astrology and Reincarnation
- Gansten/Primary Directions: Astrology's Old Master Techniques
- Garner/A Cosmic Dialogue
- Garrett/Health in the Horoscope
- Garrett/Karma in the Horoscope
- Garrett/More About Retrogrades
- Garrett/Relationships
- Garrett/Unlocking Interceptions
- Garrison/The Lunar Gospel
- Gauquelin/Cosmic Influences on Human Behavior
- Geary (Ed) Astrology the New Generation
- Geffner/Astrological Markers of ADD and ADHD
- Geffner/Astrology for Career Success
- Geffner/Creative Step-Parenting
- Gehrz/Anthology Book One - Vettius Valens of Antioch - Not Available
- Gehrz/Astrological Remediation: A Guide for the Modern Practioner
- Geisler, Pat/Chocolate Sauce
- Geisler, Pat/The Plain Vanilla Astrologer
- Gemming/Mystical Secrets of the Stars
- George/Ancient Astrology Volume Two
- George/Asteroid Goddesses

- George/Astrology and the Authentic Self
- George/Finding Our Way Through the Dark
- Gilbert/Potential Fulfilled: Accident Pattens
- Gillen/The Key to Speculation on the New York Stock Exchange
- Glenn/How To Prove Astrology
- Goldsmith/Moon Phases: A Symbolic Key
- Goldsmith/Zodiac by Degrees
- Grail/Astrology of Dwarf Planets: The Galactic Dimension of Creation Mythology
- Grant/Vol I: Elementary Astrology
- Grant/Vol II: Analysis of the Horoscope
- Grant/Vol III: Synthesis of the Horoscope
- Grant/Vol IV: Predictive Astrology
- Grasse/Signs of the Times
- Grasse/Under a Sacred Sky
- Grebner/Decanates
- Grebner/Everything Has a Phase
- Grebner/Lunar Nodes
- Green/EA Glossary: Guiding Principles of Jeffrey Wolf Green Evolutionary Astrology
- Green/Essays on Evolutionary Astrology
- Green/Evolutionary Astrology: Pluto & Your Karmic Mission
- Green/Medical Astrology: Astrological Correlations to the Anatomy/Physiology and the Chakra System
- Green/Neptune: Whispers from Eternity
- Green/Pluto Vol 1: Evolutionary Journey into the Soul
- Green/Relationships: Our Essential Needs

- Green/Uranus: Freedom from the Known
- Green/Your Horoscope in Your Hands
- Greenbaum/Temperament: Astrology's Forgotten Key
- Greene/Horoscope in Manifestation: Psychology and Prediction
- Greene/Outer Planets and Their Cycles, The Astrology of the Collective
- Grell/Keywords
- Grell/Keywords
- Gullfoss/The Complete Book of Spiritual Astrology
- Gunzburg/AstroGraphology
- Hall/Good Vibrations
- Hall/Karmic Connections
- Hall/Patterns of the Past
- Hall/The Book of Why
- Hamaker-Zondag/Aspects and Personality
- Hamaker-Zondag/Physchological Astrology
- Hamaker-Zondag/The House Connection
- Hamaker-Zondag/The Twelfth House: The Hidden Power in the Horoscope
- Hamaker-Zondag/The Yod Book
- Hannan/Predictive Techniques: Annual Harmonic Chart
- Harvey/Anima Mundi: The Astrology of the Individual and the Collective
- Hayes/Astrology of Identity
- Heimsoth/Homosexuality in the Horoscope
- Henson/Degrees of the Zodiac
- Henson/The Vertex: The Third Angle

- Hill/Vocational Astrology
- Holden(Tr)/Paul of Alexandria: Introduction to Astrology
- Holden(Tr)/Rhetorius the Eqyptian
- Holden/A History of Horoscopic Astrology, 2nd Edition
- Holden/A History of Horoscopic Astrology, 2nd Edition HB
- Holden/Biographical Dictionary of Western Astrologers
- Holden/Five Medieval Astrologers
- Holden/The Judgments of Nativities
- Hopewell & Llewellyn/The Cosmic Egg Timer - 2011 Edition
- Hopewell & Llewellyn/The Cosmic Egg Timer
- Hopewell & Llewellyn/The Cosmic Egg Timer
- Hopewell/Aspect Patterns in Colour
- Hopewell/Aspect Patterns in Colour
- Hopewell/The Living Birth Chart
- Howell/Jungian Symbolism in Astrology
- Howland/American Histrology
- Huber/AstroLog I: Life and Meaning
- Huber/Astrological Psychosynthesis
- Huber/Astrology and the Seven Rays
- Huber/Reflections and Meditations in the Signs
- Huber/Transformation: Astrology as a Spiritual Path
- Hughes/Book of Marriage Charts
- Hughes/Planetary Hour Dial
- Hunter/Black Moon Lilith
- Idemon/Through the Looking Glass
- Ishikawa/Pocket Sized Ephemeris 1900-2050 (English)
- Jakobowsky, Frank/Astrological Discoveries

- Jay/Interpreting Lilith
- Jay/Lilith Ephemeris 2000 - 2050
- Jayne/A Preface to Prenatal Charts
- Jayne/Aspects to Horoscope Angles
- Jayne/Progressions and Directions
- Jayne/The Best of Charles Jayne
- Jones/The Soul Speaks
- Kellogg/The Yod: It's Esoteric Meaning
- Keyes/Parallels to Midheaven and Ascendant
- Kimmel/Altered and Unfinished Lives
- Kimmel/Cosmobiology for the 21st Century
- Kozminsky/Zodiacal Symbology
- Lavoie/Alphee's Horary Astrology - The Master's work
- Lavoie/Four Paths to God
- Lavoie/Horary at Its Best
- Lavoie/Horary Lectures
- Lavoie/Lose this Book and Find it With Horary
- Lehman/Astrology of Sustainability
- Lehman/Classical Astrology for Modern Living
- Lehman/Magic of Electional Astrology
- Lehman/Martial Arts of Horary Astrology
- Lehman/The Book of Rulerships
- Lehman/The Ultimate Asteroid Book
- Lehman/Traditional Medical Astrology
- Levin/The Manual of Harmonics
- Levine/Breakthrough Astrology
- Lilly/The Astrologer's Guide

- Lindanger/Your Sun's Return
- Lineman & Popelka/Compendium of Astrology
- Lineman/Eclipse Interpretation Manual
- Lineman/Eclipses: Astrological Guideposts
- Lineman/Your Prenatal Eclipse
- Llewellyn's 2022 Daily Planetary Guide
- Llewellyn's 2022 Sun Sign Book
- Llewellyn's 2023 Daily Planetary Guide
- Llewellyn's 2023 Moon Sign Book
- Lustrup/Pluto: Transforming the New You
- Lyons/Astrology Beyond Ego
- Lyons/The Machine Stops: The Mayan Long Count
- Lyons/Your Hidden Face: Projection in the Horoscope
- Mann/Astrology for the Absolute Beginner
- Marr/Prediction I
- Marshall/Understanding Children Through Astrology
- Martin/Your Destiny Discovered Astrology for Believers
- Masha'allah (Holden Tr)/Six Astrological Treatises
- Mason/Art of Forecasting Using Diurnal Charts
- Mason/Aspects Between Signs
- Mason/Delineation of Progressions
- Mason/Forecasting with New, Full, and Quarter Moons
- Mason/From One House to Another
- Mason/Lunations and Predictions
- Mason/Understanding Planetary Placements
- Mason/You and Your Ascendant
- Maternus (holden Tr)/Mathesis

- Maternus (holden Tr)/Mathesis
- Maternus (holden Tr)/Mathesis HB
- Mayeda/Ten Key Features of Fame and Fortune: Astrologers Look into the Celestial DNA of Celebrities
- McClung/The Hyperion Symbols
- McCormick/Deductive Interpret. of Natal Horoscope
- McDevitt/Why History Repeats
- McDow & Graziano/ACD/LD Method of Progressions
- McRae/Understanding Interceptions
- McWhirter/McWhirter Theory of Stock Market Forecasting
- Mercury Retrograde Cards - (3 cards)
- Michelsen/Uranian Transneptunian 1900-2050
- Milburn/Progressed Horoscope Simplified
- Miller/Astrology's Twelve-Planet Tree of Life
- Miller/Designs for a New Age
- Miller/Intercepted Planets: Possibilities for a New Age
- Miller/Interceptions: Heralds of a New Age
- Miller/Pagan Astrology for the Spirit and the Soul
- Miller/Saturn: Redrawing the Outlines of Our Lives
- Miller/The Lunar Nodes to Pars Fortuna: Journey and Goal
- Morin (Tr J Holden)/Book 23 Astrologia Gallica - Revolutions
- Morin (Tr J Holden)/Book 24 Astrologia Gallica - Progressions and Transits
- Morin (Tr J Holden)/Book 26 Astrologia Gallica
- Morin (Tr J Holden)/Books 13,14,15,19 Astrologia Gallica
- Morin (Tr LaBruzza)/Book 18 Astrologia Gallica - Strengths of the Planets
- Morin (Tr. Holden)/Astrologia Gallica Book 16: The Rays and

Aspects of the Planets

- Morin (Tr. Holden)/Astrologia Gallica Book 17
- Morin (Tr. Holden)/Astrologia Gallica Book 25
- Morin(Tr. J Holden/Book 22 Astrologia Gallica Direction...
- Morinus/Astrologia Gallica Book 21 (Horoscope Interpretation)
- Munkasey/Astrological Keywords Signs of the Zodiac
- Munkasey/House Keywords and More...
- Murphy & Rosato/The Math of Astrology
- Nagle/Winning with Astrology
- Negus/Interpreting Composite & Relationship Charts
- Newman/Declination in Astrology
- Noel/Reinventing Astrology
- Nolle/Chiron: New Planet in Your Horoscope
- Noonan/Classical Scientific Astrology
- Noonan/Fixed Stars and Judicial Astrology
- Palmer/ABC Basic Chart Reading
- Palmer/Astro-Guide to Nutrition and Vitamins
- Palmer/Astrological Compatibility
- Palmer/Gambling to Win
- Palomaki/Pluto: Key to the Expansion of Consciousness
- Paul-Wolf/Personal Lunation Charts
- Pearce/The Textbook of Astrology
- Penfield/Bon Voyage
- Penfield/Horoscopes of Africa
- Penfield/Horoscopes of Europe
- Penfield/Horoscopes of Latin America
- Penfield/Horoscopes of the Asia, Australia and the Pacific

- Penfield/Horoscopes of the USA and Canada, 2nd edition
- Penfield/Stars Over England
- Phillipson/Astrology In The Year Zero
- Porphyry (Holden Tr)/Porphyry the Philosopher
- Randall & Campbell/Sacred Symbols of the Ancients
- Richards-Wheatcroft/Astrology for Self-Healing: The Essential Guide
- Richards-Wheatcroft/Discovering Faith in Neptune's Ocean
- Richards-Wheatcroft/One Body Many Illnesses
- Richards-Wheatcroft/Pluto's Season for Ashes
- Riske/Astrometeorology
- Roberts & Borkowski/Signs and Parts in Plain English
- Robertson/Cosmopsychology: Engine of Destiny
- Robertson/Eighth House
- Robertson/The Moon in Your Life
- Robertson/Transit of Saturn: Critical Ages
- Rodden/Mercury Method of Chart Comparison
- Rodden/Modern Transits
- Rodden/Money: How to Find it With Astrology
- Rowland/True Crime Astrology
- Rudhyar/Astrology of Transformation
- Ruiz/Interpreting Empty Houses
- Ruiz/Prediction Techniques Regarding Romance
- Sakoian & Acker/Astrological Anthology
- Sakoian & Acker/The Inconjunct
- Sakoian & Acker/The Transiting Planets
- Sakoian and Acker/Decanates and Duads
- Sakoian and Acker/Transits Simplified

- Sargent/How to Handle Your Human Relations
- Sasportas/Twelve Houses
- Sehested/Vol 2: Chart Interpretation
- Sehested/Vol 3: Tables and Reference
- Sharman-Burke and Greene/The Astrologer, the Counsellor and the Priest
- Silva/Astrology and Psychology
- Silveira de Mello/Declinations
- Silveira de Mello/Decumbitures and Diurnals
- Simmonite/Horary Astrology
- Simms/Astrology and the Power of Eight
- Simms/Twelve Wings of the Eagle
- Simms/Your Magical Child
- Sky, Sylvia/Tetrabiblos for the 21st Century - "The Bible of Astrology"
- Smith/Transits of the Planets
- Solibakke/The Mahabote Families
- Stacey/Uranus Square Pluto
- Stiopei/Pluto the Power of Transformation
- Stone/Delineation with Astrodynes
- Swatton/From Symbol to Substance
- Terry/The Progressed Moon Around the Zodiac
- Tompkins/The Contemporary Astrologer's Handbook
- Van Toen/The Mars Book
- Von Klockler/Astrology and Vocational Aptitude
- Wakefield/Cosmic Astrology
- Watters/Horary Astrology and the Judgment of Events
- Watters/Sex and the Outer Planets

- Weber/Arabian Parts Decoded
- Weber/Astro-Geology of Earthquakes and Volcanoes
- White/The Moon's Nodes and Their Importance
- Wickenburg/In Search of a Fulfilling Career
- Wickenburg/Journey Through the Birthchart
- Wickenburg/Your Hidden Powers
- Williams/Financial Astrology
- Williams/Simplified Astronomy for Astrologers
- Willner/The Rising Sign Problem
- Wilson-Ludham/Power Trio: Mars, Jupiter and Saturn
- Wilson-Ludlam/Dear Mae R
- Wilson-Ludlam/Healing Thru the Centers
- Wilson-Ludlam/Horary, The Gemini Science
- Wilson-Ludlam/Interpret Your Rays thru the Planets
- Wilson-Ludlam/Letters to 22 Astrologers
- Wilson-Ludlam/Living the Good Life
- Wilson-Ludlam/Ten Lessons in 7 Universal Rays
- Wilson-Ludlam/Yielding to Spirit
- Wilson/Astrology of Theosophy
- Wise/Houses of the Zodiac
- Wynn/Key Cycle
- Yacoubian/Psychid Self-Defense and the Zociac
- Ybarra/Emotional Dimensions of Astrology

This list reflects the current catalog and is subject to additions or deletions.

www.astrologers.com

For Celeste

We are the lucky ones
We shine like a thousand suns
My heart and I have wandered aimlessly
All those years drifting in space
I have known you well, yet
I have never seen your face
You are the stars in my darkest night.

You are one of the kindest and wisest souls I have encountered on my evolutionary journey.

With much love and admiration

Alan

www.ingramcontent.com/pod-product-compliance
Lightning Source LLC
Chambersburg PA
CBHW050244170426
43202CB00015B/2915
* 9 7 8 0 8 6 6 9 0 6 8 8 3 *